The Transformation of Governance

INTERPRETING AMERICAN POLITICS
Michael Nelson, series editor

The Transformation of Governance

Public Administration for the Twenty-First Century

UPDATED EDITION

Donald F. Kettl

Johns Hopkins University Press
Baltimore

© 2002, 2015 Johns Hopkins University Press

All rights reserved. Published 2002, 2015

Printed in the United States of America on acid-free paper

9 8 7 6 5 4 3 2 1

First edition published as *The Transformation of Governance: Public Administration for Twenty-First Century America*, 2002

Johns Hopkins University Press
2715 North Charles Street
Baltimore, Maryland 21218-4363
www.press.jhu.edu

Library of Congress Cataloging-in-Publication Data

Kettl, Donald F.

 The transformation of governance : public administration for the twenty-first century / Donald F. Kettl. — Updated edition.

       pages cm

 Includes bibliographical references and index.

 ISBN 978-1-4214-1635-9 (pbk. : alk. paper) — ISBN 978-1-4214-1636-6 (electronic) — ISBN 1-4214-1635-2 (pbk. : alk. paper) — ISBN 1-4214-1636-0 (electronic)   1. Administrative agencies—United States—Management. 2. Bureaucracy—United States.   3. United States—Politics and government. 4. Public administration—United States.   I. Title.

 JK421.K483 2015

 351.73—dc23   2014024705

A catalog record for this book is available from the British Library.

Special discounts are available for bulk purchases of this book.
For more information, please contact Special Sales at 410-516-6936
or specialsales@press.jhu.edu.

Johns Hopkins University Press uses environmentally friendly book materials, including recycled text paper that is composed of at least 30 percent post-consumer waste, whenever possible.

Contents

Series Editor's Foreword to the Updated Edition

The United States may be the only country in the world whose constitutional plan of government can be read in the map of its capital city. The Constitution's separation of powers, for example, was expressed physically by the city's planners when the Capitol and Executive Mansion were separated from each other by a considerable distance. The idea that Washington's main reason for being was to represent the rest of the country was displayed in the wide avenues that radiate from the city in all directions, inviting citizens to come and be heard. No space was left for the construction of large commercial enterprises. Just as constitutional government was to rest on the consent of the governed, so would Washington survive as a city only through their financial support.

Yet the original capital plan was hazy about where the administrative departments would be housed. To locate the departments on the outer reaches of the various avenues would suggest that they would take their direction from the people and the states, implying a bottom-up model of bureaucratic accountability. To cluster the departments together in their own part of town would suggest that they would be largely self-governing, an inside-out model of accountability. To place them near the president and Congress would suggest a top-down model, in which the departments would take their marching orders from their elected superiors.

In practice, the approach taken by the new government during Washington's early years as a city favored the last of these three strategies of building and governing the bureaucracy, the top-down model. As Donald F. Kettl shows in the new edition of this book, the top-down model of bureaucratic accountability continued to dominate American public administration for more than a century and a half, reigning supreme at least until the time of the Allied victory in World War II. The way top-down administration worked, Kettl writes, was that "elected officials made decisions on behalf of the people, and they delegated responsibility for carrying them out to agency heads." In turn, these agency heads "subdelegated responsibilities through the bureaucracy to the floor, where bureaucrats met citizens." Public administration was meant to work almost like "a vending machine: insert tax dollars, push the policy lever, and wait for government agencies to dispense goods and services."

As Kettl demonstrates, the last three-quarters of a century have witnessed great strains on the top-down model of bureaucratic accountability. "Hyperpartisanship" has created gridlock within and between the elected branches, with unfortunate consequences for the bureaucracy. Public trust in government has been in steep decline, a condition that government seems better at aggravating than remedying. Most of the programs created by elected policymakers in recent decades have been designed to be implemented by units outside the federal government, with little attention to the attendant complexities. "Twenty-first century governance in the United States and around the world," Kettl argues, "is increasingly a matter of boundary-crossing between the public, private, and nonprofit sectors, and between home and abroad." Because those outside Washington were given a share of the responsibility for making the policies work, these programs necessarily implied a weakening of the top-down accountability in favor of bottom-up accountability. A further weakening has come from the contemporary idea, imported from the business world, of making the customer (citizens) the boss.

Policymakers have also injected doses of inside-out accountability into the workings of public administration in recent years. Most prominently, the "reinventing government" movement that caught fire in the 1990s was, as Kettl points out, "a strategy founded on an assumption that managers know how to do their jobs and that top officials ought to get out of the way and let them perform."

To complicate matters even more, the emergence of the inside-out and bottom-up models has not displaced the traditional top-down model of public administration. In times of crisis, such as the September 11, 2001, terrorist attacks on New York and Washington or Hurricane Katrina, which struck New Orleans and the Gulf Coast on August 29, 2005, the universal impulse is still to put someone in charge of the government's far-flung activities and then hold that person accountable for the government's performance. In short, Kettl demonstrates that modern bureaucracy, like the map of contemporary Washington, is the furthest thing from simplicity and coherence. Although visitors to the city will still find some departments and agencies located near the Capitol and the White House, they also will find others headquartered on the broad avenues leading out of town and still others clustered in neighborhoods of their own.

Michael Nelson
Fulmer Professor of Political Science
Rhodes College

Series Editor's Foreword to the First Edition

The United States may be the only country in the world whose constitutional plan of government can be read in the map of its capital city. The Constitution's separation of powers, for example, was expressed physically by the city's planners when the Capitol and the Executive Mansion were separated from each other by a considerable distance. The idea that Washington's main reason for being was to represent the rest of the country was displayed in the wide avenues that radiate from the city in all directions, inviting citizens to come and be heard. No space was left for the construction of large commercial enterprises: just as constitutional government was to rest on the consent of the governed, so would Washington survive as a city only through their financial support.

Yet the original capital plan was hazy about where the administrative departments would be housed. To locate the departments on the outer reaches of the various avenues would suggest that they would take their direction from the people and the states, implying a bottom-up model of bureaucratic accountability. To cluster the departments together in their own part of town would suggest that they would be largely self-governing, an inside-out model of accountability. To place them near the president and Congress would suggest a top-down model, in which the departments would take their marching orders from their elected superiors.

In practice, the approach taken by the new government during Washington's early years as a city favored the last of these three strategies of building and governing the bureaucracy, the top-down model. As Donald F. Kettl shows in this book, the top-down model of bureaucratic accountability continued to dominate American public administration for more than a century and a half, reigning supreme at least until the time of the Allied victory in World War II. The way top-down administration worked, Kettl writes, was that "policymakers, elected by citizens, would craft public decisions and delegate responsibility to administrators." In turn, these "higher-level bureaucrats would use authority to control what their subordinates did" in carrying out the decisions of the elected policymakers.

Public administration was meant to work "almost like a vending machine, into which [policymakers] put money and out of which they expected results."

As Kettl demonstrates, the last half-century has witnessed great strains on the top-down model of bureaucratic accountability. Most of the programs created by elected policymakers in recent decades have been designed to be implemented by state and local governments, or by private contractors. Because those outside Washington were given a share of the responsibility for making the policies work, these programs necessarily implied a weakening of top-down accountability in favor of bottom-up accountability. A further weakening has come from the contemporary idea, imported from the business world, of making the customer (citizens) the boss.

Policymakers have also injected doses of inside-out accountability into the workings of public administration in recent years. Most prominently, the "reinventing government" movement that caught fire in the 1990s was, as Kettl points out, "a strategy founded on an assumption that managers know how to do their jobs and that top officials ought to get out of the way and let them perform."

To complicate matters even more, the emergence of the inside-out and bottom-up models has not displaced the traditional top-down model of public administration. In times of crisis such as the September 11, 2001, terrorist attacks on New York and Washington, the universal impulse is still to put someone in charge of the far flung activities of, in this case, homeland security, then hold that person accountable for the government's performance. In short, modern bureaucracy, like the map of contemporary Washington, is the furthest thing from simplicity and coherence. Although visitors to the city will still find some departments and agencies located near the Capitol and White House, they also will find others headquartered on the broad avenues leading out of town and still others clustered together in neighborhoods of their own.

Michael Nelson

Preface to the First Edition

Public administration is built on the foundation of a theory of hierarchy and authority that is clear and straightforward, with a tradition that has continued for millennia. The actual work of public administration, however, has grown increasingly out of sync with the theory guiding it. While the theory is built on the foundation of hierarchy and authority, the structure of public work has become less and less hierarchical. Managers manage less through authority and more through a wide variety of other strategies. Moreover, the very nature of American democracy—the force that makes American public administration *public*—has shifted dramatically as well.

As a result, public administration—in theory and practice—has sagged under the strain. Managers have cobbled together new approaches without sufficient theoretical support. Many managers have followed what appeared to be lonely pathways only to discover other managers on the same road. Other managers have wandered down blind alleys. The field's lack of a guiding compass has thwarted the pursuit of efficiency that long was its reason for being. Even worse, the "ad hocracy" that emerged from the erosion of the theoretical foundation has posed huge challenges to democratic accountability. Elected officials find themselves delegating authority in traditional ways but discovering that the old mechanisms for ensuring accountability often work poorly, if at all. Instead they work increasingly through loose networks of service providers, but often, as government practitioners, they struggle to maintain government's legitimacy—to retain their roles as the leader of the network instead of just one participant among others.

The challenge to public administration theory thus is more than just an academic exercise. It has profound implications for the effectiveness and efficiency of government. It defines the conduct of American democracy. It shapes the relationship between government and its citizens. Public administration is in trouble because it does not match up well, either in theory or in practice, with the problems it must solve.

Public administration, especially in the United States, has for a long time been built on a tight theory of hierarchy and authority. Citizens elect officials to govern them. These elected policymakers frame policy and delegate the administrative details to unelected administrators. Delegation is inevitable—the work of government is too complex for elected officials to supervise every detail. Even if they had the time, they could not possibly have the skill or training to oversee the wide-ranging work of government. Relying on a career civil service allows government to build the capacity it needs to get the job done, and to get it done efficiently. Holding public administration responsible for that delegation, moreover, is the keystone of democratic accountability—for limiting the power of administrators and ensuring that administration pursues the goals that policymakers set. But as public administration has become less hierarchically organized and authority controlled, the shifting realities have challenged its traditions.

Such intellectual struggles, of course, are nothing new to American administration or democracy. Since the nation's first years, America's leaders have recognized that public administration is a fundamental manifestation of governmental power. They have advanced different—and conflicting—ideas about how to shape and control it. Over the centuries, policymakers and theorists alike have periodically reexamined which values and practices deserve the most emphasis. The process was much like the maddening Rubik's cube, a puzzle cube with different colors on different sides that could be rearranged in a vast number of combinations—43,252,003,274,489,856,000, in fact. What has changed is that public administration is no longer simply a matter of rearranging the dominant values of the American system. Rather, public administration has changed so fundamentally, if quietly, that the traditional values provide weak guidance.

Consider, for example, the September 11, 2001, terrorist attack on New York's World Trade Center and Washington's Pentagon. Traditional bureaucratic strategies proved a poor match for detecting and preventing such attacks or for deploying a coordinated response. The burning and collapsing buildings demonstrated that effective management of the crisis depended on coordinating very different agencies. In probing possible intelligence failures before the attacks, analysts quickly focused on the old rivalries between the CIA and the FBI. They poked into the historic division of responsibility, between the FBI's emphasis on domestic terrorists and the CIA's focus on international problems. The proposals for a single national antiterrorist agency to coordinate terrorist policy recall the challenges that came from the post–World War II plan that combined the various military services into a single Department of Defense.

During the attack and its aftermath, the coordination problem boiled over. Federal officials bluntly admitted that they had no procedure for notifying federal agencies in Washington about a possible attack. Washington Mayor Anthony A. Williams complained that federal officials failed to inform him quickly enough about critical decisions they were making, while District of Columbia officials discovered they lacked a citywide antiterrorist plan. New York's emergency management officials discovered that they had planned for many contingencies but didn't anticipate having their communications system virtually wiped out. Creative managers there proved almost unimaginably inventive in salvaging communications. Around the country, local officials discovered that their emergency response plans, devised for hurricanes or floods, were inadequate to manage a terrorist threat.

The terrorist attacks and the government responses were unprecedented. This book argues, however, that they were especially tragic examples of a far broader and deeper problem: that the way we think about and study public administration is out of sync with the way we practice it. The result of this disjunction is a serious challenge to the cost, effectiveness, and responsiveness of American government.

At the core is an emerging gap between *government* and *governance*. *Government* refers to the structure and function of public institutions. *Governance* is the way government gets its job done. Traditionally, government itself managed most service delivery. Toward the end of the twentieth century, however, government relied increasingly on nongovernmental partners to do its work, through processes that relied less on authority for control. We have advanced theories about government, how it works, and how we can make it work better. Our theory for understanding the relationship between government and the nongovernmental partners who play a critical role in executing government policy, on the other hand, is underdeveloped. The gap between how we have traditionally thought about government and governance itself has widened. That poses fundamental challenges to ideas that reach back to Jefferson and Hamilton—and to management practice that stretches out into the twenty-first century. Sorting through those challenges is the aim of this book.

The book's principal aim is to examine the historical traditions of American public administration, to identify the challenges facing it, and to chart the tensions between what it has to do and its capacity to do it. This volume will not attempt to offer comprehensive solutions, although it concludes with a blueprint of ten basic strategies for building a new approach to the field. Rather, its goal is to frame a research agenda: why theory and practice have increasingly failed to connect with the problems of American public administration—and why attacking these problems head-on is a critical and inescapable challenge for twenty-first century American government.

Acknowledgments to the First Edition

In preparing this book, I was fortunate to have received generous financial assistance from the Smith Richardson Foundation, the University of Wisconsin–Madison's Robert M. La Follette School of Public Affairs, and the university's Graduate School, for support of the book's research and writing. I am deeply indebted to them for their assistance.

Two anonymous readers contributed the kind of thorough comments about which authors can only dream. They forced me to think even more carefully about the book's themes and arguments, and I am truly grateful to them for prodding me to straighten the furrows the book has plowed. Moreover, my editor at Johns Hopkins, Henry Tom, has proven more patient and helpful than any author has a right to expect. Series editor Michael Nelson contributed great insight and unflagging support. The book's copyeditor, Alice Honeywell, discovered the hidden meanings of some phrases that were struggling to see the light. They all have my deep thanks.

An earlier version of chapter 6 appeared as "The Transformation of Governance: Globalization, Devolution, and the Role of Government," in *Public Administration Review* 60 (November/December 2000): 488–97. This paper, in turn, grew out of work done by the Priority Issues Task Force of the National Academy of Public Administration. The Task Force engaged in spirited and stimulating debate about the future of the field. Its members spurred me to consider carefully the links between the field's deep traditions and its emerging challenges: Mark Abramson, Donald Borut, Jonathan Breul, Peter Harkness, Steven Kelman, Valerie Lemmie, Naomi B. Lynn, David Mathews, David Mathiasen, Brian O'Connell, and Susan Schwab.

Finally, my wife, Sue, provided constant support and encouragement. I'm more grateful to her than she could know.

The Transformation of Governance

Chapter One

Administrative Paradoxes

Toward the end of 2000, junkfoodaholics suffered through a major crisis. The puffy corn munchies adored by millions of snackers suddenly disappeared from store shelves. Why? Producers feared that genetically engineered corn, approved for animal feed but not for human consumption, had found its way into the manufacturing process. Rather than risk harm to consumers—and a public relations debacle—the producers took the puffs off the market until they could check the manufacturing lines. Some consumers complained of a "puff paucity," but grocery store owners reassured buyers that crunchy snacks were still available, and they outsold the puffy ones by a ratio of twenty to one.[1] Snackers were relieved, but recalls of corn-based products swept the nation's grocery stores. Kellogg's shut down production at a Memphis plant, Kraft asked that its taco shells be removed from the shelves, and even Japanese merchants soon joined the product recalls. The cheese puff problem had become a genuine foreign policy crisis.

The problem flowed from the invention of a new genetically engineered brand of corn named "StarLink." Farmers had long been plagued by the European corn borer, a pest that devoured the grain before it could reach market. American farmers annually lost hundreds of millions of dollars in corn to the insect's voracious appetite. Organic farmers, however, had discovered that a natural insecticide called "Bt" would kill the corn borer, and long-term research had shown Bt to be safe. Genetic scientists at Aventis, a biotech company employing upwards of 95,000 people in more than 120 countries, discovered a way to implant a bacteria gene in corn to produce Bt. Farmers could simply plant the new breed of corn—StarLink—and allow the grain's genes to do the work instead of using an expensive hit-or-miss spray that also carried greater environmental risk.

Although farmers saw the seed as a huge boon, health experts worried that the corn could cause harm. In addition to the Bt, the bioengineered corn also contained a protein, Cry9C, which had caused allergies in some people. Aventis scientists did not believe that the small concentrations of Cry9C posed any real health danger, but to be on the safe side, government regulators initially approved the seed for use only as animal feed. In addition, the Environmental Protection Agency (EPA) mandated a 660-foot buffer zone around all fields containing Star-Link to prevent cross-pollination with corn grown for human consumption.

In marketing StarLink, Aventis had counted on a long-term winner. By 2000, the bioengineered seed already accounted for about 1 percent of the 80 million acres of corn grown in the United States. Soon, however, the reports of contaminated corn chips began, followed by recalled corn tortillas and shutdowns of the corn flakes line among cereal producers. Some farmers complained that seed salespeople never told them of the mandated buffer zone. Some farmers even said that the salespeople never informed them that StarLink was not yet approved for human consumption. Because of careless planting, some of which was inadvertent, pollen from the StarLink corn blew into fields with corn being grown for human use. Some corn grown for human consumption became cross-pollinated with StarLink, while other corn that had been separated from StarLink was later shipped on barges or in rail cars or stored in silos that, in turn, contained contaminated corn. Once any StarLink corn became mixed with corn certified for human consumption, screening tests for Cry9C would show that the entire shipment was suspect.

Some of this corn found its way into American factories. Other supplies spread through the food and grain transportation systems as well. Japanese officials, for example, discovered that a corn flour mix sold for home baking contained StarLink residue. That was triple trouble for American farmers. Japan was the single biggest importer of U.S. agricultural products. Japan had approved StarLink for neither human nor animal consumption, and Japanese citizens were especially leery about bioengineered food products. The domestic problem thus quickly became an international crisis as well.

Aventis managers saw the problem primarily as a technical one that they could solve through a regulatory waiver. If the EPA would temporarily permit

StarLink to be sold for human consumption, they would no longer risk violating the regulations. Because of the low concentrations of Cry9C, the company's scientists suspected that the corn was highly unlikely to cause any problems for humans in any event. They thought they could resolve the international issues by having the U.S. Department of Agriculture (USDA) test all corn shipments bound for Japan for StarLink residue. The Japanese government, in addition, pledged to conduct random tests to ensure that no StarLink corn entered the country. This combined strategy, Aventis hoped, would end the embarrassing headlines and get the corn back to market.

But the problems continued. Even after the import ban, traces of StarLink were found again in Japan. In the United States, the product continued to pop up throughout the food chain. Archer Daniels Midland (ADM), one of the largest U.S. agricultural giants, announced that its plants would no longer accept bioengineered crops that did not have worldwide approval. In many European nations, citizen concern about bioengineered crops was rising. Governments were considering proposals to require more labeling about the source and content of food items, and ADM simply did not want to risk its worldwide business by purchasing StarLink products.

Aventis argued that the health worries were overblown, but the international complaints had created an escalating public relations disaster. In January 2001, Aventis staged a retreat: It announced that it was asking the EPA to cancel StarLink's registration, which would effectively withdraw the product from the market. Aventis also announced a plan, costing hundreds of millions of dollars, to compensate farmers and grain elevators in seventeen states whose crops were contaminated with StarLink and were thus unmarketable. These steps, Aventis hoped, would put the problem quickly behind them. Japanese officials, however, soon discovered even more StarLink in imported corn. American brewers found traces of StarLink in cornmeal used in making beer. Once the corn crept into the human food chain, Aventis officials found it unexpectedly difficult to remove. StarLink researchers argued that normal food processing would destroy any Cry9C residue that might make its way into supply chains, but the science failed to reassure worried consumers. Food producers had no wish to risk their reputations on corn that might provoke a consumer backlash and backed away from StarLink.

The StarLink episode was the quintessential twenty-first century policy problem. New technology offered great advances, but it also created huge uncertainty and potential risk. Faced with scientific uncertainty and political attack—some critics labeled bioengineered products like StarLink "Frankenfoods"—the ground shifted under food producers. No matter how small the risk, the *perceptions* of danger drove the policy agenda. When scientists discovered even small traces of Cry9C in corn used for corn chips and other products, worried manufacturers recalled the product. Once recall fever started, further scientific research mattered little. From Japanese corn to American cheese puffs, public concern about the safety of the food supply pushed the issue squarely onto the policy agenda, and citizens literally around the world demanded that their governments respond.

The StarLink problem defied any effort to assign responsibility for solving it. StarLink was produced by Aventis, a French-based global corporation, and marketed by its agricultural division, Aventis CropScience, with American operations based in North Carolina's Research Triangle. In announcing the creation of CropScience in December 1999, the company's president proudly said, "Our objective is to bring to the North American farmer the innovative and effective products that are solutions to the challenges he faces—and in the process, create an effective partnership with him."[2] Within a year, the StarLink problem had seriously scarred its reputation, and the company's efforts to market the new product ended, at least for a while.

Within American government, multiple agencies regulated the product. The EPA granted the initial approval to use StarLink for animals but not for humans. The USDA's Grains Inspection, Packers, and Stockyards Administration oversaw corn shipments, including exports to Japan. Its Kansas City laboratories tested samples for traces of Cry9C. The Food and Drug Administration (FDA) conducted voluntary screening of bioengineered food and, in general, monitored the safety of the food supply. The Centers for Disease Control, part of the U.S. Department of Health and Human Services, along with the FDA, examined the cases of forty-four people who blamed Cry9C for allergic reactions along with possibly life-threatening anaphylactic shock. These regulators shared jurisdiction. In addition, unlike in most countries around the world, the EPA sometimes granted "split approval," which could approve the use of a product for animal feed but not for consumption by humans. The EPA said the decision was a halfway step that allowed initial production of StarLink as researchers completed research into the grain's effects on humans. Critics, however, worried that corn approved for animals would find its way into the human food chain. The result, however, was a public relations nightmare for Aventis. It was a biotech scare for many consumers. It was a foreign relations dilemma for American regulators.

And it was an extraordinarily complex regulatory problem for three federal agencies.

The Study of Administration

The StarLink case was, in short, the prototype for twenty-first century management problems. It was a problem that demanded a solution, but no agency had the responsibility or the leverage to solve it. Government's response by necessity had to involve teamwork among a host of regulatory agencies as well as cooperation of private companies, from Aventis and food manufacturers to food shippers and individual farmers. Americans had to satisfy both the Japanese government and Japanese consumers. Even these efforts could not truly "solve" the problem. The Americans could only contain the problem and, in the end, hope it would ebb as StarLink gradually disappeared from the food and distribution chains. Those hopes were frustrated by continuing discovery of StarLink corn in the food chain, even months after regulators thought they had solved the problem.

Government agencies thus could not truly solve, control, or even manage the problem. At best, they could collaborate in framing a response. Neither was it an issue for which the theories of public administration offered an adequate solution. For a century, the field had built its approach on service delivery, basing that service delivery on theories of hierarchy and authority. The StarLink case grew out of a complex problem that simply did not fit standard hierarchical, authority-based systems. As a result, the case presented policymakers with problems for which neither they nor the theory on which they operated were prepared. Government found itself ill equipped for the problems it had to solve, and administrative theory proved a poor match for the world in which it attempted to operate.

BOUNDARIES AND PUBLIC ADMINISTRATION

The theory and practice of modern American public administration date from the end of the nineteenth century. The rise of the industrial age had gradually pushed aside the agrarian lifestyle and put large, complex private corporations at the center of American economic life. As the market grew for cheap, standardized goods, the budding corporations developed new systems of mass production, including the assembly line and other new processes. Entrepreneurs discovered the advantages of monopoly. Citizens complained that the muscle of corporate trusts drove prices up, limited market choice, and weakened citizens' autonomy. They complained that private utilities ignored some neighborhoods and that other companies produced unsafe products. Tough market competition produced wildly fluctuating interest rates, especially between the heavy borrowing season (for spring planting) and the heavy repayment season (during fall harvest). The concentration of capital, especially in the East, enraged those who needed it for development, especially in the West. In these and scores of other cases, the rise of corporate power created new demands for a stronger government.

The Progressives responded by arguing for a more powerful government, one powerful enough to tackle these demands and yet be insulated from political influence. In 1883, Congress took the first step toward forming a modern public administration by creating the federal civil service system. By the turn of the twentieth century, this modern public administration was in full flower.[3] Frank J. Goodnow, whom Paul P. Van Riper views as "the effective founder of academic public administration in the United States," wrote influential works on administrative law and the relationship of politics and administration.[4] The Taft Commission, which recommended a consolidated executive budget in its 1912 report, included such public administration notables as Frederick A. Cleveland (as chairman), W. F. Willoughby, and Goodnow.[5] Congress later enacted the commission's key recommendations. As governor of Wisconsin, Robert M. La Follette pressed the Progressive agenda, which embodied a positive role for government and the need for an effective government to play that role. In 1911, a training program was created to prepare public administrators to meet government's new responsibilities. That program later grew into Syracuse University's Maxwell School of Citizenship, now the oldest academic public administration program in the country.

The Progressive movement espoused a belief in strong government, a government that pursued both administratively efficient and politically accountable strategies. Furthermore, the Progressives aimed to create a government that solved public problems at the lowest cost for taxpayers—and that ensured government would ultimately be accountable to citizens, not to large corporate interests. The Progressives' belief in effective government led, in turn, to a theory of public administration built on principles of technical professionalism and political neutrality. The Taft Commission's proposal for a comprehensive executive budget, for example, advanced the norms of rational-comprehensive analysis and executive-centered control. Goodnow's work underlined the role of administrative law as a way of establishing clear, uniform, procedural standards for administrative action. Following on the Teapot Dome and other late-nineteenth-century scandals, the field's early thinkers insisted on strong ethics.

The rise of public administration also brought new technologies to government, like the Burroughs adding machine, punch cards for automating the census, typewriters, and a decimal system (invented by Melvil Dewey) for classifying library books—a system later adapted for filing papers in the War Department. Army engineers accomplished what had been thought nearly impossible—digging a canal across the Panamanian isthmus. The result, in the early part of the twentieth century, was what Paul P. Van Riper has called "an heretical and explosive idea," the thought "that the modern administrative state, properly directed, could accomplish almost anything it might envision and at reasonable cost."[6]

They built a new civil service system and created independent regulatory agencies. They constructed a unified executive budget that pulled decision-making into one place and gave the president power to shape the government's overall fiscal policy. In many ways, for better or worse, they built the foundation for the modern federal establishment—on a commitment to a strong government that worked well but that ultimately was accountable to elected officials. They were not devoted to an expansion of government power as much as they were committed to solving the people's problems. Well schooled in the warnings of the founders about the potential abuse of executive power, they nested the more-powerful executive in the balance-of-powers system created to ensure that no branch of government could misuse its power at the expense of the citizenry.

But if they were not devoted to expanding administrative power as an end in itself, the direct product of their work was indeed a stronger executive. They were cognizant of the risks, so they drew elaborate boundaries to prevent, they hoped, the strong executive from straying too far into political decisions or abuses of individual liberty. In fact, the creation of orthodox public administration by the Progressives at the turn of the twentieth century was as much about building boundaries as strengthening administrative structures—restraining government power to make it accountable while empowering government to make it effective.[7] Its proponents struggled with a central dilemma—how to make government administration strong enough to cope with the increasingly complex problems of the modernizing world. On the other hand, they shared the worries of the nation's founders—worries well founded in their experience with the British king—that strong government could rob citizens of their liberty. The Progressives thus struggled first to define and then to solve the central problem of the modern administrative state as it operated in a democracy: How could it be made strong enough to work without risking tyranny? Their answer, in general, was to strengthen administration but also to limit its power.

For the Progressives, the most important boundary was between policy-*making* and policy *administration*. Policymakers, elected by citizens, would craft public decisions and delegate responsibility to administrators. They defined clearly what each agency's job was and, by extension, what it was not. The principle of hierarchy defined clearly each administrator's responsibilities. Complex missions could be separated into their individual components, each component could be assigned to individual administrators, and administrators would know what they were—and were not—charged with doing. The principle of authority would hold everyone in the system accountable. Policymakers delegated authority to the bureaucracy, and higher-level bureaucrats could use authority to control what their subordinates did. The application of these two principles—hierarchy and authority—would promote efficiency by allowing the creation of sophisticated bureaucracies full of highly skilled workers. It would promote accountability by specifying the relationship of each worker to policymakers. It would remove administration from the political chaos that had often crippled it in the past. And it would do all of these things by carefully structuring the work within clear boundaries.

This approach dominated both the theory and practice of American public administration throughout most of the twentieth century. When the Depression brought a new wave of problems, Franklin D. Roosevelt's New Deal created new government reforms in the Progressive spirit. New problems led to new government programs, and new programs spawned new government agencies. When the Brownlow Committee concluded that "the president needs help," the new Executive Office of the President emerged to supervise better the executive branch's expanded domain.[8]

World War II helped bring orthodox public administration to the apex of its influence. Its experts built the Pentagon in an extraordinarily short time and then worked from the Pentagon to manage the war effort. Many of the nation's best public administrationists—professionals trained in the art and science of managing government programs—came to Washington to help run the war effort. They ensured that the Progressives left an indelible mark on American government. Their success in the vast complexity of mounting and winning a two-front war sealed the Progressives' legacy. So it was scarcely surprising that, when the war ended, President Truman, a Democrat, appointed Herbert Hoover, a

Republican engineer-as-president-as-government-efficiency-expert, to chair two long-running commissions, which, in turn, transformed how government worked.[9] It had become unthinkable to build a government without simultaneously worrying about how to make it work, to plan government policy without thinking about how best to manage it, or to consider how best to manage it without consulting the best thinkers of American public administration.

The postwar high point of orthodox public administration, however, did not anticipate emerging crises, both pragmatic and intellectual. The field had few good answers about how to manage new programs intended to eliminate poverty or urban blight. Frustrated elected officials began turning to other sources for advice in designing and running programs. Meanwhile, beginning in the 1950s, the social sciences in general devoted themselves to becoming more scientific. Orthodox public administration, long as much art as science and as much philosophy as theory, found itself increasingly squeezed from the central role it had played for three generations. Its scholars lamented the erosion of respect, while practitioners looked far more broadly for guidance. Public administration was suffering from a genuine intellectual crisis.[10] The boundaries that had limited both theory and practice for three generations no longer seemed appropriate for the nation's emerging problems.

BOUNDARIES AND POLITICAL SCIENCE

Among public administration theorists, this crisis could not have been more jarring. Public administration, after all, had been one of the original subfields of the American Political Science Association when it was established in 1903, along with comparative government (as applied to the governance of colonies), public law (through constitutional law and jurisprudence), international law, and political theory. The association's first president was perhaps the most prominent public administrationist of the day, Frank J. Goodnow. Goodnow preached the critical connection between theory and practice.[11]

For the next generation, public administration helped shape the emerging discipline of political science. The field proved attractive to students, and in 1940, public administration accounted for one-fifth of all Ph.D.'s awarded in political science.[12] Franklin D. Roosevelt gave the field's thinkers a front-line education by bringing them to Washington to help run the New Deal and World War II. All in all, it had been a stunning half century: one that helped to give birth to a new discipline, shaped that discipline's development, and brought the field's knowledge to policymakers.

By the 1960s, all that had changed. The social sciences put a far greater emphasis on the development of scientific knowledge. That, in turn, shifted the focus of much administrative theory from the traditional focus on organizational structure to human interactions, especially the power relationships and motivations that drive them. Herbert Simon, a social scientist who won the Nobel Prize for economics, argued that decision-making, not organizational structure, was the central problem of administration.[13] The emerging focus on decisions and power ran counter to orthodox public administration's focus on organizational structure and process. Rooted so deeply in that orthodoxy, public administration found it hard to change, and even sympathetic analysts despaired about whether public administration could ever truly become a science.[14]

These worries about public administration surfaced precisely as political science, sociology, and especially economics together sought a more scientific footing. A new generation of postwar social sciences wanted more rigor: theories that produced predictions, predictions that could be tested, tests that could be replicated. The search for more science in the social sciences brought, in particular, new statistical methods. These methods were especially hard on public administration. Public administration researchers had been used to working at the organizational level and, within the organization, on administrative process. To be valid and reliable, the new statistical methods demanded large numbers of units to study. Organizations typically occurred in groups of just a few, and organizational processes proved hard to model. The traditional study of public administration thus did not match the new analytical techniques sweeping the social sciences, so as they rose in influence, the study of public administration became more marginal.

At that high level of analysis, moreover, the same circumstances rarely repeat themselves. Unlike the scientific approaches the other social sciences were beginning to champion, traditional public administration rarely sought to predict outcomes. Rather, public administration grew from the "scientific management" movement of the late nineteenth and early twentieth centuries, which was led by analysts like Frederick W. Taylor.[15] The legacy of the scientific management approach infuriated the postwar social scientists. They tended to view public administration as little more than a collection of fuzzy proverbs that sometimes conflicted and that, in any event, provided weak guides for both theory and action.[16] The new social scientists looked longingly at their colleagues in the natural sciences, where advances in everything from biochemistry to nuclear physics fueled an explosive growth in theory and in government financial support.

In political science, this new work focused on the behavior of individuals. Berelson, Lazarsfeld, and McPhee's classic 1954 study, *Voting*, brought statistical research to voting behavior.[17] Dahl's *Who Governs?* shaped the study of small-scale pluralistic influences on political life.[18] Analysis of institutions, especially of the bureaucracy, fell in prestige within political science. In the view of the emerging orthodoxy, bureaucracies were too few to be analyzed statistically, whereas there were millions of voters whose decisions could be studied. Public administration theory yielded too vague a set of hypotheses for careful testing. As statistical methods and individual-level analysis became more popular in political science, public administration dramatically slipped in prestige. One of the field's giants, Dwight Waldo, sadly noted the split between the emerging political science orthodoxy and the traditional approach to public administration. That, Waldo believed, was ironic, given public administration's central role in helping found the discipline of political science: "It is now unrealistic and unproductive to regard public administration as a subdivision of political science. . . . The truth is that the attitude of political scientists (other than those accepting public administration as their 'field') is at best one of indifference and is often one of undisguised contempt or hostility. We are now hardly welcome in the house of our youth."[19]

At the beginning of the twentieth century, public administration and political science were inseparable. By the century's midpoint, the two fields were asking different questions (searching for predictability instead of prescription) using different levels of analysis (individuals instead of institutions) and different analytical methods (statistics instead of common sense). In a little more than half a century, the two fields went from seamless connection to a strained relationship. In the view of some public administration scholars, the stress was leading to an outright divorce.

BOUNDARIES AND PUBLIC POLICY

Similar problems plagued public administration's efforts to train practitioners. The practical side of the field had always had an uneasy place within political science. In the American Political Science Association's first decade, public administrationists made an abortive effort to launch a training program. In the end, they decided to stay within political science, in part because they had no other discipline to which they could go. Still, public administrationists worried that political scientists had little appreciation for the need to train individuals in the practice as well as the study of government. For their part, political scientists worried that a focus on training would deflect energy from the more important task of building the intellectual foundation for the new field. They made an uneasy but highly productive truce, and in every major university around the country, public administration proved one of the cornerstones of the political science department.

The New Deal and its administrative challenges scratched the pragmatic itch of many public administrationists. In 1939, these pragmatists formed the new American Society for Public Administration (ASPA), largely because they believed they needed a new institutional home in which to train public servants more effectively. Faced with the enduring question of whether they were pursuing science or practice, the ASPA embraced all the competing perspectives by dedicating itself to the "science, process, and art of public administration." ASPA leaders played critical roles in governments throughout the country, especially during World War II.

The same forces that eroded public administration's place in political science soon reduced its influence in training public servants as well. In the early 1960s, the Kennedy administration's "whiz kids" brought a new commitment to policy analysis and an argument that microeconomics provided a powerful—indeed, a superior—analytical tool for producing efficiency. Orthodox public administration sought efficiency through structure and process. Microeconomics pursued Simon's argument that decisions mattered most and sought to use rigorous methods to prescribe the right policy judgments. At the very least, microeconomics had a patently reassuring feel to it. It was exacting. It grew from a straightforward theory and led to relatively unambiguous prescriptions. As public administration was criticized for offering flimsy proverbs and platitudes, microeconomics rose to present clear guidance. That is not to say that the guidance was always useful or correct. One of the whiz kids' central projects, the development of a new tactical fighter to be shared by the navy and the air force, thus slashing development and procurement costs, failed. Both services continued to add requirements until the plane eventually worked for neither. But in the face of public administration's reputation for fuzziness, there was something powerful and persuasive about an approach that gave clear answers.

Many major universities had long-established public administration programs that became the centerpieces of orthodox public administration. Syracuse University's Maxwell School of Citizenship and Public Affairs, for example, began in 1924 with six students. The program focused on training "teachers of citizenship" and "practitioners of public affairs."[20] The Maxwell program, and scores like it, produced thousands of graduates who went into government service. Such programs also housed the field's best scholars and produced a generation of scholarship that defined the field and helped run the country.

In the 1960s, however, the desire for stronger economics-based prescriptions fueled the rise of public policy schools in direct competition with—indeed, rejection of—public administration programs. For example, Harvard's Littauer Graduate School of Public Administration, established in 1936 with the same mission as Syracuse's Maxwell School, gradually shifted to the Simon-based decision-making approach. In the spirit of the Kennedy administration's whiz kids, the program incorporated more microeconomics and policy analysis. Friends of the Kennedy family created the Institute of Politics and, eventually, a school renamed in the assassinated president's honor.

The public policy movement grew from an assumption that orthodox public administration had reached a dead end. Its enthusiasts agreed with Simon that decisions were central and that most of the field's theory was excruciatingly simplistic. The field's scholars started essentially from scratch by creating a new approach, which they named "public management." The field rejected the orthodox public administration focus on organizational structure and process. The public policy movement rejected the field's emphasis on the organization of the unit of analysis as its method of drawing insights from common sense. Instead, public policy focused on public decisions (What fighter plane should we buy? How does the State Department shape foreign policy?) and individual policy areas (like transportation, welfare, housing, or defense). It drew its method from the business school practice of extracting insights from close analysis of cases.

The touchstone of public policy was Richard Neustadt's *Presidential Power*. He built on the decision-based approach of Herbert Simon and the power-based approach of Norton Long. Neustadt's preface was seductive to scholars seeking to build a new field: "My theme is personal power and its politics: what it is, how to get it, how to keep it, how to use it."[21] The president's power built on the "power to persuade." For the new students of public policy, that focused their work on the personal interactions of high-level players, instead of the front-line activities of administrative minions. To gain insights about how this worked, they wrote case studies that provided rich detail of such decisions.

Graham Allison's classic on the Cuban missile crisis, *Essence of Decision*, became the model for how case analysis could illuminate the study of public decisions. He developed three alternative models for explaining decisions in the crisis. "Model I" presented a classical model of rational actors making rational decisions. "Model II" explained decisions in terms of basic organizational theory and standard operating procedures. "Model III" put the case in the context of bureaucratic politics. Allison quite carefully explained that these were alternative models and that none of them presented the "correct" approach.[22] Nevertheless, his readers—especially in the new public policy community—immediately gravitated to Model III. Model I's "rational actor" approach conveyed the basic journalistic who-what-when-how story and provided few new insights. Model II's "standard operating procedures" approach laid out the pathologies of bureaucratic action, especially how the standard operating procedures of the military on both sides almost led to major irremediable miscalculations—and nuclear war. It was Model III that produced the new insights: central players make the important decisions; the places where they sit affect the decisions they make; and government decisions can be understood as political results. It was clear that the political instincts of the key players, especially John and Robert Kennedy, had helped shape the key decisions at the critical moments, and it was also clear that these instincts ran against the interpretations suggested by Models I and II.

In one stroke, Allison portrayed the behaviors stimulated by orthodox public administration as pathologies to be managed—that management had to come through skilled leaders who could negotiate bureaucratic politics. This approach proved a serious, nearly fatal blow to orthodox public administration. It reinforced the emerging belief that orthodox public administration had led to inflexible, rules-oriented organizations that frustrated the ability of leaders to lead. It strengthened the case of analysts who argued the need for stronger leaders who could cure the pathologies of administration. It supported the budding movement toward a decision-based, case-driven management approach.

In fact, analysts argued that there was a "missing link" in the study of public policy—bringing decisions to action.[23] Pressman and Wildavsky's instant classic, *Implementation*, sealed the argument. They explained that in preparing the book, they assumed that "there is (or there must be) a large literature about implementation in the social sciences. . . . It must be there; it should be there; but in fact it is not."[24] That surprised orthodox public administrationists, who had always believed that their field had been exploring these questions for generations. If the problem was not new, the movement and its approach were. The implementation movement rejected the primarily structural and procedural approach of orthodox public administration in favor of a policy-based approach. And it began with an assumption that the fledgling movement needed to start from scratch.

Some of the problem, moreover, flowed from how public administration tended to approach administrative problems. Rooted far more than most political science in pragmatism, public administration focused much more on *prescriptions*. And much more than most political actions, administration is full of vast complications, irresolvable conundrums, and eternal dilemmas. Should managers decentralize to increase the responsiveness of their programs or centralize to improve accountability? Should they organize by function to improve specialization or by area to strengthen coordination?

Even in its more recent search for theoretical rigor, pragmatic imperatives have driven the field. In part, this is because many of the scholars who craft its literature also teach students who have (or seek) public-sector jobs. Trying to build theory from the work of public managers has always proven difficult, Behn argues, because managers manage by "groping along."[25] The complexity of public problems and the multiple strategies of the public officials who wrestle with them have made finding, or even imposing, predictable patterns difficult. The constant tensions between administrative theories and public events have, on one hand, always kept public administrationists busy. On the other hand, struggling with difficult problems and uncertain solutions has made the search for predictable patterns an endless and, ultimately, frustrating one. It seeks to give practitioners grounding in coping with their daily lives; students a foundation for the careers they hope to explore; and scholars a precision in how they understand administrative action.

Every academic discipline, and especially every social science field, grapples with such problems. Fields constantly search for "the next big idea," a concept that can both resolve ongoing theoretical battles and powerfully shape future work. Sociology, for example, has dealt with structuralism, deconstruction, poststructuralism, psychoanalysis, post-colonialism, historicism, and empire.[26] Within economics, the study of macro-level behavior ebbed as microeconomics rose—and critics complained that the model-driven approach of some microeconomics had torn the soul out of the field. Political science, torn between an instinct to become more scientific and the urge to ground itself more deeply in the realities of politics, felt the pressure from both sociology and economics. These pressures affected public administration as well, where the simplifying urge of more formal social science theory was at odds with the growing complexity of administrative action. Theorist Edgar H. Schein argued that the "theory in use" tends to endure until reality intervenes with problems and scandals "that cannot be hidden, avoided, or denied."[27] When theories and problems fall out of sync, pressures build for recasting the theory. Among all the areas of social science, public administration has perhaps taken pragmatic problems most seriously. It has always sought a theory to guide practice.

Toward the end of the twentieth century, the growing complexity of public policy problems and the governmental response increasingly confounded theory. In particular, these trends challenged the field's roots in hierarchy and authority; boundaries that once seemed secure became porous. At the same time, public administration's sister fields—political science, economics, and sociology—all pressed toward more rigorous theories. Public administration found itself trying to span growing gaps: between its own intellectual heritage and the emerging realities of twenty-first century administration; and between its own intellectual pursuits and those of the other social sciences.

The tensions have also come from the search for *prescriptions* amid academic pursuits based on *predictions*. The goal of political science—and related fields, like public management—is to have a strong analytical framework that generates replicable propositions. What are the central, repeating patterns of political life? How will voters vote, judges decide, legislators legislate—or administrators manage? Predictions build on an effort to simplify reality. Prescriptions, on the other hand, flow from an understanding of the rich complexity of political and administrative life. The search for answers to the basic questions—What do we know? What should we do?—lead in opposite directions. Those seeking prescriptions are often surprisingly comfortable with ambiguity and complexity; they often look for *how to think about* issues as much as *what to do*. The search for simple, straightforward, replicable, verifiable propositions leaves little room for ambiguity and the "It's complicated!" approach to analysis.

That, at its core, defines public administration's basic problem. For a century, it has sought both an accepted place in academic theory and a voice in the debate over important policy puzzles. These goals have always pulled public administration in opposite directions, toward theoretical parsimony and pragmatic richness. In the last half of the twentieth century, these tensions pushed public administration near the breaking point. The social sciences have worked to make their research more scientific. The policy world has become more intricate, with more federal-state-local partnerships, more public-private linkages, and more transnational action. The demands for parsimony have grown even as complexity has increased. Rooted fundamentally in difficult theoretical puzzles, public administration has struggled as well with practical problems that have become even harder.

It is tempting to attack these problems by moving away from public administration's roots—by seeking *either* pragmatic policy advice *or* theoretical rigor. That course is surely the road to intellectual defeat, however. Theory without the ability to predict and understand something real and important is not worth having. Political action without theoretical structure is dangerous, especially in the American political system, where political traditions and ideas have always had great sway. Public administration without a guiding theory is risky; administrative theory without connection to action is meaningless. That dilemma is the foundation of a genuine intellectual crisis in public administration.

This is more than just a quaint intellectual debate among academics. Public trust in government depends, at least to some degree, on government's ability to produce results. Effective oversight of administration by elected officials hinges on their ability to understand the management systems they create to implement policy. Global economic and political systems pose challenges that participants only dimly understand. Solving tough problems thus requires substantial intellectual capital. Efforts to govern without investing in that intellectual capital will inevitably be impoverished. That is surely all the more true as tight budgets make it harder for governments to devise new programs and where much of the action lies inevitably in making existing programs work better.

Meanwhile, new interdisciplinary public policy programs sprang up in the late 1960s and early 1970s. These programs focused sharply on how to improve the performance of public programs and on how to make public managers more effective in managing these programs. Traditional public administration had focused, for nearly a century, on the structure of government organizations and the processes (especially budgeting and personnel systems) that drove them. The intellectual leaders of the new public policy movement did not find the traditional approaches useful, and they self-consciously pushed them aside in creating their new programs.

While some public policy scholars like Pressman and Wildavsky worried about "why it's amazing that federal programs work at all," as the subtitle of their book read in part, others asked how effective leaders could produce strong results. Implementation scholars focused on the program as the unit of analysis (just as public administrationists looked at structure and process). In many of the new public policy schools, analysts used case studies to understand how individuals—especially high-level officials in government agencies—could make a difference. "Leadership counts" was the watchword.[28] Unlike the implementation scholars, they saw the solution in individual leadership rather than analysis of programs. Like the implementation scholars, however, they found public administration sorely lacking. They developed, instead, a new focus—"public management"—to replace a discipline they found tired and disconnected from the theoretical challenges facing both theory and practice.

In addition to dodging salvos from political science and public policy, public administration found itself under attack from the practitioner community as well. Public cynicism, rising expectations, more complicated programs, and political crossfire combined to create imposing challenges for government managers. Many of the old theories seemed to fit poorly, and hard-pressed managers scrambled for fresh insights. When they looked to public administration theory, they found few answers that fit their new challenges well. Many managers, in fact, felt strangely alone, jury-rigging tactics to fit their own situations. They had little sense of which managers shared their problems and which solutions fit which problems best. While many public administration scholars rejected the lively arguments in Osborne and Gaebler's *Reinventing Government,* many practitioners eagerly embraced their message of hope. The result was a growing gap between those who *taught* public administration and those who *lived* it.

Private managers and business theorists have seized the intellectual lead in management practice. They invented new ideas like total quality management, customer service, reengineering, and a host of others. Some produced quick results. Others soon failed. Many proved to be fads that ebbed away. Regardless of their ultimate success, however, the energy created a flood of new ideas—and, with the vacuum of engaging new approaches in public administration, the private sector ideas quickly swept through public management as well. The more private sector ideas took hold, the weaker public administration's theoretical claims became. At the same time, many of the private ideas worked no better in government agencies than they had in corporations. That left public administration adrift, without a strong set of its own cutting-edge theories yet saddled with private sector ideas that, at best, were a poor fit.[29] Administrative theory often found itself not one but two bounces behind.

It was scarcely the case that administration had become less important, either in American society or in the academy. If anything, policy goals had become more ambitious, tight budgets made it harder to create new programs, and the execution of existing programs became more complicated. Administration was more, not less, central to the aspirations of citizens and elected officials alike. Public administration, however, was less sure about how to speak to these issues.

In a century, public administration had gone from playing a central role in academic research to being a relatively marginal player. Political science's push toward behavioralism and formal theory left public administration on the sidelines. Practitioners complained that it provided weak guidance to those on government's front lines, and they sought solutions elsewhere. To provide better training—and, they would argue, better research—scholars in the public policy schools put most of public administration aside in favor of new approaches to implementation, leadership, and public management.

It is hard to dispute the sense that the field lost its intellectual footing—that it struggled for respect from those for whom, a century before, it had been vital and central. Indeed, public administration found itself stranded between two problems: it possessed a theoretical tradition that no longer fit reality, and it faced tough new policy problems for which the theory had few good answers. To make matters worse, it was hard to escape a nagging sense that public administration was lagging behind the intellectual curve, with ideas and innovations from the practice of administration far in advance of most of the field's literature. That, in fact, was the underlying message of the StarLink problem.

Public administration scarcely slid away. It continues to claim one of the largest contingents of scholars within the American Political Science Association. The American Society for Public Administration continues to publish a first-rate journal, *Public Administration Review,* and its annual meetings continue to attract hundreds of practitioners and scholars alike. New journals, like the *Journal of Public Administration Research and Theory,* have produced significant theoretical advances. Even a casual look at the academic scholarship shows that the field's intellectual energy and dynamism continues to grow. Intellectual inquiry in public administration, in fact, began an important renaissance as the twentieth century ended.

Along with the rise of the public management movement came greater compartmentalization of the field. Political scientists focused on the study of elected executives, especially presidents, governors, and mayors. Public management scholars focused on appointed executives, like cabinet officials, senior advisers, and other key policymakers. Public administrationists focused on career executives and front-line administrators. The same compartmentalization occurred within the respective disciplinary homes of these scholars: the American Political Science Association for students of the executive; the Association for Public Policy Analysis and Management for students of appointees; and the National Association of Schools of Public Affairs and Administration for students of careerists. As Laurence Lynn Jr. has perceptively noted: "The partitioning of the domain distorts the study of public management and, ultimately, our understanding of it. Scholars in the two largest academic provinces, public policy and public administration, have tended to be—there is no better word for it—provincial. Sociologically they fraternize or collaborate infrequently, and intellectually they cite each other's work irregularly."[30]

This fragmentation has created new boundaries in the field's research and training. Political scientists studying executives have focused on broad historical trends as well as more systematic analysis of presidential decisions. They have not worried much about training. For public management scholars, leadership by political appointees is what counts, so they have concentrated heavily on understanding the personal attributes and skills of effective leaders.[31] Public administration continues doggedly to train thousands of public servants a year, but its struggles to regain a toehold in political science, cope with the rising tide of public management, and compete with the public policy schools have led to genuine soul-searching.[32]

BOUNDARIES AND CIVIC LIFE

The different approaches to analysis have rarely intersected, and the proponents of each one have stuck to what they knew. In part, this fragmentation reflects the increasing balkanization of academia in general. In part, it also reflects public administration's instincts for self-preservation. Within political science, the pressure for a more formal, more scientific, model-driven approach has become increasingly powerful. In the 1980s and 1990s, public administrationists occupied a stronger place within political science, but they rarely found their way into the field's governing councils. And within public policy schools, public management scholars encountered serious problems as well. Policy analysis, driven by microeconomics and microeconomists, became increasingly influential. The field offered a clear, persuasive theory of decision. It was a theory derived from widely accepted assumptions, like the individual pursuit of self-interest, and it provided a scheme for both understanding and shaping public decisions. While public policy schools accepted the need to offer public management, it was no secret that many microeconomists viewed public management as a theoretically weak sibling to be tolerated out of necessity but not fed with new resources. As the twenty-first century dawned, each of the major approaches to the study of administration was struggling for legitimacy: struggling with each other for intellectual primacy, struggling within their disciplinary homes for respect, and struggling for a foothold in the public mind.

One sign of this tug-of-war was the rise of the "reinventing government" movement. The best-seller by Osborne and Gaebler became a phenomenon—at least within government circles.[33] It provided ten steps for transforming government, making it more innovative and improving its responsiveness. It fueled the Clinton administration's sweeping reform, led by Vice President Al Gore, and a host of similar initiatives throughout the country. The book had an impact on government unlike anything since the Hoover Commission reports of the 1950s. But unlike the studies produced by academic experts during the heyday of orthodox public administration, *Reinventing Government* was the product of a journalist—David Osborne—and a former city manager—Ted Gaebler. Academics had little to do with either the book or its implementation throughout government. When asked about which academics they relied on for insights, though, Elaine Kamarck, Gore's senior domestic policy adviser, paused, thought carefully, and replied, "Well, really—none."[34]

Thus, the study of administration, management, implementation, and public policy became fragmented and neglected, and it no longer had the impact on decisions that had prompted the development first of public administration and later of public management. This intellectual laryngitis could not have come at a worse time. America's effort to reinvent government was in fact part of a global management reform movement that struggled to help government do more with less. That movement had begun a decade earlier, first in New Zealand and then spreading through the United Kingdom, Canada, international organizations like the World Bank, and even into developing nations.[35] Governments were reforming their administrative systems, simultaneously and on a massive scale, unlike anything seen since the turn of the twentieth century. Unlike in the transition to the twentieth century, led by the Progressives and orthodox public administration, public officials were charting their own course into the twenty-first century, largely without intellectual or moral support from academia.

The Future of Public Administration

The challenge facing government administrators in the twenty-first century is that they can do their jobs by the book and still not get the job done. They can issue regulations as required by Congress and discover that the problems they were seeking to prevent occur nonetheless. They can audit taxes only to discover that they upset taxpayers when they get it right and enrage members of Congress when they get it wrong. They can produce programs that work better and cost less only to discover more demands that they work even harder and spend even less. They can run airport security systems by the book only to have terrorists slip by and crash airplanes into office buildings. The challenge is to rewrite the book to get the job done.

Complicating the task is the fact that government administration—and public administrators—have never remained very popular for very long. Even Jesus raised local eyebrows when he chose a local bureaucrat, Matthew the tax collector, as one of his twelve apostles. Administrators tend to make people happy only when they are providing services (and usually only when the level of service is generous and the cost is low). When services are lower than people expect, or if the costs are too high, people complain. In fact, while wandering in the desert, the Israelites constantly grumbled about Moses' leadership. Why had they not remained in Egypt? they asked.

Administrative reformers move between tinkering and transforming institutions fundamentally. In the American political tradition, the transformations occurred with the creation of the executive branch by the founders; with the Progressive period along with its new processes and structures; and with the generation-long changes that followed World War II. As America entered the twenty-first century, another transformation was in the works. It was subtler than its predecessors. The founders and the Progressives each contributed long tracts to provide intellectual leadership for their reforms. By contrast, the twenty-first century transformation emerged from the triumph of bottom-up pragmatism. Front-line administrators struggled to cobble together new tactics for solving the problems they faced, but new problems often surfaced faster than their solutions could be applied. Administrative orthodoxy became increasingly disconnected from administrative realities. The twenty-first century reformers faced nothing less than the intellectual and governmental crises of the Progressives, and they reached to frame solutions that would prove just as enduring.

Food and Drug Administration (FDA) regulators discovered the problem the hard way. For eight years during the 1990s, the FDA had warned pharmaceutical companies not to use products from cattle in countries plagued by mad cow disease, a fatal brain-based illness that spread from cows to humans in some European countries. Despite the warnings, however, the FDA discovered that five drug companies had continued to use bovine-based ingredients from these countries. In some cases, blood might have been used to grow cultures in the lab.

In other cases, vaccine manufacturers might have made gelatin from the hooves or bones of cows. The FDA also worried that suspect ingredients might have found their way into supplements for humans that claimed to improve memory or stimulate sexual vitality. Even though scientists calculated that the risk was very small, "it's just insane not to have greater safeguards," one senior FDA official said, especially for the supplements. A wide variety of vaccines, including polio, diphtheria, and tetanus administered to children, were affected.[36]

The FDA had recognized the risks very early. It had warned manufacturers not to use the suspect ingredients. In fact, some companies complained they had a hard time keeping up with the FDA's advisories. The FDA had done its job as it was supposed to—yet problems occurred despite its work. As with the StarLink corn episode, a mismatch occurred between how the government did its work and the problems it was trying to solve. As with StarLink, government managers had made clear what they expected private companies to do, but for a variety of reasons, serious problems developed. Citizens and policymakers alike, in the treasured tradition of holding government managers accountable for the results of government programs, had not reduced their expectations.

Policymakers tend to think of government management as a matter of framing decisions, delegating responsibility to administrators, and holding government administrators accountable for results. That approach, of course, defines two centuries of American democracy as well as the driving theory for bureaucracy in most of the world's governments, democratic or not. Policymakers tend to convey a simple and straightforward view of how the administrative process works—almost like a vending machine, into which they put money and out of which they expect results. When the desired product does not pop out of the machine, their instinct is to summon the machine's builders and mechanics and demand to know why. In the early decades of the Progressive period, this model proved a reasonable fit. The builders could construct a machine that operated through hierarchy and authority; the mechanics could fix problems by adjusting the machine's structure and process.

In the last decades of the twentieth century, however, government's policymakers retained the same expectations, but its machinery worked far differently. More of what government—especially the federal government—did no longer fit the hierarchical model of authority-driven government. As in the StarLink and vaccine cases, government needed close and active partnerships with nongovernmental partners to accomplish its purposes. Government could do its part, but without effective partnerships it could not achieve the results it desired.

Because policymakers rarely looked inside the machines responsible for public policy, they had little sense that the insides had so dramatically changed. Their instincts remained the same: When trouble brews, haul the responsible government managers before legislative committees and demand an accounting. In the early decades of the Progressive period, these managers were responsible for the results and could adjust the machines to produce better outcomes. In the last decades of the twentieth century, however, they had control over only some elements of the machine and relied increasingly on their partners to produce results. Thus, not only did administrative theory become more distant from administrative reality; so, too, did political decisions become more distant from the results of those decisions. Policymakers—elected officials—understandably became more critical of the administrative system as the growing complexity of the administrative process frustrated their ability to transform their bold ideas into results.

These problems did not fit well with the approaches of orthodox public administration or its more modern challengers. To an increasing extent, from regulating StarLink corn to finding a way to make government work better while costing less, government officials and academic theorists worked on different planes. The problems are not just the field's struggles to adjust to maturity and some hardening of the intellectual arteries. They are more fundamental and flow from the roots of American approaches to public administration. They flow as well from the mismatch of a system created on principles of control—and an administrative system that can no longer control the problems it was fashioned to solve. Public administration grew on the principle of establishing boundaries, especially around hierarchy and authority. New issues, however, strained the existing boundaries and challenged public administration's theory and practice. The "theory in use," as Schein put it, ran headlong into problems it did not fit.[37]

It is time to reclaim public administration and refashion it for a new century's problems. Its deep historic roots establish the field—and its questions—as among the oldest and most important in human inquiry. Its centrality to politics makes understanding its functions essential to understanding government. Its role in bringing government decisions to life constructs a framework for understanding the relationships between government and society. Public administration is inescapably central to both academic inquiry and government practice. The field's difficulties in cracking both problems are not so much a sign of its intellectual weaknesses—though problems have abounded throughout its history—but, rather, are a reflection of the challenges society must solve.

Reclaiming public administration requires matching these new problems with new approaches. Finding the new approaches requires adapting the great administrative traditions to new issues. It requires understanding that fundamental transformations have occurred in governance, and that these transformations challenge both administration and politics. They pose stark challenges for the administrative traditions as well. Exploring these traditions and transformations, and their implications for the transformation of governance, is the aim of this book.

Chapter Two

Administrative Traditions

Public administration—the art of turning big policy ideas into solid results— ranks among the very oldest of intellectual disciplines. Public administrators were managing government programs long before Plato and Aristotle worried about how they *ought* to do so. Aaron Wildavsky's lively study of the Torah powerfully makes the case that Moses needs to be understood not only as a religious leader but also as a political leader, one who struggled to transform the Jews from runaway slaves into a coherent nation.[1] Much of the Bible's first five books is a study of organization, rule-making, and other forms of bureaucratization to ensure that the Israelites walked in God's ways. Caesar's commentary on the Gallic wars describes the administrative and political challenges he faced in subduing the Gauls, conquering Britain, and keeping strong the lines to Rome. Indeed, as long as humans have been writing, they have been writing about administration. It is a safe bet that they were worrying about administration long before they started writing about it.

Administration is about organizing people to do complex jobs. *Public* administration is about organizing people to do complex jobs in pursuit of a broader, government-defined interest. It is, in short, about applying the public interest to the management of work. The thread of public administration has wound through human history from its beginning, as long as difficult social jobs and multiple players have required coordination. In fact, public administration—its study and practice—predates democracy and its debates. Its very centrality, however, has also ensured constant conflict. Public administration is not only about getting government to work well, but it is also about managing—both promoting and limiting—the exercise of governmental power. Through the centuries, despots have sometimes misused that power. Ineffective leaders have produced poorly managed programs, which caused their citizens to suffer. Over the centuries, citizens have frequently disagreed over what government should do—and how. They have wanted a strong and effective government, but they have resisted a government so strong and effective as to threaten their liberty.

Political conflict has thus always been an inevitable component of public administration, around the world and especially within the United States. So too are complaints about administrative mismanagement. Those who think that complaints about waste, fraud, and abuse in government programs are a new phenomenon have only to look at General George Washington's letters from the field. Officers in units at the rear often stopped wagons heading for the front. They unloaded the supplies they needed for their own men and left front-line troops chronically undersupplied. Some of the government's own purchasing agents encouraged defense contractors to bid up prices, which increased their own commissions.[2] The much-repeated news reports of the last decades of the twentieth century—of overpriced screws and toilet seats—have a rich tradition in American political history.

Americans, on the other hand, have always called on government at the first sign of trouble. When nineteenth-century riverboat steamers exploded, citizens demanded that government toughen safety standards. More recently they complain about government spending, but they plead with elected officials not to cut Medicare. They criticize IRS tax collectors, but they insist on good weather forecasts, safe air-traffic control, and effective treatment of anthrax. Since the days of King George III, Americans have loathed public administration because it represents the exercise of governmental power. New innovations constantly create the demand for rules, Deborah Spar argues.[3] As columnist David Wessel explains, it is an eternal cycle. On the other hand, Americans have expected high levels of public service in exchange for the taxes they dutifully paid: "A revolutionary new technology emerges—the compass, the telegraph, the radio, the Internet, the mobile phone, the science of cloning. Pioneers profit, enjoying the gold rush. Pirates arrive. Pioneers seek to protect their property rights. Problems of coordinating emerge. Government looks impotent." Eventually, the demand for rules of the game becomes inescapable and government typically supplies them.[4]

Public administration thus is paradoxical, caught between citizens' antipathy toward government and their insistence on government services and protection. It is an eternal paradox for all public administration, but it is especially deeply rooted in American democracy. In part this is because armed revolt against government power gave birth to the nation. In part, though, it is because fierce individualism has long driven American culture. And in part it is because conflicting expectations between tax collections and government services, between the abuse of government power and the benefits of using it, have been particularly fierce in this nation. Citizens—especially American citizens—resent the exercise of government power almost as much as they rail at its inefficiency.

This paradox also appears in the academic study of public administration. On one hand, there can be no understanding of government and politics without a study of public administration. Ambitious public goals are empty without the capacity to meet them, so it is impossible to study government adequately without also studying how it is administered. On the other hand, the study of public administration has long struggled to find a seat at the academic table. In part, this is because its work is mundane, especially in comparison with more lofty debates about the meaning of human rights and the tragedy of the commons. In part, this is because its work is messy, because it deals with the constant complications of human behavior in complex organizations. In part, this is because the complexity of administrative action creates enormous methodological problems that frustrate the creation of robust theory.

Orthodox public administration conquered these problems long enough to enjoy a truly golden age in the first half of the twentieth century. By the end of the century, however, both the theory and practice of public administration had fallen onto hard times. As an academic field of study, public administration had an uncertain intellectual home. Its students struggled for acceptance within traditional academic disciplines (although by the 1990s public administration began a notable resurgence). In practice, public administrators struggled to cope with rising expectations of performance, declining public enthusiasm for taxes, growing complexity in doing ever-harder things, and increasing calls for fundamental "reinvention" of their operations. From ending welfare as we know it to providing a healthy cradle-to-grave environment, public administrators have found themselves constantly exhorted to do more with less. They have sought more insight from theory just as theory struggled to reestablish its former prominence.

The founders created American constitutional government to limit government's power. Public administration is about making the exercise of government power effective. Governments and citizens everywhere, at all times, have quarreled over the use of such power. While Moses spent forty days on Mount Sinai receiving the Ten Commandments from God, his people broke God's law by building a golden calf to worship. They had found the law too hard to follow, and they rejected Moses' attempts to enforce it. Of course, these were the same people who had previously welcomed God's power, exercised through Moses, to lead them out of bondage in Egypt.[5] In twenty-first century consultant-speak, Moses' first try to promulgate the commandments failed because of the lack of constituent buy-in. For millennia since then, people have sought the exercise of political power to advance their aims but have struggled against that power when its burdens limited their freedom. Add to this age-old mix America's special antipathy toward government power and its historic devotion to the motto "give me liberty or give me death." The result is the profound tension within the peculiarly American form of public administration.

The tension springs from four fundamentally different intellectual traditions: a *Hamiltonian* tradition that seeks an effective government, that promotes top-down government, and that favors a strong executive; a *Jeffersonian* tradition that celebrates America's agrarian roots, that promotes bottom-up government, and that seeks a weak executive; a *Madisonian* tradition that tries to balance political power among competing forces; and a *Wilsonian* tradition that prefers to concentrate administrative power in hierarchically structured organizations.[6] In this chapter and the next, we examine these traditions.

The Hamiltonian Tradition

Administrative historians credit Alexander Hamilton as the true founder of the American administrative state.[7] Leonard D. White's sweeping history of American bureaucratic development, for example, concludes simply, "Hamilton was the administrative architect of the new government."[8] While many leaders shaped the new republic, Hamilton's voice was loudest when it came to devising an administrative scheme for the new nation. He made a forceful case for a strong executive—a case, in fact, he often made so strongly that he stirred anger among many political leaders. At the Constitutional Convention in 1787, he made an impassioned case for an elected monarchy. When the delegates rejected that idea, he continued to argue for a strong and powerful national government.

Hamilton built his case on the manifest failures of the Articles of Confederation. The confederation was a masterpiece of over-devolution. The Continental Congress had rejected John Dickinson's plan for a strong national government and in its place constructed a plan to give the states maximum discretion. It took the states years even to ratify these limited rules, and in the meantime, they quarreled over everything from boundaries to commerce. After the victorious new nation won the Revolutionary War, its leaders were embarrassed by their failure to get the states to live up to the terms of the Treaty of Paris, which had ended the war. Some states created their own foreign policies while others disputed who had control of the western lands. The states squabbled over paying for an army, and some leaders worried that this type of spending might open the frontier to poaching by the Spanish and British. By 1787, nearly everyone agreed that the Articles had not worked and that some stronger national government was needed.

The central problems proved the enduring ones: making the national government strong enough to be effective; creating an executive powerful enough to make the government strong; yet preventing a concentration of power that would threaten liberty. Hamilton's was the most important voice in making the case for a strong executive. As the nation's first treasury secretary, he wrote reports on public credit, national banking, and manufacturing that ultimately created the framework for the modern executive branch.

Three basic principles drove Hamilton's views on public administration: independence, power, and responsibility.[9] He recognized that the law, as passed by Congress, bound the executive branch. He also strongly believed that the executive needed independence in implementing the law. Within its own sphere, he said, the Constitution gave the executive freedom of action. In *Federalist* 71, he pointed out that "it is one thing to be subordinate to the laws, and another to be dependent on the legislative body." In essence, Hamilton was making two points. One was the need for separation of powers. A too-powerful legislature could thwart government just as could a too-powerful executive. He embraced the notion of balance to counter this danger. The other was the need for delegation. Once Congress passed a law, Hamilton believed, it needed to allow the executive flexibility in determining how best to administer it. He recognized that one of the most important roles for the executive was concentrating the expertise required to administer the law well. If the executive was to do so, it needed to rely on this expertise as it managed public programs.

From there, Hamilton argued the need for executive power. In perhaps his most-quoted passage, Hamilton contended in *Federalist* 70 that "energy in the executive is a leading character in the definition of good government." The Articles had clearly demonstrated that weak government produced poor policy and worse results. The new Constitution, he believed, required a government that could act decisively over the long haul to pursue the national purpose. Failing to do so—creating a government that was ineffective—was unwise and ultimately threatening to democratic government. If the people were to rule and be served, Hamilton argued, they needed a government strong enough to protect their interests and fulfill their ambitions.

In *Federalist* 70, he outlined what "energy in the executive" required. His analysis was perhaps the first textbook in American public administration, and it set the foundation for public administration orthodoxy that emerged in its fullest form a century later. Energy first requires *unity*, he said. There must be a single top administrator, the president, with clear lines of authority to those charged with managing government programs. This executive must have *duration*. There must be consistency in administration over time. The argument for duration was, of course, a not-so-subtle suggestion that the legislature, driven by popular opinion, could not produce a sufficiently strong foundation for effective government management. Finally, he said, there must be adequate *competence*. The executive needed to have enough expertise to know how to carry policy ideas forward to achieve effective results.

On one level, of course, *Federalist* 70 lays out the central elements of any effective administrative system, elements that the Progressives rediscovered a century later. On another level, however, Hamilton's argument raised many of the same worries that had stalled Dickinson's argument for a strong central government a decade before. A unified, long-term, highly competent executive brought worries about the risks of a too-strong executive—worries that were to surface periodically throughout American history.

Hamilton's third basic principle, in addition to independence and power, was responsibility. This was his argument about keeping administration accountable and preventing it from becoming too powerful. If the executive was to be empowered to act independently of Congress, it would also ultimately be subject to its oversight. For example, Hamilton accepted the power of Congress to investigate the executive departments' actions and to impeach the chief executive. He clearly was not happy about surrendering authority to the legislature; he would surely have preferred a far stronger executive branch and less chance of congressional intrusion into legislative affairs. But he accepted these provisions as central tenets in the new system's balance-of-powers structure.

Hamilton worked hard to translate these principles into practice. As treasury secretary, he led the battle for national assumption of the states' revolutionary war debt and the creation of the First Bank of the United States. His "Report on Manufactures" laid out his long-term vision for a manufacturing-driven economy, one strongly supported by government. James Madison observed that his views were a coherent package that came together "like the links of a chain." Hamilton biographer Richard Brookhiser explained, "Settling America's debts would fortify its credit; credit would allow manufactures to develop; a diverse and flourishing economy would generate the revenue that would ensure the debt's proper funding."[10] Underlying it all was a grand vision for a brash, ambitious new country. It was a country that would rise above its agrarian foundation to play a major role in global commerce. A strong national government, led by a powerful executive, would support this economic transformation and, in turn, generate jobs and economic growth for citizens.

This ambitious vision caused Hamilton unending problems, especially with the Jeffersonians. In the end, it led to his death in a duel with Jefferson's vice president, Aaron Burr. As Brookhiser puts it, "He had been trading partisan shots with the man who killed him for twelve years before they traded real ones."[11] His personal life, from a high-profile sex scandal to his ongoing feud with the Jeffersonians, was puzzling. But his long shadow across American government is unmistakable. He made the case for strong government, structured with unitary command and managed with skill. He recognized, if reluctantly, the need for a balance of power while asserting the executive's preeminence. He contended that unlike the legislature, with elected representatives moving in and out, the executive needed long-term capacity and leadership. He made the case for a strong executive branch, run from the top down but also responsible to the other branches and, ultimately, to the people. In vision, writing, and practice, Hamilton truly was the father of the modern administrative state.

The Jeffersonian Tradition

If Hamilton shaped the American administrative state, Thomas Jefferson cast a vastly longer shadow over the American political tradition. The gentleman farmer from Virginia is well known as author of the Declaration of Independence, president of the United States, and founder of the University of Virginia, as his tombstone says simply. His home, Monticello, is a notable tourist attraction and great architectural achievement—one celebrated, in fact, on the back of the nickel, with Jefferson's own image on the other side. Hamilton trumps Jefferson in the currency department: His image on the ten-dollar bill is better known, by contrast, than Jefferson's on the little-seen two-dollar bill. But Hamilton's statue in front of the Treasury Department pales in comparison with Jefferson's impressive memorial on the shore of Washington's Tidal Basin. Daniel J. Boorstin notes, "The vitality of Thomas Jefferson is one of the striking features of modern American history. He always has something to say to us, and the nation always seems ready to listen."[12]

On government, Jefferson's view was simple: It was not, according to Boorstin, "the expression of political theory, but the largely unreflective answer of healthy men to the threat of tyranny."[13] The threat of abuse of power—especially executive power—hung heavy over Jefferson. Unlike Hamilton's early background in commerce and accounting, Jefferson came of age as a gentleman farmer in Virginia. He drew his strength from the love of the land. The British crown was a very long way from his mountaintop house. The exercise of its power had perennially poached on his freedom, and he was determined that the new American nation would never again risk losing liberty. His Declaration of Independence is a ringing expression of his rejection of tyranny.

When the new Constitution replaced the Articles of Confederation, Jefferson joined George Washington's cabinet as secretary of state. His relationship with treasury secretary Hamilton was constantly tumultuous. They engaged in a long-running policy feud over the question of federal power. For Jefferson, power came from the land and from the people. Hamilton distrusted popular rule out of his fear that it would retard commerce and industry. When Hamilton proposed the creation of a national bank, Jefferson fought it thinking that the bank would encourage speculation and undermine agriculture. Hamilton believed the bank would provide the federal government with the power it needed. Jefferson was a staunch advocate of the limitations on federal power embodied in the Tenth Amendment. The differences helped spawn the first American political parties, Hamilton's Federalists and Jefferson's Democratic-Republicans. Yet despite their differences and because Hamilton despised Aaron Burr, Hamilton supported Jefferson in the 1800 presidential campaign.

Jefferson and Hamilton could not have been more different. If Hamilton celebrated the nation's commercial, manufacturing, and banking future, Jefferson venerated the nation's agrarian roots. Where Hamilton argued vigorously for a strong national government with a powerful executive and a limited citizen role, Jefferson believed in local government, a strong legislature, and popular control. Jefferson argued for limited government, while Hamilton pursued an energetic government. Their philosophical disagreements erupted over the Bank of the United States and continued for more than a decade until Hamilton's death.[14]

Jefferson's almost religious belief in limited government has resonated throughout American history. His instinct, especially as captured in his early writings, was to keep as much power in the people's hands as possible. If government needed to exercise power, it ought to be state and local governments, he argued, not the federal government. And if the federal government needed to exercise power, Congress, with its roots in popular will, ought to be supreme. Jefferson championed federalism because it established the predominance of state governments in the American system. He was a champion of the separation of powers because it provided checks on executive functions. Like many of the founders, he worried constantly that monarchy might reassert itself, and he saw a monarchist threat in Hamilton's incessant arguments for an energetic executive. The foundation of society, he believed, ought to be individual liberty. Government's foremost responsibility was to promote that liberty. Accountability in the system had to come from the bottom up.

In practice, however, Jefferson's philosophical approach did not much inform his approach to public administration. Jefferson had a "speculative rather than an administrative mind," Leonard D. White concluded. In fact, he writes, "Jefferson was not interested . . . in the normal process of day-by-day administration." Jefferson, in his own words, believed "there are no mysteries in it." It simply calls for "common sense and honest intentions." He compared government administration to running a farm, and "we all know that a farm, however large, is not more difficult to direct than a garden, and does not call for more attention or skill." White was incredulous and argued that such a statement could scarcely have been made by anyone familiar with the difficulties of keeping even a modest government running.[15] The model fit neither practical reality nor Jefferson's own approach to the presidency. He feared power, but "he nevertheless found himself forced to exercise it ruthlessly," White noted. "His preferences were frustrated by circumstances that compelled him to abandon his own theories."[16] He enforced the embargo extending the Alien and Sedition Acts. He negotiated the purchase of Louisiana, whose constitutionality was questioned, and he dispatched Lewis and Clark to survey that vast expansion of American territory. As a philosopher, Jefferson believed in a weak government and in strong individual liberty. As president, however, he was truly Hamiltonian in supporting a strong and energetic presidency.

These conflicts—between Jefferson and Hamilton as political philosophers, and between Jefferson the philosopher and Jefferson the president—have long engaged historians. Over time, however, the Hamiltonian foundations of Jefferson's presidency have largely been forgotten. A romantic reading of his intellectual tradition, of his reverence for liberty, and his life as the gentleman farmer of Monticello have more powerfully defined the Jeffersonian tradition. His almost theological arguments for limited government have echoed in conservative minds throughout the centuries. These themes drove the South's revolt against Lincoln during the Civil War as much as they did the conservative congressional Republicans' short-lived Contract with America during the 1990s. In these cases, as in Jefferson's life, the romantic themes have always collided with pragmatic realities. The North bitterly fought to preserve the Union in the 1860s, and in the 1990s Americans discovered that they did not really want the more limited government that the congressional Republicans promised. One can debate— endlessly—the struggles between Jefferson's ideas and actions. One can also debate how to factor his thoughts into the quest to make government, whatever its size and reach, truly effective. Jefferson's paradoxical life helps underline two big quandaries—what government *ought to do* and *how best to do it.* But throughout the ensuing debates, Jefferson's ideas have held sway. His ideas have made a lasting case for limiting government power, for keeping governmental power more in the hands of the legislature than in the administration, and for maximizing individual liberty. They have defined a counterpoint to Hamilton's argument for a powerful executive branch.

The Madisonian Tradition

James Madison's work defines a third American administrative tradition. It is, in fact, not so much a theory of administration as a more general approach to politics in America's republican government. Madison was the architect of America's balance-of-power system and thus a designer of the tactics that Americans have used for centuries to keep an uneasy peace between the conflicting Hamiltonian and Jeffersonian forces. Madison's influence on the Constitution is unquestioned. The notes he kept on the Constitutional Convention's deliberations remain the best record of the debate. His was the most influential voice in crafting the Constitution and the strongest voice for developing the separation of powers. Later, he joined with Hamilton and John Jay to write the *Federalist Papers*, but his contributions are perhaps the best known. In particular, *Federalist* 10 is the definitive explanation of the linkage of government power and economic power. Economic differences among the states could breed conflict. A strong, effective, well-balanced national government, on the other hand, could bring stability and prosperity.

Like Jefferson, he differed with Hamilton over just the how strong the executive ought to be. But unlike Jefferson, whose more doctrinaire position held that power ought to be left in the hands of the people and the local governments, Madison developed a subtler approach that hinged on balancing power among the major players. He worried about the "mischiefs of faction" and the risks that economic and political competition could undermine both social order and the new federal government. He also worried about the risk that a too-strong government could promote tyranny. To resolve these problems, he hewed a pragmatic middle position between Hamilton and Jefferson. The new system was a larger and more complex republic than thinkers had often considered wise, but he concluded that the system offered more internal balance, more diverse institutional roles, and more factions—all the better to balance the ambitions of any faction and block its ability to exercise monarchical power.[17]

In *Federalist* 51, Madison argued, "It is evident that each department [that is, branch of government] ought to have a will of its own." To prevent "a gradual concentration of the several powers in the same department," he contended that the key lies in "giving to those who administer each department, the necessary constitutional means, and personal motives, to resist encroachments of the others. The provision for defense must in this, as in other cases, be made commensurate to the danger of attack. Ambition must be made to counteract ambition." Then comes the most famous piece of *The Federalist*: "If men were angels, no government would be necessary. If angels were to govern men, neither external nor internal controls on government would be necessary. In framing a government which is to be administered by men over men, the great difficulty lies in this: You must first enable the government to control the governed; and in the next place, oblige it to control itself." The legislature, he argued, ought to predominate in a republican government. To prevent legislative tyranny, legislative power was divided between two houses. His biggest worry, however, which he shared with most of the founders, was preventing renewed executive tyranny. Separating government powers provided dual checks, through the legislative and judicial branches, on executive power.

In fact, of course, the founders never fully subscribed to a complete separation of powers among the branches. For them, it was more a matter of blending powers. The president can veto acts of Congress, Congress can impeach and remove a president, the president appoints Supreme Court justices, and Congress confirms them. In *Federalist* 48, Madison pointed to the "partial mixture" of powers as a safeguard—indeed, an enhancement—of republican government.[18] The inherent messiness of the American constitutional system prevented the abuse of power. That also made its effective exercise difficult, as Hamilton often later pointed out. But it provided the safeguards for which a new nation yearned.

Madison devoted most of his contributions to *The Federalist* to reassuring his fellow citizens that the new Constitution did not create a government so strong as to threaten their liberty. He pointed to the risks that continuing the Articles of Confederation would bring, and he energetically led the charge for the new form of government. Like Jefferson, however, he worked to protect liberty by ensuring that no part of this new government became too powerful. He saw great virtue in federalism, especially as stated in the Tenth Amendment, which reserved powers to the states. Most of all, Madison devised an approach to government founded on a separation—actually a blending—of powers. Administration and bureaucracy did not preoccupy him. Like Jefferson, he did not focus heavily on the execution of government powers but worried more about government's overall architecture.

Like Jefferson, Madison had bitterly fought Hamilton's plans for a strong national government. In part, as with Jefferson, his differences lay along North-South lines, with Hamilton championing commerce and the two Virginians, Jefferson and Madison, promoting agrarian interests. He opposed Hamilton's proposal for federal assumption of state debts. Virginia had retired most of its debt, but Hamilton's New York had not. He objected to Hamilton's plans for a new tariff and a national bank. By the end of his presidency, however, Madison, like Jefferson, had become more Hamiltonian. He came to support both the national bank and a tariff to protect American industries. In the broad sweep of American political thought, however, Madison's separation-of-powers ideas have had much more influence than his more pragmatic adaptation of Hamilton's views to the presidency.

Unlike Hamilton, who had an administration-based view of government, Madison's ideas were fundamentally political. The basic political features of the system—the institutions created to exercise government power and how to balance power among them—were for Madison its most important elements. Thus, he did not develop an explicit theory of administration. Rather, he built a political theory in which administration was subservient, in practical operation and in theoretical understanding, to political power. He was a political scientist to Hamilton's public administrationist and Jefferson's political theorist.

The Wilsonian Tradition

The fourth major theme of American administrative thought did not develop until more than two generations later. Toward the end of the nineteenth century, American government had suffered embarrassing breakdowns. Development of the West presented new opportunities for corruption, and greedy developers eagerly took advantage. Stunning new technologies, from electric lights to the telegraph and telephone, offered new conveniences, but market competition left some areas unserved and other areas tangled with spaghetti-like masses of wires. Corporate trusts brought huge concentrations of private power and new threats to public well-being.

In response, a new political movement, Progressivism, sprang up with twin messages: Government had a positive role to play in shaping, balancing, and controlling corporate power; to play that role, government needed to be strong enough to be effective. In many ways, the Progressives were children of Hamilton. It had taken a century for Hamilton's vision of a mercantile America to emerge. When it did mature, however, it came with a concentration of power and threat to republican government that Hamilton had not anticipated.

Unlike the theorists of a century before, the Progressives had a tightly integrated approach to the relationship between political and administrative power. With the American Revolution a distant memory of more than a century before, the specter of George III was not so frightening. But with the emergence of corporate monopolies, the threats of unfettered market competition loomed large indeed. In the face of those monopolies, the Progressives argued the need for a stronger government, both to rein in the abuses of corporate power and to bring Americans a better life: quicker transportation, better communication, protection from an ever-more-dizzying collection of external threats. With American "manifest destiny" secure—with the United States stretching from the Atlantic to the Pacific Oceans—the next step lay in developing the land between. That meant a government that could secure a continental railroad, make credit available for citizens who needed to borrow for their businesses, and redefine the historic commitment to the common welfare.

The Progressives saw a strong government as a balance to the corporate world and as the natural next step to prosperity. They worried, however, that building a stronger government would open a new route for private power to capture control of the public agenda. Political machines celebrated their invention of "honest graft" and profoundly dishonest tactics for gaining leverage over municipal governments. If government was to be stronger, the Progressives needed to keep it from being captured by narrow interests. They found themselves squarely in the middle of the same debate that had preoccupied the founders. This time, however, instead of fears that a monarchist administration might dominate American government, the Progressives worried that king-like corporate titans and corruption might control the political system. They saw a stronger, better-organized government—and a more effective public administration—as essential to a new balance of political power.

A stronger federal government, however, raised the familiar problem of how to keep a more powerful government from undermining democratic government. In response to this issue, a thirty-one-year-old professor at Princeton University, Woodrow Wilson, wrote an article suggesting how this balance ought to be struck. The author was not yet famous and the 1887 article, "The Study of Administration," was not much read. Only when Leonard D. White's famous 1950 textbook discussed it extensively did scholars pay it serious attention.[19] Since then, however, Wilson's article has become a classic as the first American statement of modern public administration. Scholars have celebrated his argument about the relationship between political institutions and public administration. "It is the object of administrative study," he wrote, "to discover, first, what government can properly and successfully do, and, secondly, how it can do these proper things with the utmost efficiency and at the least possible cost either of money or of energy."[20] Determining what government could do best and how it could best do it were the central questions for the Progressives' approach to government.

Wilson began his article by noting that "at the same time that the functions of government are every day becoming more complex and difficult, they are also vastly multiplying in number."[21] As he famously pointed out, "It is getting harder to *run* a constitution than to frame one."[22] That is why, Wilson argued, "there should be a science of administration which shall seek to straighten the paths of government, to make its business less unbusinesslike, to strengthen and purify its organization, and to crown its duties with dutifulness."[23]

American government, he suggested, had grown quickly, like a child who had become taller but more awkward at the same time. For clues about how to manage a modern state effectively, Wilson looked to Europe, especially the Prussians and French. The English and Americans, by contrast, had "long and successfully studied the art of curbing executive power to the constant neglect of perfecting executive methods." The concern had been far more with making government "just and moderate" than "well-ordered and effective."[24] Wilson sought to marry the Anglo-American strategies for controlling administrative power with Franco-Prussian strategies for enhancing it.

The lesson that Wilson drew from these other nations was that "the field of administration is a field of business . . . removed from the hurry and strife of politics."[25] To be sure, the great truths that drive the political process lie at the core of administration as well. But Wilson believed that "administration lies outside the proper sphere of *politics*. Administrative questions are not political questions. Although politics sets the tasks for administration, it should be not suffered to manipulate its offices." His evidence? Wilson pointed to the Germans, for example, who had made such a separation the bedrock of an effective administrative system.[26] That did not mean Wilson wanted to make the American system more German, or more like any other system dominated by monarchist traditions. "If I see a murderous fellow sharpening a knife cleverly, I can borrow his way of sharpening the knife without borrowing his probable intent to commit murder with it." He concluded that we could learn from others how to administer our own system more effectively without "getting any of their diseases into our veins."[27]

Wilson's formulation, especially his argument about separating administration and politics, has defined the central battle of modern public administration. He argued that public administration could be made stronger and more effective by borrowing the best practices from administrators around the world. It could be made more accountable by separating administration from politics, empowering administration to follow political direction, and making administrators ultimately responsible to policymakers. In making this argument, he sought to resolve the field's eternal dilemma. Separating administration from politics could free administrators from political interference in their work and thus enhance administrative efficiency. Separating politics from administration could strengthen the ability of elected officials to oversee administration and thus enhance accountability.

Orthodox public administrationists seized on Wilson's formulation. Wilson's argument made the case for a separate field of study in public administration and suggested, at least implicitly, a methodology. It was one that fit neatly into the orthodoxy that had emerged in the first half of the twentieth century: focus on the process and structure of government organizations; explore strategies to make them more efficient; keep them separate from political institutions to ensure their effectiveness; but ultimately hold them accountable to elected officials for their exercise of power. As powerful as some public administrationists found the argument, many political scientists argued it was hopelessly naive to pretend that one could actually separate administration from politics. If public administrationists used Wilson's article as a manifesto to define the field, many political scientists seized on it as a justification for dismissing it. The emerging public policy schools likewise saw in Wilson's article—and the field's embrace of it—a validation of their efforts to invent a new approach. To his critics, Wilson neither got to the core of effective program implementation nor made the critical linkages to bureaucratic politics.

Wilson's small article was barely read for sixty years, but it emerged in the intellectual debates just as critical boundaries were beginning to form. If his article did not broadly shape the Progressive tradition, it certainly captured its most important administrative ideas. It explained the Progressives' efforts to strengthen bureaucracy without threatening democracy. At the same time, it clearly defined the target at which political scientists and public policy scholars shot when they took aim at the field.

What should we make of Wilson's politics-administration separation? Even a casual observer of politics and administration would quickly reject the idea that the two are truly separate. A senior official in a major American city once told me that his department had a special plan to help Democrats in case of a major snowstorm on election day: city plows went first to the wards that had the highest percentage of Democratic voters to make sure they made it to the polls. There can be no clearer case of administration having political impact—or of political incentives shaping administrative decisions.

Moreover, the administration of law inevitably involves the exercise of discretion. Exercising discretion inevitably requires value choices, and value choices are without doubt political decisions. No law can ever detail all the decisions that administrators on the front lines must make, and sometimes even the smallest of front-line decisions can have great political implications. Witness the election-day snow removal plan: which streets get plowed first can influence which voters end up at the polls. Other administrative decisions, from how to translate tax legislation into regulations or which road proposals to fund, involve both discretion and value choices. For many observers, therefore, Wilson's argument was not only naive, but it hid the implicit (or explicit) political judgments made by administrators and limited the ability of elected officials to hold them accountable for the exercise of discretion.

Wilson's argument, actually, was much more fundamental. Like other Progressives, he believed that government needed to play an important role in a society that was becoming ever more complex. To play that role, public administration needed to be strong and effective. He argued that Americans, preoccupied with high-profile constitutional issues, had paid far too little attention to figuring out how to *run* their constitution, especially by comparison with many European nations. He believed that Americans could learn important lessons from the European experience while maintaining American democratic principles. Perhaps most important, he believed that effective democracy required competent, politically impartial administrators, who could work free from political interference.

Wilson was scarcely naive. Nor was he alone in asserting the politics-administration dichotomy. Indeed, the American Political Science Association's first president, Frank Goodnow, wrote a book in 1900 that made the same argument.[28] Wilson, Goodnow, and their colleagues grew out of a tradition in which public administration had received relatively little attention, either from elected officials or from scholars. New social problems were emerging that the existing administrative system could not solve effectively. Special interests were infiltrating government administration and were threatening to steer government action to private, not public, interests. Their argument was not so much to wring politics from the study or practice of administration, though. Wilson quite explicitly recognized the role of constitutional politics in the administrative system, and he had earlier written a more famous work, titled *Congressional Government*. For Wilson, Congress was "the central and predominant power of the system."[29] His argument, rather, was that, to be effective, administration had to be protected from political interference. Just *how* that ought to be done remained a constant dispute. In fact, it ultimately caused a fundamental schism between public administration and rest of political science and a break between the field of public administration and the public policy community.

Wilson's work nevertheless was—and continues to be—an enormous influence on American public administration. It was fully compatible with Madison's separation-of-powers argument, but unlike Madison's approach it had an explicit role for administration. Like Jefferson, he recognized the importance of responsiveness and local governance, but Wilson shared with Hamilton a strong belief in effective administrative power. Wilson had much in common with Hamilton, but he came to the issue with less commitment to *national* power and with the more subtle sense of government's complexity that a century of experience helped nurture. Like Hamilton, he laid an important cornerstone in the intellectual construct of public administration.[30]

Irreconcilable Differences

These four traditions represent the basic approaches that have framed both the study and practice of American public administration since the beginning of the twentieth century. Over time, these traditions have risen and fallen in importance and emphasis. Indeed, the history of American public administration has identified three recurring themes. First, at the core of public administration rests important and enduring ideas. Second, these ideas push both theory and practice in opposite directions. Third, the balance among these ideas has shifted over time, so no approach has defined orthodoxy for long. It is scarcely surprising, then, that the field of public administration has always found itself amidst political conflict and intellectual tumult. The conflicts center in part on whether the bureaucracy is seen, by both practitioners and scholars, as the primary actor or a supporting cast member in public affairs. They focus as well on whether the approach to the bureaucracy presumes a relatively strong executive insisting on top-down accountability, or whether the approach builds accountability from the people—from the bottom up—and presumes a weaker executive. Hamilton believed in a strong executive managing from the top down; Jefferson argued for a weak executive held accountable from the bottom up. Madison's balance-of-powers model made the executive just one of the players, and the bureaucracy did not play a role; Wilson concentrated on the role of the permanent bureaucracy in making the case for the separation of policy and administration. Jefferson and Madison shared their concern over the broad architecture of the American system, while Hamilton and Wilson concentrated on the mechanisms of administrative action.

As table 2.1 shows, these four traditions produced radically different, and fundamentally irreconcilable, administrative traditions. These traditions, in turn, have fueled centuries of debate and conflict in American public administration. Where should power be centered? How should executive power be balanced with other institutions? How should accountability work? The conflicting traditions have resulted in very different answers to these questions.

Table 2.1   Administrative Ideas in the American Political Tradition

	Wilsonian Bureaucracy centered	Madisonian Balance-of-power centered
Hamiltonian Strong executive/ Top down	Centered on executive Principle: strong executive function Top-down accountability Hierarchical authority	Centered on nonbureaucratic institutions Principle: separation of powers Focus on political power Top-down accountability
Jeffersonian Weak executive/ Bottom up	Centered on local control Principle: weak executive with devolved power Bottom-up accountability Responsiveness to citizens	Centered on nonbureaucratic institutions Principle: federalism Focus on local control Bottom-up responsiveness

Americans have struggled for more than two hundred years to resolve these differences—and they have proven singularly unsuccessful in doing so. The conflicts are likely to continue as long as American democracy does because the American approach to bureaucracy embodies two important sets of tradeoffs: about how bureaucracy ought to work—from the bottom up or from the top down; and how bureaucracy ought to be integrated into American republican government—whether bureaucracy is central or peripheral. These issues shape the arguments in the chapters to come. In the meantime, three questions frame the conflict.

Administration and Hierarchy

First, *what is the role of hierarchy in public administration?* Strong bureaucracies have always built on strong hierarchies. They provide a highly organized way of completing complex tasks—structured along a chain of command and controlled by authority. Ancient Rome's conquest of much of the Western world, and its ability to maintain control for centuries, hinged on the strength of its military power and the hierarchical structure that directed it. The Roman centurion, for example, was the linchpin of the imperial army, the critical "middle management" man in charge of 100 soldiers. The Middle Ages that followed suffered, at least in part, because that powerful arrangement disintegrated.

Since the earliest days, American public administration has always had a hierarchical structure. The structure, moreover, has built primarily on functionally organized departments—Departments of State, Treasury, War, and Post Office, with others added in the centuries since the Washington administration. As the government grew, the practice of organizing by function and managing through hierarchy became strongly entrenched. In the early years of the twentieth century, however, this foundation came under assault. Social psychologists conducted experiments that suggested hierarchy was not the only—or even the most important—tool to use in shaping administrative action. For example, researchers at Western Electric's Hawthorne plant found in the late 1920s that behavioral incentives could radically affect productivity.[31] The Hawthorne experiments stunned managers because they established, for the first time, the case for managing complex organizations through mechanisms other than hierarchical authority. New government programs further eroded the roles of authority and hierarchy as the basic building blocks. The pragmatic demands for fighting World War II led the federal government to create GOCOS—government owned, contractor operated facilities—to manufacture weapons. The GOCO was an administrative hybrid, with the government producing goods and services through an indirect contractor network.

In the decades that followed the war, the pattern continued. In the 1950s, the federal government managed urban renewal through grants to local governments and built the Interstate Highway System through grants to state governments. It fought much of the 1960s War on Poverty through grants to local governments that ultimately went to nongovernmental organizations, like neighborhood associations. Private contractors managed most of the Medicare and Medicaid programs, while the 1970s federal effort to restore the environment operated largely through contractors and the states. In the 1990s, the federal government "ended welfare as we know it" by giving the job to the states. In fact, the federal government managed every major post–World War II policy initiative through nonhierarchical, nonauthority-based strategies. To a lesser but still substantial degree, this movement toward using indirect tools of government spilled over into state and local governments as well.[32]

These trends sharpened a tough problem: How could its hierarchically structured, authority-managed agencies effectively manage increasingly nonhierarchical, nonauthority-based administrative systems? Hierarchy and authority worked, more or less well, in an era in which the government produced most of its goods and services itself. As government employed more indirect tools, however, the management strains grew. So, too, did the challenge to ensuring the accountability of administration.

POLITICS AND ADMINISTRATION

Second, *what is the linkage between politics and public administration?* Wilson's article is most famous for framing the battle lines. The question, however, dates back to Hamilton's battles with the Jeffersonians, who quarreled for decades over the proper spheres of administrative and political power. If administration is central to government, as Wilson argued in the less-cited portion of his famous paper, neither political science nor public administration can be complete without embracing the other. At least since World War II, however, political science and public administration have been on uneasy terms with each other. The public policy schools, increasingly grounded in microeconomics and policy analysis, have grown uneasy with politics. Are politics and administration truly inseparable? If so, how have analysts managed so successfully to separate them? And if they are to be joined, what linkages make the most analytical and practical sense?

The reform tradition in American politics, always bubbling but especially strong in the Progressive period, has long sought to prevent political interference in administration. Toward the end of the twentieth century, reformers led by the "reinventing government" movement sought to empower bureaucrats and, thus, to give administrators more political discretion. The field's efforts to provide prescriptions have often been ignored by politicians, while politicians have frequently criticized administrators for their inability to deliver results. Some academics, in their search for stronger predictive theory, have moved further from practical prescriptions. Other academics see little need for theoretical predictions from which pragmatic implications have been wrung. Understanding these linkages remains one of public administration's toughest problems.

ADMINISTRATION AND THE PEOPLE

Third, *what is the connection between public administration and citizens?* Evidence abounds that public trust and confidence in government declined significantly in the last half of the twentieth century. In 1964, three-fourths of Americans said that they trusted government to do the right thing. By the end of the twentieth century, the number dropped to one-fourth. Cultural and political conflicts, worsened by a cynical news media, had deepened public cynicism and reduced trust.[33] Most Americans were frustrated with government, especially with its elected officials. Citizens in 1998, for example, trusted federal workers more than elected officials to do the right thing (by a margin of 67 percent to

16 percent). More citizens held a favorable view of government workers than in the past—69 percent favorable in 1998, compared with 55 percent in 1981. Nevertheless, the eroding public trust in government corroded government's ability to perform—and performance problems undermined public confidence.[34] Meanwhile, Robert D. Putnam wrote tellingly of the decline of "social capital" and community in American society.[35] How, he asked, could we rebuild the bonds between citizens and social organizations, especially government?

The trust-in-government scores shot upward in the aftermath of the September 11, 2001, terrorist attacks. Of those surveyed, 64 percent trusted the government in Washington to do what was right, three times the proportion in a 1994 poll.[36] In their heroic response to the attacks, firefighters and police officers renewed Americans' faith in at least some government workers. Analysts carefully watched the surveys to determine whether this marked the end of a decades-long slide in public trust of government or a short-lived response to the tragedy. Either way, the polls made clear, popular opinion about government was closely tied to the public's sense of how government, pragmatically and effectively, helps citizens solve problems.

Administration and Politics

In its early years of the twentieth century, public administration sought strength by insulating itself from politics. Indeed, its leaders presented a strong public administration as a defense from corruptions of political power. By the end of the century, political problems had soiled administration along with the rest of the American political system. Politicians have discovered great success in mounting antigovernment (read: antibureaucracy) campaigns. Reformers tried to "reinvent" bureaucracy, but they did so with unorthodox strategies and tactics. The century began and ended with a quarrelsome linkage between administration and politics, with deep uncertainty about whether both were stronger or weaker if tied together theoretically and pragmatically. Critics and analysts alike were uncertain about how administrative pathologies might have weakened public trust in politics—and how the behavior of political institutions might spawn administrative problems.

These issues are both profound and inescapable, for they lie rooted in the enduring tradeoffs of the American political traditions. The tensions have only been worsened by new trends, discussed in the next chapter, that layer new dilemmas on top of old ones. The connection between politics and administration, on one level, is clear. Without an adequate administrative foundation, bold policy ideas will fail in execution, or at least will stumble erratically in ways that further erode the public's trust in government. Theories about political relationships and institutions will be fatally flawed without an understanding of how administration shapes political possibilities and results. Moreover, in ways that even elected officials often fail to appreciate, changes in administration are redefining fundamental political relationships: between and among nation states, between the national and state and local governments; and between government and the private and nonprofit sectors.

Nevertheless, both academics and politicians have lurched ahead without adequately thinking through these connections. Elected officials—and especially candidates for elected office—launch bold policy proposals without thinking through how they will carry them out. The mass media rarely hold them to account for the mismatch of their ambitions and their results, and when problems occur, they blame the administrative machinery instead of its policy designers.

Many of the key players work from a vending-machine model of public policy. They frame big ideas. They then assume that they can carry them out by putting money into the top of the machine and waiting for services to pop out the bottom. The failure of this model in describing either how public administration *does* or *should* operate helps explain the mismatch between public problems and the administration we use to solve them.

That is why reclaiming public administration is so essential. Without a theory of administration that is a theory of politics, and a theory of politics that is informed by administration, the basic connection between citizens and their government simply cannot be understood. Meeting that challenge means grappling with the three central linkages—of administration with hierarchy, politics, and citizens. It also means understanding the fundamental transformation that occurred in governance at the end of the twentieth century and how that transformation undermined the sense of boundaries that had helped sustain public administration for a century. We turn to that puzzle next.

Chapter Three

Administrative Dilemmas

The four enduring traditions of public administration paint a rich tableau against which Americans have developed their dreams. The traditions, however, have provided weak guidance about just *how* to fulfill those dreams. Compared with some other social science theories, theories of public administration have often been lacking. Microeconomics, for example, holds an explicit theory of efficiency built on markets and how individuals use markets to maximize their preferences (although economist Arthur Okun warns that conflicting values about efficiency and equality plague microeconomics more than its advocates typically admit).[1] The pursuit of efficiency in microeconomics leads to a single best approach for problem-solving.

By contrast, public administration builds on recurring tradeoffs: responsiveness and efficiency; centralization and decentralization; strong executives and separation of powers; federal control and federalism. Resolving those tradeoffs in the short run has always been difficult; settling them permanently has been impossible. America's leaders and citizens have traditionally wanted both responsiveness and efficiency, both centralization and decentralization, and so on—and they have wanted different measures of each at different times. While microeconomics built its theory on maximizing one value—efficiency—public administration has grown up struggling with multiple and conflicting values. There is no prospect that either theorists or politicians will find an enduring balance among these values any time soon, so there is little hope that public administration will ever be able to match the theoretical precision of microeconomics. The inherent conflicts buried deep in these traditions have long posed big problems for theorists and practitioners alike: finding short-term accommodations among the four traditions; developing theoretical insights to bring clarity to the complexity of administrative action; and offering practical guidance to improve how government works.

New Trends in Old Traditions

The field's four major intellectual traditions each built on basic assumptions about how public administration can pursue efficiency in a democratic republic. Hamilton's case for a strong executive assumed that executives could command without threatening accountability. Jefferson's argument for responsive local government assumed that the governments could be insulated from large-scale pressures. Madison's balance-of-power proposition assumed that the delicate political balance would produce workable policy, while Wilson's case for accountability rested on an assumption of a bureaucracy shaped by hierarchical authority. The traditions still powerfully shape the way Americans think about and act upon American public administration. Within each of these traditions, however, new challenges have arisen that pose fundamental problems.

THE WILSONIAN DILEMMA

Wilson's approach to public administration laid out a neat strategy for organizing administrative work: elected officials defined policy and delegated the details to top-level administrators; these administrators worked within a hierarchy to organize the work; and authority within the hierarchy ensured that the exercise of administrative discretion remained consistent with policymakers' goals. His theory guided public administration for a century. He intended it as a mechanism for promoting both efficiency (by building hierarchies and controlling them through authority) and accountability (by separating elected officials who make policy from administrators who carry it out). Even though analysts have long attacked this approach as a thin reed on which to build theory or practice, Wilson's ideas have dominated the public administration community.

In the last third of the twentieth century, however, government began relying on new tools, especially grants, contracts, and loans, which undermined Wilson's theory.[2] Unlike direct delivery of services by government bureaucracies, these tools operated more through incentives and partnerships with nongovernmental players than through governmental management with hierarchical authority. With the erosion of traditional tactics, government managers had to devise new mechanisms to ensure effectiveness and accountability. As Lester M. Salamon put it, "Instead of the centralized hierarchical agencies delivering standardized services that is caricatured in much of the current reform literature and most of our political rhetoric, what exists in most spheres of policy is a dense mosaic of policy tools, many of them placing public agencies in complex, interdependent relationships with a host of third-party partners."[3] For example, one study of human service programs in sixteen communities revealed that government itself delivered only 40 percent of public programs in 1982. As partnerships for welfare and other social service programs spread in the 1990s, the government's direct service provision shrank further. The more such indirect tools rose in importance, the less traditional theory provided guidance for managing the already problematic traditions of public administration. Such tools were often more complex to manage, and government found itself struggling to manage them without the reassuring intellectual framework that a century of administrative theory had provided for directly managed programs.

Getting a clear fix on the scale of this movement is difficult because government keeps its books according to how much it spends, not who does its work. Moreover, the full financial implications of some indirect tools, like loan and tax programs, do not show up in standard budget scorekeeping. In fact, that is one of the political attractions of these new tools. Policymakers can expand government programs without their full cost appearing in the budget. Nevertheless, by the end of the twentieth century, indirect tools had become the dominant form of federal administrative action. In 1999, Lester M. Salamon analyzed the full range of federal activity that year, including spending, loan, insurance, and regulatory programs. He estimated that at least 83 percent of all federal financial activity occurred using indirect tools like contracts, grants, loans, and regulation. Of the 17 percent of the federal government's remaining financial activity, 9 percent went for income support (mostly for Social Security) and 4 percent went for interest on the debt (for payments to individuals and organizations holding federal securities). That left only about 3 percent of all federal financial activity for goods and services, from air-traffic control to management of the national parks, that the federal government administered itself.[4] In the last two decades of the twentieth century, federal spending through indirect methods has increased while federal spending through direct provision of goods and services has shrunk—probably by half.[5] Direct spending for goods and services at the state and local levels is greater, since a much larger share of their budgets goes for police, fire, emergency, and education services, all of which are provided by government employees. However, even in local government, contracting out has grown significantly, especially for road construction and maintenance, social services, and support services.

Wilson's administrative tradition was founded on the direct government administration of public services. The government's changing strategies and tactics, therefore, pushed the actual management of public programs out of sync with the theories that had long guided them. The sources of this trend vary greatly. Ideologues have argued that shifting service provision from government to the private sector would improve efficiency and reduce the incentives for an ever-burgeoning government. Pragmatists have argued the need for greater flexibility in service delivery.[6]

But beyond its roots, three things are clear. First, in many ways, there is nothing new here. Governments have relied on contractors for millennia. Indeed, the Roman legions relied on their own defense contractors as they conquered most of the land within reach. The "ideal type" of direct government administration has never really described the full range of scope of governmental activity.

Second, even though governments have always relied on contractors, the scope and scale of this contracting out increased significantly in American government toward the end of the twentieth century. The balance between indirect and direct governmental tools significantly shifted, and American governments showed no signs that the trend would reverse. The linkage between the dominant Wilsonian idea and reality thus became increasingly strained, and more public administration occurred outside the fundamental theoretical framework.

Third, this change brought significant administrative implications. Analysts have debated whether indirect tools are harder to manage than direct ones. However, at the very least, managing government's set of indirect tools requires a *different* collection of people skills, organizational processes, and control mechanisms. These different tactics, in turn, require different people skills and, perhaps, even different people. The comptroller general of the United States, David M. Walker, called this issue the government's "human capital problem" and found that the government's "human capital management has emerged as the missing link in the statutory and management framework that Congress and the executive branch have established to provide for more businesslike and results-oriented federal government."[7]

Authority still matters, but at the start of the twenty-first century it mattered less than a century earlier, when Wilson's tradition ruled.[8] At the same time, it continues to provide the basic framework for the structure of government agencies and how they relate to other political institutions. The intellectual challenge lies in updating government's tools to fit these new realities. The Wilsonian tradition simply could not account for most of how the federal government—and, to a growing degree, state and local governments as well—performed its functions. As a result, American government increasingly found itself focused on governmental tools that had become much less important. It was poorly equipped to handle the emerging tools that increasingly dominated government activity. As the twenty-first century dawned, a yawning gap had emerged between government's dominant management technologies, founded on traditional Wilsonian principles, and the tools it used to deliver government services, which were distinctly non-Wilsonian. That poses the Wilsonian dilemma: *How can we secure efficient and responsive public administration when there is no chain of hierarchical authority linking policymakers with those who deliver public services?*

THE MADISONIAN DILEMMA

American public administration has always struggled to accommodate its pursuit of efficient management with the political system's idiosyncratic diffusion of power. Managerial efficiency seeks strategies to produce high value at the lowest costs, but for any of the strategies to work, managers must know what goals they are seeking. That is always a tall order in the public sector, but it is all the more the case in the United States.

In part, this is because the American separation-of-powers system is exquisitely balanced to ensure that no one ultimately is in charge of anything. The founders worried about an over-concentration of power in any branch of government. In particular, a too-strong president would raise the old worries about monarchical power; a too-strong Congress would bring to the surface worries about the recurring ineffectiveness that plagued the Articles of Confederation. The founders balanced power among the institutions and put the judiciary in a position to keep an eye on both the other branches. That has indeed secured a remarkable political balance over the centuries, but it has created an ongoing administrative predicament. The balance-of-powers approach builds on the art of compromise, and compromise blurs the objectives of public policy.

Compromise, of course, is part of politics everywhere, but the Madisonian features of American democracy introduce peculiarly American dilemmas for public managers. The interplay of the three branches means that no decision is ever truly final. Congress passes a bill, usually after negotiating at least quietly with the president and his staff. The executive branch administers the law, but rarely without at least subtle consultation with Congress and its committees. Anyone who disagrees with the way a law emerges from Congress can take the case to the executive branch and hope to bend rules and procedures more to his or her liking. And anyone who disagrees with those twists can seek leverage through congressional oversight and budgetary action. Those who lose in either forum can seek redress through the courts. As a result, decisions are rarely ever absolute. Every decision is subject to reinterpretation and revision as administration evolves. This dance of implementation has helped the government adapt and endure, despite the huge problems the nation has encountered and the vast pluralism of the interests at play. But it regularly proves frustrating to administrators who seek a clear sense of direction to guide their work.

The great genius of the Founders, captured in Madison's elegant arguments for balance, lay in creating a system that could survive, even thrive, among the pressures and counterpressures of modern society. The system's great administrative problem, however, grew directly from its political strength. The very elements that promoted political steadiness made it difficult to strengthen the system's administration and improve its results. As the Clinton administration sought to "reinvent" American government, for example, administration officials and analysts compared their efforts with the New Zealand reforms, widely viewed as the world's most aggressive.[9] In New Zealand, the connection between political decisions and administrative action was relatively straightforward. Parliament set the policy goals and delegated implementation to government ministers. The ministers signed management contracts with chief executives, who had great flexibility in managing the programs as long as they delivered the outputs defined in the contracts. As the New Zealand Treasury argued in a report to help guide the 1987 transition for a new prime minister:

> Making the right choices about the nature and form of government intervention is the key to effective economic and social management. . . . Where the Government makes an intervention in some area it is important that it be done well. The design of efficient and effective institutions is difficult. Careful consideration must be given to the specification of objectives (to avoid ambiguous or conflicting objectives), to the scope of the authority given to managers (it must be sufficient to allow the manager to manage effectively), to effective lines of accountability, an effective way of assessing performance (which is not easy if the institution's shares are not publicly traded), and above all else to the

way in which incentives can be designed to ensure that the objectives of managers and other employees are aligned with the institution's objectives.[10]

The contrast with the American system could scarcely be greater. The New Zealand reforms built on the clarity of goals and accountability of managers. The American reforms built on the search for political consensus. Some American reformers wistfully visited New Zealand and wished for the opportunity to import that system to the United States.[11] New Zealand reformers visited the United States and wondered how the country managed to run anything at all.

This is not to say that the New Zealand system—or, indeed, any other system—is superior to the American one. Indeed, the New Zealanders have constantly tinkered with their reforms. They have struggled, in particular, to link the output-based focus of management—what should agency managers do?—to the outcome-based focus of politics—what results do these programs have? None of the management reforms introduced around the world during the 1990s proved stable because all of them struggled to balance the connection between policy and its administration. No system proved inherently superior—and every nation struggled to strengthen the connection between its political decisions and its management processes.

Compared with virtually any other nation's, America's political and administrative systems are highly fragmented. That does not necessarily mean that the quality of management is worse in the United States. It does mean that the separation of powers and federalism place extra burdens on both elected officials and administrators: to translate broad, sometimes conflicting political goals into goals clear enough for administrators to follow; to hold administrators accountable for goals that often shift underneath them; and to link administrative structures with the peculiarly American diffusion of responsibility. That shapes the Madisonian dilemma: *How can we secure efficient and responsive public administration, which presumes clear lines of authority, when the constitutional separation-of-powers system diffuses responsibility? Who is in charge when no one is in charge—or if everyone is in charge?*

The Jeffersonian Dilemma

That brings in the Jeffersonian dilemma. As president, even Jefferson was not a Jeffersonian. Through the Louisiana Purchase, the gentleman farmer from Virginia produced the greatest expansion of federal reach in American history. That only underlines the profound irony of Jefferson's administrative tradition. Perhaps none of the four administrative traditions has historically been more honored but less followed.

Nowhere has that been truer than in the ongoing debate over devolution of responsibility within American federalism. As the federal role expanded, so too did its partnerships with state and local governments and the opportunities for leveraging policy decisions. The antipoverty programs of the 1960s, the pollution control programs of the 1970s, the social service programs of the 1980s, and the welfare reform of the 1990s all relied heavily on state and local government implementation of federal standards. In each case, the argument was that governments closer to the people could be far more politically and administratively responsive to local needs. Furthermore, these strategies allowed a substantial growth in federal programs without increasing federal employment or multiplying the number of federal agencies. Federalism, of course, has been an underlying principle of American government since its inception. Conflict over federalism has been just as deeply rooted, whether the conflict was armed (as in the Civil War) or legal (as in the struggle over civil rights).

In vastly multiplying the loci of action, in explicitly giving state and local governments authority to adjust national goals to local conditions, and in adding their contributions to federal money, the federalism strategy has made it far more difficult to determine what the "goal" of any program is or to assess what results they produce. This process provides an uncommon level of flexibility, one of the central virtues of the American system. In the federal Medicaid program, for example, different states add different supplements to fund different levels of service. No two states, in fact, have identical versions of the same federal entitlement program. The same is true of welfare reform, environmental policy, and other national programs. The counterpoint to local flexibility is wide variation in the goals pursued and the results achieved, and that further fogs accountability in the process. The enduring reality—the great political strength and administrative nightmare—is that no policy decision in the United States is ever final.

Jefferson anticipated neither the hyperdevolution that has resulted in so many national responsibilities being shared with local governments nor the intrusion of globalization into the fabric of American government. Jefferson's bucolic image of local self-government was of a self-contained government. The facts of twenty-first century governance have removed the few remaining bits of romance from that idyllic vision. That shapes the Jeffersonian dilemma: *How can we secure efficient and responsive government in an era when the federal government devolves so much responsibility to state and local governments and, at the same time,*

finds itself swept along by broader globalizing trends? Is it possible to secure account-
ability when there is no locus for accountability and where responsibility is spread
across the entire political landscape?

THE HAMILTONIAN DILEMMA

Hamilton imagined a pragmatic solution to Jeffersonianism. He never believed
that Jefferson's reverence for local self-government could ever work in practice,
and he sought instead to strengthen the nation's ability to craft and sustain a
strong commercial footing. Hamilton was a pragmatist and viewed his argument
for a strong federal executive as the essential and inevitable prerequisite for a
strong national economy and for a rich quality of life for America's citizens.

In many ways, Hamilton anticipated America's future. If the Constitution created a three-way separation of powers, the president has clearly become first
among equals. If the Tenth Amendment reserved powers to the states, the federal government has set the agenda for much state action (even if the states pursue infinite variations on that agenda). The federal executive—especially the
presidency—is the fulcrum on which American government sways. The power
of different players might rise and fall, but the president is never far from the
center. As the twentieth century wore on, American government increasingly
became presidential government, to the point that Nixon's critics fretted over
his "imperial presidency."[12] Concentrated on a single person, in contrast to
Congress, which has 535 members, and with unequaled ability to command the
media, the presidency is both the symbol and focus of American government.

If Americans have almost all become Hamiltonians, Hamiltonians have struggled to make sense of fundamental changes in governance. Hamilton argued the
need for a strong government to shape commerce and a strong president to command the government. What he never anticipated was the government's broad
sharing of its power with nongovernmental partners and the difficulty of integrating them into the conduct of public policy. Neither did he anticipate the
flood of global influences into American public policy. He always saw government shaping commerce, not the other way around. In short, what Hamilton
never expected was the importance of *governance* as well as *government*.

As Hamilton had hoped, the executive has become the center of American
government. But the executive does not hold sway over American governance.
Power has become broadly shared with nongovernmental partners; federal power
is shared with state and local partners; and no important problem remains within
the boundaries of any local government for long. Transnational problems intrude

constantly on American government. Citizens expect government to respond, but government cannot control the tools of action. These changes frame the Hamiltonian dilemma: *How can we secure efficient and responsive government when government is only one player among many? No matter how efficient and responsive government might be, how can it solve problems it cannot control?*

Fuzzy Boundaries

Each of these four dilemmas presents a common problem—"fuzzy boundaries." The administrative orthodoxy of the twentieth century depended on drawing clear lines of responsibility, especially who was in charge of setting policy and who was in charge of implementing which pieces of policy. The four dilemmas all demonstrate different difficulties in setting boundaries. These problems, of course, have affected nations around the world, and because American government was founded with deliberate sharing of responsibility and multiple channels of access, it was better positioned than most of the world's governments for the transformations that occurred at the dawn of the twenty-first century. American government nevertheless faced the challenge of devising new strategies to cope with the administrative implications of this transformation.

The fuzzy-boundary problem confounds the central task of administration—building coordinated efforts to solve complex problems. Administration, in both public and private life, is a search for coordination. It is about how leaders pull together widely disparate resources—money, people, expertise, and technology—to do complex things. The implementation of public programs requires an intricate performance, whether it is the dispatch of highly trained firefighters to the scene of a disaster or the high-tech ballet that safely separates planes in the air-traffic control system. Indeed, as Harold Seidman points out, coordination is the "philosopher's stone" of public management.[13] Medieval alchemists believed that if they could find the magic stone, they would find the answers to human problems. Coordination, Seidman argues, has the same appeal for managers and reformers. "If only we can find the right formula for coordination," he writes, "we can reconcile the irreconcilable, harmonize competing and wholly divergent interests, overcome irrationalities in our government structures, and make hard policy choices to which no one will disagree."[14] Coordination becomes the answer to government's problems; the lack of coordination is the diagnosis for its failures.

As responsibility for implementing public programs has become more broadly shared, however, devising effective coordination strategies has become more difficult. Moreover, as authority has become a less effective tool with which to solve problems, managers have struggled to determine what can best replace it. Twenty-first century bureaucracy thus faces a host of new coordination problems. With responsibility for management so broadly shared, no bureaucracy can completely encompass, manage, or control any problem that really matters. Pursuing either efficiency or responsiveness is far more difficult when no one is fully in charge of anything.

When partners share responsibility for managing programs, how well the programs work depends on how well the partnerships work. Managing government programs effectively thus increasingly depends on bridging the fuzzy boundaries that separate those who make policy from those in the complex interdependent chain of those who share responsibility for implementing it. Six fuzzy boundaries, in particular, are important in managing public programs:

1. *Policymaking versus policy execution.* With responsibility for policy so diffuse, where does the boundary lie between policymakers and policy administrators?

2. *Public versus private versus nonprofit sectors.* With responsibility for results fundamentally shared among the sectors, where do the boundaries between the sectors lie?

3. *Layers within the bureaucracy.* With efforts afoot to flatten the bureaucracy and trim middle management, where does responsibility for the critical management and administrative decisions lie?

4. *Layers between management and labor.* Tensions between management and labor in government, as in the private sector, abound. How do these tensions affect the performance of public programs?

5. *Connections between bureaucracies.* With service recipients and policy reformers alike demanding more service coordination between and among bureaucracies, how can managers sort out the responsibilities of each bureaucracy?

6. *Connections with citizens.* With reformers seeking to treat citizens more as "customers," what is the proper relationship between government agencies and the citizens they serve?

POLICYMAKING VERSUS POLICY EXECUTION

Wilson, Goodnow, and their colleagues set the stage for the century-long battle over whether one can truly distinguish policy execution from policymaking. Since then, of course, scores of political scientists have contended that political decisions have meaning only in administrative action. Matthew Holden Jr., for example, argued in his 1999 American Political Science Association presidential address, "If students of politics, in this country and around the world, wish to observe power in action, then the crucial focus is discretion regarding the actual use of information, money or its surrogates, and force." Indeed, Holden argued simply, "administration is the lifeblood of power."[15] It is one thing to declare that safe streets or high-quality public education ought to be available to all citizens. It is quite another to make it happen. To do so requires discretion—whether to do more of one thing than another or to decide which thing is appropriate to do first. The exercise of discretion, in turn, requires a choice among competing values, and that means administrators inevitably make political judgments in managing programs.

The government reform movements of the 1990s took very different routes toward resolving this problem. The reforms launched in Australia, the United Kingdom, and especially New Zealand, built on the assumption that politics and administration can—and should—be separated. The American reforms, by contrast, drew no such sharp line between politics and administration. The Clinton administration's "reinventing government" effort, for example, argued the need to give front-line managers more flexibility so they could better meet the needs of citizens. It was a strategy founded on an assumption that managers know how to do their jobs and that top officials ought to get out of the way and let them perform. It built on a blurring of the lines of policy and administration.

The differences in the reform techniques underline just how slippery a concept "policy" has become. A definition of "policy" limited to the decisions of elected officials is ludicrously inadequate. On the other hand, a definition extended through the long chain of decisions required to carry it out would be impossibly broad. This has complicated the task of separating administration from policy and of determining who is responsible for what.

Public, Private, and Nonprofit Sectors

Even more than citizens in most countries, Americans have never much liked government. Since the dawn of time, taxing has never been popular, and no level of public service is ever really adequate. But the American republic was founded on a rebellion against government, even if it was a monarchical government, and its framers wrote the American Constitution to put strong limits on government's power. In many but certainly not all parts of American society, the instinct has been to criticize government endlessly for its failings and to contend

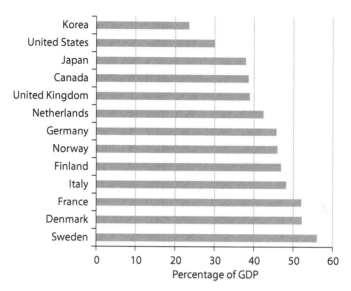

Figure 3.1. General Government Total Outlays
Source: Organisation for Economic Co-operation and Development, *OECD Economic Outlook* 68 (December 2000): 236.

continuously that the private sector could do any job better. Despite the criticisms, Americans over time have asked government to take on an ever-lengthening list of responsibilities. Nevertheless, as figure 3.1 shows, American government, at least as measured by the percentage of the gross domestic product devoted to public spending, ranks almost at the bottom of industrialized nations. With government spending at 30 percent of its gross domestic product compared with Sweden, which spends more than 50 percent, the United States has still found itself criticized for its size of government despite being among the smallest of the world's leading governments. It has taken on more responsibilities without growing disproportionately.

The public-private sector dichotomy likewise has obsessed both analysts and policymakers in the United States. Americans have never much liked government and, like reformers around the world, have often argued that markets produce better solutions than public power does. If government seemed inefficient or unresponsive, then market competition might offer the hope of giving consumers more choice at lower cost. The Reagan administration produced a report, based on a private sector survey, on how the government could reduce its costs through more privatization.[16] The Clinton administration's "reinventing government" campaign continually re-echoed the need to teach the government lessons from the nation's best-run private companies.[17] Both Bush administrations aggressively pursued public-private partnerships, tax cuts to shrink the government, and turning more responsibility over to the private sector. Other nations have likewise expanded government's relationship with the private sector. Reformers have not only copied the British and New Zealand strategy of converting state-owned enterprises to market-driven private companies or public-private hybrids. They have also followed the American contracting-out model even more aggressively.

Americans, in particular, have long argued the need to fix clear boundaries between public and private power. Such boundaries offered the Jeffersonian hope of protecting individual liberty from the threat of governmental tyranny, but the reality has never matched the rhetoric. In the eighteenth century, settlers asked for government protection on the frontier. In the nineteenth century, travelers clamored for government regulation of private enterprises, from steamboats whose boilers blew up far too often to trusts whose monopolies gouged consumers. In the twentieth century, calls for a stronger governmental role occurred even more often than complaints about overreaching public power. By the end of the century, television newsmagazines regularly alternated "give me a break!" features about government gone amuck with plaintive stories of citizens in need—along with a tag line such as "Why isn't the government protecting us?" The calls for more government, in fact, reached unprecedented levels following the September 11, 2001, terrorist attacks on New York and Washington.

As government's reach expanded with stronger public-private partnerships, government sought to retain its sovereignty over crucial decisions while sharing more power with nongovernmental partners. It worked to ensure that its partners managed programs efficiently while it lost the traditional leverage that came through hierarchy and authority.[18] The rhetoric calling for sharper boundaries between government and the private sector continued to grow out of the Jeffersonian tradition. The administrative tactics, however, produced boundaries between government, business, and nonprofit organizations that were ever fuzzier.

LAYERS WITHIN THE BUREAUCRACY

Fuzzy boundaries exist within the bureaucracy as well as outside it. For example, the 1986 space shuttle *Challenger* tragedy stemmed in large part from communication problems across boundaries—between NASA and its contractors but also across boundaries within NASA. The night before the fatal launch, engineers working for Morton Thiokol, the contractor that built the shuttle's solid rocket motors, warned that launching the shuttle in freezing weather posed serious risks. These warnings, however, never reached top NASA officials charged with the launch decisions. Low-level NASA engineers shared the worries of their Morton Thiokol colleagues, but mid-level NASA managers decided that the concerns were not serious enough to stop the launch and did not inform top agency officials. The project had suffered a series of embarrassments, from an inability to keep to the schedule to, on one occasion, difficulty in finding the right tools to pop open the shuttle's hatch following a launch cancellation. Top officials worried that more such problems would erode public support, and they put heavy pressure to get the *Challenger* into orbit. These internal boundary problems in the end proved tragically fatal.[19]

James Q. Wilson's classic, *Bureaucracy*, argues that most government agencies must cope with these three very different internal cultures. "Operators," Wilson wrote, perform the basic work of government agencies. What they do and how they do it define the organization's culture. "Managers" help organizations cope with the constraints imposed by the political environment. "Executives," finally, seek to maintain their organization's "turf" and autonomy.[20] These three levels are important because the roles of officials at each level are different. These different roles lead to different organizational perspectives.

Because officials at each organizational level have different functions, sociologist Talcott Parsons concluded, the gaps between the levels can interrupt the chain of command.[21] As the *Challenger* accident illustrated, these different perspectives can in turn hinder communication—by making lower-level officials cautious about speaking and higher-level officials deaf in hearing. The boundaries separating operators from managers and managers from executives are certainly fuzzy, but the three cultures are very real and important for the management of public organizations. Bridging those boundaries is one of the most critical jobs that government officials have. Moreover, as the tasks and relationships of public management become more complex, the gaps between the three cultures have threatened to expand, and the job of bridging them has become more important.

When the "government bureaucracy" interacts with its external partners, therefore, it is not just as a monolithic entity. The "bureaucracy" is really composed of different individuals at different levels with different instincts and goals. These officials interact, in turn, with counterparts in other bureaucracies who share similar characteristics. Officials at different levels tend to behave differently; as they interact with other officials at different levels in different bureaucracies, problems in communication, performance, and accountability often arise. Top-level executives must manage the programs for which they are responsible. They must also span the boundaries between different types of officials within the bureaucracy to prevent failures that could prove politically embarrassing. Mid-level managers must ensure that the operators perform their tasks and serve as a shock absorber between external forces (transmitted from top-level executives) and internal pathologies (generated by operators). The operators must do the organization's work within the resource limits imposed on them. Failure to bridge the boundaries between levels can create temporary breakdowns, chronic performance problems, political embarrassments, and, sometimes, great tragedies.

LAYERS BETWEEN MANAGEMENT AND LABOR

With the exception of the occasional outbreaks of labor-management tensions like the 1981 air-traffic controllers strike, the federal government has been spared the virulent worker-management battles that have plagued many private companies, some state and local governments, and many foreign governments. The lack of high-profile struggles has tended to hide enduring labor-management tensions, however. When congressional hearings in 1997 and 1998 highlighted problems in the IRS, treasury officials struggled with reforms because of the monumental task of changing the behavior of the service's 95,000 employees. In the 1980s and 1990s, downsizing the Pentagon became enmeshed in ongoing disputes over protecting the jobs and transforming the work of civilian employees. The Clinton administration's "reinvention" effort centered on shrinking the federal workforce and on reducing the number of bureaucratic layers. While the number of federal employees who belong to public employee unions is closely held, the percentage of federal employees represented by unions is especially high in agencies like the IRS, Social Security Administration, and other agencies with large numbers of clerical employees. Federal managers tend to view the unions as an impediment to flexible operations, and it is a constant refrain among federal managers that labor-management tensions span a set of very well-protected boundaries.

The Clinton "reinventing government" initiative recognized the importance of these tensions: the substantial number of employees covered by collective bargaining agreements; the tremendous political problems that Ronald Reagan had after breaking the air-traffic controllers union; the special bonds that the Democratic Party had enjoyed with unions, especially public employee unions; and the damage that strong union opposition could have inflicted on the National Performance Review (NPR) at its very start. To counter these problems, the administration created the National Partnership Council, composed of top-level managers and union representatives. Charged with reinventing labor-management relations as the administration tried to reinvent government, the council in fact accomplished relatively little beyond defusing the potential of initial strong union opposition to the NPR's downsizing. Many government managers, moreover, complained that downsizing disrupted labor-management relations and made it even harder to manage effectively.

The George W. Bush administration tried a different tack. In 2000, the Office of Management and Budget (OMB) ordered agencies to develop plans to reduce the number of layers between top policymakers and citizens and to put more workers into positions where they could serve citizens.[22] The goal certainly was admirable: Who could object to structuring government agencies so that they best served citizens? In many federal agencies, however, from the Federal Aviation Administration to the Centers for Disease Control and from most of the State Department to the National Institutes of Health, most federal employees do not have contact with citizens. Their job is to do the background work that makes programs function. Moreover, the government is most thickly layered at the very top, with many levels of political appointees, and the administration did not propose to reduce the layers by trimming the number of these appointments.[23] The OMB's directive simply did not match the changing realities of federal management.

Other nations included more explicit labor-management changes in the 1980s as part of their reforms. New Zealand, for example, dramatically changed those relationships along with the move to government-by-contract and, in 2000, launched a "partnership for quality" between government and its employees.[24] In the United Kingdom, the government pursued a more collaborative effort as part of the "Next Steps" initiative. The strategy, among other things, decentralized bargaining substantially and gave a great deal of negotiating authority to agency officials.

No nation's management reforms have solved the labor-management conundrum. New dilemmas, moreover, lay over the horizon. Given the limits on public employee unions' rights within government, could the unions find new strength by organizing workers in nongovernmental organizations that have come to play a larger role in service delivery? Can managers devise innovative ways to motivate and discipline employees to improve their ability to deliver results? Can government develop a better match between its management needs and the capacity of its employees? As Comptroller General David M. Walker argued, "No organization can maximize its economy, efficiency, and effectiveness without having up-to-date, state-of-the-art, human capital strategies that are integrated with its overall strategic plan. People are assets in which one has to invest, in which one expects a return, in which one has to manage the risk. People are not an unlimited resource one can consume and throw away."[25] Americans, like the citizens of most nations, have never much liked bureaucrats, but the importance of good managers, well-trained, has never been greater.

CONNECTIONS BETWEEN BUREAUCRACIES

The policy-administration, public-private-nonprofit, bureaucratic-level, and labor-management fuzzy boundaries create substantial coordination problems. But the biggest coordination problem—the one for which organizational alchemists have for millennia sought the philosopher's stone—is coordination *between* bureaucracies. If this coordination problem is ageless, it increased in the last third of the twentieth century as a product of both the growing ambition of government and the transformation of governance in seeking to serve that ambition.

Some coordination problems occur within government. In the aftermath of the September 2001 terrorist attack, for example, President Bush named Pennsylvania Governor Tom Ridge to head a new Office of Homeland Security. Ridge's mission was to coordinate both the government's intelligence information and its operational response. Critics pointed, for example, to the problems of pulling together facts and analysis from such disparate sources as the FBI, the CIA, and the National Security Agency. A unified response required uniting the efforts of the Coast Guard, Border Patrol, and the Immigration and Naturalization Service, among other agencies. The problem was clear and the need was great. On the other hand, many government agencies shared responsibility for pieces of work, and no agency had responsibility for it all. Like most public problems, the government's antiterrorist policy played out through a network of agencies. Each agency, in turn, was part of multiple networks working on a host of different problems. If there were but one problem, policymakers could simply reorganize government agencies to focus on that problem. But as problems proliferated, so too did the networks—and the impossibility of drawing clear boundaries around any of them.

Other coordination problems occurred between government and its nongovernmental partners—and among those partners as well. The American welfare reform initiative of the 1990s, for example, depended on moving welfare recipients to productive long-term employment. That required assessing a welfare recipient's job skills; providing job training to help the recipient be more employable; securing transportation to get the recipient to training and, eventually, to a new job; finding a good job to put those new skills into practice; securing day care for the recipient's children; and frequently ensuring health care, subsidized housing, and Food Stamps through the transition to work. The recipient's children might be troubled at school and require remedial work, and too often the children stumble into problems with the law and require attention from the juvenile justice system. Children of newly working parents might need after-school care and could well benefit from new recreational and educational help. Welfare reform thus was not one program but the complex amalgamation of perhaps a dozen or more different programs, each run by a different agency. It could not succeed unless each of those programs supported the overall mission, much as different pieces of an orchestra combine to produce fine music—except that in the case of welfare reform and other complex programs, the orchestra plays without a conductor.

Recurring jokes focus on how much time government managers spend in meetings. Everyone agrees that managers spend more time in meetings than they need to, but one of the reasons meetings have proliferated is that officials need face-to-face conversations to resolve the nonroutine issues that routinely develop across organizational boundaries. That is where much of any organization's hardest work takes place—and where, if the boundaries are not understood well and spanned carefully, citizens can fall through the cracks.

Relationships with Citizens

Reformers, finally, have eagerly sought to redefine government's relationships with its citizens. The Clinton administration built its strategy on the notion that "taxpayers are customers too." Private-sector managers and consultants, in fact, challenged the federal government to become "raging inexorable thunderlizard evangelists of customer service," as management guru Tom Peters put it.[26] In fact, turning citizens into customers and making the customer's—not the bureaucracy's—needs the goal of government agencies was the centerpiece of the reinventing government movement. Reinvention advocates David Osborne and Ted Gaebler argued that "while businesses strive to please customers, government agencies strive to please interest groups." As a result, citizens become irritated with "the arrogance of the bureaucracy." Reform, they concluded, requires "getting close to the customer" and "putting the customer into the driver's seat."[27]

In other nations, the customer service movement has been even more aggressive. The British government created "citizens' charters," which sought to guarantee citizens a prescribed level of service. Signs at British railway stations listed the on-time performance of different trains, and regular riders received rebates if a train's performance did not meet standards. Similar customer-service initiatives drove reforms in both New Zealand and Australia. Improving citizen satisfaction with government programs was a central goal of most government reform efforts.

The customer-service movement, however, enraged many academic analysts.[28] Individuals are citizens and taxpayers, not "customers," the argument went. It would be hard to suggest that government should not be as responsive as possible to the needs of its citizens, and surely anything that improves the quality of government services is a good thing. Shorter waiting lines at customs and immigration facilities and more on-time delivery from the Postal Service can scarcely be a bad idea. Simple IRS forms and friendlier Social Security offices would certainly receive warm taxpayer welcomes. But such notions only begin to explore the issues implicit in the customer-service approach. Five unresolved problems make it difficult to use "customer service" as a touchstone for management reform.[29]

1. *Who is the customer?* The customer-service advocates typically proceed as if everyone knew just who government's customers are and what they want. That, however, is rarely the case. There are at least four different perspectives on the citizen-as-customer. As *service recipients*, citizens naturally want large (sometimes even unlimited) high-quality services at low (even no) cost. If it snows, citizens want their streets plowed—immediately. If a pothole develops, they want it filled before they break an axle on their car. They want parks that are clean and safe, schools that teach kids to read and write well, police that arrest criminals quickly, and food inspection services that keep dangerous germs away from their stomachs. In short, they want a responsive government. This perspective most closely matches the total-quality-management approach of the private sector: find out what customers want and find a way to give it to them.

Citizens, however, often are *partners in service provision* as well. More government programs, from welfare reform and social services to environmental protection and recreation, require citizens to be active participants in the process.

As these partnerships grow, the need for coordinating services among the partners multiplies. Citizens want programs that work effectively, where service provision is seamless regardless of bureaucratic boundaries. As customers of these services, citizens must play a strong role very different from the more passive role suggested by the customer-as-service-recipient one.

Third, citizens are *"owners" of the government* and expect accountability. If there are problems, they expect that they will be solved. In the American system, this means acting through the formal process of republican democracy: elections, administrative oversight, judicial review, and the other strategies and tactics that drive American political life. The relationship is not as direct as it is in transactions between a business and its customers. The relationship, rather, is more like that between a company's stockholders and its management. Stockholders can be customers, too, but the relationship and expectations are different.

Finally, citizens are *taxpayers*, and as such they pay the government's bills. As service recipients, they might expect virtually unlimited service; as taxpayers, they expect tough management, high efficiency, and minimal waste, fraud, and abuse. These standards, moreover, are as much political as managerial. Fraud is a legal term, but "waste" often is in the eye of the beholder. One person's waste is often money that flows into someone else's favorite program. Senior citizens sometimes criticize agricultural subsidies, while farmers wonder why Medicare costs so much. Thus, not only do the interests of citizens-as-service-recipients often conflict with their interests as citizens-as-taxpayers, but citizens rarely agree on how their tax dollars can best be spent.

It is clear that government should try hard to serve the needs of its citizens and to do so responsively. It is also clear that government has a long way to go. But it is often deceptively difficult to define clearly what "customer service" truly means. The relationships between citizens and their government in a democratic society are far more intricate and difficult than those between a customer and the private organization seeking the customer's business. Customer service thus is a valuable target but in actuality is perhaps only one of several.

2. *How should connections with customers be designed?* The customer-service model, drawn as it is from the private sector, presumes a straightforward connection between customer and organization. In the private sector, the market transaction is the fundamental building block for customer service. In the public sector, however, the transactions not only are typically not market-based, but the connections between elected policymakers, government agencies, and the proxies who produce many of government's goods and services are at best attenuated.

Most federal agencies and many state agencies do not deal directly with citizens. Their business, rather, is with each other and with government's proxies. In most public programs, moreover, organizations do not have a choice about which services they will provide customers. Programs and priorities are fixed in law.

That scarcely makes the customer-service concept useless. Many imaginative public managers, for example, have created the notion of "internal customers" to describe those within government whose needs they are responsible for meeting. They suggest, for example, that personnel managers must think of the needs of the agencies for which they recruit personnel instead of the dictates of their own procedures. They suggest that contract managers must work toward high performance by their contractors instead of mere compliance with internal paperwork. The nature of government's administrative strategies and tactics, however, make it hard to import private-sector notions of customer service to its operations. Many private-sector companies, of course, work through proxies as well. But the multiple boundaries within areas of public service provision create stark and very different challenges.

3. *How can government avoid hypersensitivity to customers' wishes?* Much of government's problem is not so much insensitivity but hypersensitivity to citizens' demands. Elected officials, naturally, wish to please their constituents. Indeed, one of Congress's first acts upon learning that the budget was to be balanced in fiscal year 1998 was to pass a massive transportation bill that provided highway improvements to virtually every congressional district. From higher Social Security checks and new dams to cleanup of waste dumps, the relationship between voters and elected officials can swell government spending and make it hard to judge where customer service stops and waste begins. The 2001 debate over a fiscal stimulus plan brought forth ideas to funnel tax cuts and spending increases to virtually every political constituency.

These pressures, of course, are scarcely a phenomenon limited to the United States. Moreover, some critics have suggested that government is already hyper-tuned to microlevel needs yet lacks the capacity or incentives to deliver broad, sustained, high-level performance.[30] George Frederickson has contended that genuine reinvention of government that focuses only on reinventing the administrative process will fail. He argues for "total quality politics" to supplement "total quality management."[31]

4. *How can government balance top-down and bottom-up pressures?* Historical notions of governmental accountability, along with traditional public administrative practice, build from the top down. In the traditional model, citizens vote

for elected officials. These officials make policy and delegate administrative responsibility to executive-branch agencies. These agencies implement their own policy in accordance with the policy set at the top. If citizens object to administrative behavior, the standard course of action is to work through their elected officials. Redress of grievances is a top-down affair, which turns tradition on its head. It argues that front-line government workers ought to identify and respond directly to citizens' needs. It contends that the rest of the bureaucracy ought to be structured to make this connection as effective as possible. Most important, it makes accountability bottom-up instead of top-down.

This raises two difficult problems. First, it squeezes government managers between two perspectives—the traditional top-down approach to rational-legal accountability and the bottom-up approach to greater citizen satisfaction. Such a squeeze often proves uncomfortable at best and creates impossible dilemmas at worst. Second, it raises a stark challenge to the rule of law and accountability on which American government is based. The more grassroots administrators adjust their practice to accommodate the needs and demands of citizens, the more elected officials can become marginalized. The more elected officials insert themselves into the transactions between front-line administrators and citizens, the more administrators often struggle to provide customer service. Elected officials thus can find themselves squeezed between the top-down process (citizens as voters) and the bottom-up process (citizens as customers). The customer-service approach makes their role anything but clear and creates the potential for great tension.

Especially when coupled with the other problems surrounding the customer-service movement, the top-down or bottom-up dilemma is a difficult one for public managers. Improved responsiveness of government to citizens/customers/taxpayers is, of course, an ideal toward which all democratic governments strive. The customer service movement, however, complicates as much as it guides by leaving critical questions unanswered and boundaries even fuzzier.

5. *How should government balance responsiveness through customer service with other governance objectives?* It is impossible to argue that government should not provide services in a responsive and friendly way. It is equally impossible to suggest that government does so all the time. Responsiveness, however, is not the only goal that Americans expect government to achieve. They expect an efficient government as well; maximizing responsiveness (for example, ensuring that every telephone call from a citizen is answered within two rings) does not necessarily maximize efficiency (since building enough slack into systems to provide rapid telephone response can prove very costly).

Moreover, citizens expect government to treat citizens equitably. Although airlines accommodate their frequent flyers with special check-in lines, it would be inconceivable for the IRS to provide fast-track treatment (like a special-service telephone number or expedited refunds) for rich taxpayers.[32] Applying the private sector's customer service approaches to government would often violate the public's expectations of how the government ought to behave, at least in part. Add to that the fact that, in public programs, the "sellers" have no choice of what to sell, and the "buyers" frequently have no alternative place for buying. The metaphor thus becomes unrecognizable. Indeed, it is the public's multiple and often-conflicting expectations that make public management fundamentally different, and harder, than private-sector management.

Assessing the Fuzzy-Boundary Problem

American public administration thus finds itself swirling. Four great administrative traditions shape both the practice and theory of public administration, but the traditions lead in conflicting directions. One cannot simultaneously embrace Jeffersonian and Hamiltonian principles, or Madisonian and Wilsonian principles. Just as Americans have always simultaneously sought the advantages of centralization *and* decentralization, administrators and administrative theorists must eventually make strategic choices that emphasize some values over others. No choice has ever endured for long because Americans' preferences among the underlying values have shifted over time. The one sure feature of every new presidential administration, for example, is a new "new federalism" that swings back and forth between national dominance and local discretion. Similar swings have driven reform in all areas of administrative practice.[33] By the end of the twentieth century, it was not only impossible to find a comfortable middle ground between Madisonian and Wilsonian ideas, or between Hamiltonian and Jeffersonian impulses, but it was also impossible to embrace and follow *any* of the traditions because the transformation of governance, in each case, undermined each tradition's guiding principles. That further confounded the search for both practical and theoretical guidance.

At the core of this issue lies the fuzzy-boundary problem. Each of the four traditions grew from efforts to draw lines defining the roles and responsibilities of each of the players. The transformation of governance, in each case, blurred those historic boundaries. It proved impossible to draw useful new boundaries to replace the old ones. Moreover, experience in both the United States and other nations soon proved that the transformation was unlikely to be a short-lived phenomenon. As first the United Kingdom, then Europe, and finally the rest of the globe struggled to deal with "mad cow" and hoof-and-mouth disease in the first years of the twenty-first century, the world learned that traditional boundaries could no longer contain big problems. The world's nations learned that they could not impose solutions on problems that grew from complex interactions among hosts of players.

That, in turn, framed the central problem of American public administration. Administration, in general, is about defining the nature of work; breaking work down into its component pieces; developing expertise for managing each of those pieces; and matching expertise to the job to be done. Administration is about devising and honing routines to accomplish complex tasks. That requires fixing responsibilities and drawing boundaries. However, the American version of *public* administration, from the very beginning, dealt with these principles. The founders were political men dealing with difficult political problems. They worried about making government strong enough to protect citizens and promote the common good without making it so strong as to threaten individual liberty. Their political answer was an institutional one, founded on a separation of governmental power into three branches. They did not so much seek a long-term strategy for government management as much as a short-term balance of political pressures. Their genius lay in charting the basic cross-pressures and in devising remarkably elastic systems for resolving them—a system that could constantly bend without breaking.

For most of the founders, with the notable exception of Hamilton, determining how to manage the details of the new government was not a first-order question. It is not that they were not practical men. They were, in fact, idealists with a powerful sense of the pragmatic. Rather, it was hard enough simply crafting the new political institutions. Making the institutions work created more questions that were even more difficult, and their genius extended in not biting off too much at once. As a result, however, very different ideas emerged about just how government should administer itself. The tradeoffs implicit in the design of the institutions multiplied throughout the administrative system. Strong and fundamentally conflicting traditions grew up around basic questions: What functions should government perform? Who should perform them? As the nation grew, the four fundamental traditions— Jeffersonian, Hamiltonian, Madisonian, and Wilsonian—emerged, and American public administration shifted uneasily among them.

Administration has always struggled to create and manage the boundaries that contain it. That has been true through the ages wherever administrators have practiced, whether in private or public enterprises. The particular balancing act of the American republic, however, has put the search for administrative boundaries in a distinctive political setting. It has involved not only finding a match between administrative tasks and political values but constantly readjusting that match to the endlessly shifting balance among the political traditions.

As this chapter illustrates, the growing complexity of the administrative process has added another layer to the issue. Administrative boundaries, both within public agencies and between those agencies and the broader environment, have multiplied and become fuzzy. The old dilemmas—balancing the Jeffersonian instinct for self-government with the Hamiltonian pursuit of a strong executive; balancing the Madisonian separation of powers with the Wilsonian models of effective administration—have not disappeared. Indeed, these lasting ideas have powerfully shaped how Americans, academic theorists and public officials alike, have approached new issues. What has emerged, however, are new pressures that increasingly stress the fundamental problem of administration—balancing the instinct of administration to create boundaries with the need to pursue broad social goals of political institutions. Theorists have devised numerous approaches to accommodate the fundamentals of administration, the enduring American administrative traditions, and the emerging fuzzy-boundary problems. The next two chapters chart those approaches.

Chapter Four

Boundaries within the Bureaucracy

The fuzzy-boundary problem compounded public administration's practical difficulties. Public administration, especially in the Wilsonian tradition, built its case for strong administration on the assumption that it could devise strategies for elected officials to oversee administrative decisions effectively. These strategies all depended on drawing clear boundaries between policy-making and policy administration. Meanwhile, the number of boundaries within the system multiplied and became fuzzier. For a field founded on drawing clear boundaries, that proved a serious problem. As government relied more on partnerships with the private sector, the problems multiplied. Government not only needed to devise new techniques to manage the emerging tools, it also needed to create new strategies for securing democratic accountability.

As public administration tried to solve these puzzles, the twentieth century's advances in social sciences raised the theoretical bar. Public administration theory quite thoroughly charted the competing choices that managers faced. By the middle of the century, however, that was no longer enough. Theorists wanted to know more than that rival approaches posed contradictory implications. They wanted to know which approaches produced the best outcomes, and social scientists became increasingly impatient with the tradeoffs that traditional public administration posed.

Other models, including emerging formal models that grew out of economics, also built on tradeoffs, but they had greater respect in many quarters. In part, the difference lay in the method. Many of the social sciences favored newer, inductive approaches, derived from basic assumptions about human behavior and then formed carefully into hypotheses and theories. New social science research methods emerged, and those that allowed advanced statistical analysis increasingly gained favor. To use data analysis, researchers needed large samples. That, in turn, led researchers away from qualitative research on organizations or programs—which each presented small samples—to the behavior of individuals, especially bureaucrats and policymakers, where the numbers of research subjects were far larger. These methods posed real problems for traditional public administration, which had long relied on case studies about individual programs and analysis of public agencies. Traditional theory-building had been deductive, with propositions drawn out of such small samples. This approach tended to emphasize variations more than similarities, and it tended to produce conclusions that emphasized tradeoffs more than general theoretical propositions.

These methodological problems have proven especially difficult for public administration. The big public policy battles have brought to the surface the big political values, and scholars have often found it more alluring to examine these issues than to probe the tough, intricate process of moving from decisions to results. That has produced a stronger bias in favor of studying how public policy is made than how it is implemented.

Moreover, the scholars who have studied the administration and management of public programs have often not been at the center of their fields. Political scientists, who focus on institutions, often have not worked with public administrationists, who concentrate on organizational structure and process. Public management scholars at public policy schools give their attention to decision-making, especially by top-level officials. Economists who analyze the decision-making and evaluation processes have tended to dominate those schools. Different scholarly backgrounds lead scholars from different traditions, such as organizational sociologists, to ask different questions and use different analytical techniques. Their work crosses without a sense that they share the same problems. Not only does the work from these different disciplines fail to be cumulative, but the disagreements about basic problems, approaches, and conclusions tend to feed the more widespread belief among some cynical academics that there really is no theory in the field at all.

These conflicts also are deeply rooted in the four American administrative traditions. These traditions have powerfully guided research in public administration and related fields, even if scholars pursuing formal methods might not recognize the intellectual provenance of their work. A careful look at the state of theory, however, shows that these four traditions help organize much of what Americans have contributed to the study of public bureaucracy. In turn, the inherent conflicts in the traditions help explain the ongoing tensions in the academic literature: over the questions they ask as well as the ones they do not, the answers they reach, and the methods they use to explore. This disparate work fails to connect because of these differences—and because the instincts embodied in these traditions and the ways in which they combine tend to take scholars down very different roads.

As Norton Long once argued, administration is about power—who has it and how they use it.[1] John Gaus reminds his readers that how one feels about power depends on whether one has it: "When you are out of power, you want to limit the powers of those who are in; but your zeal (or rather, that of your wiser and shrewder leaders) will be cooled by the consideration that you want to leave a loophole through which you can respectably undertake the same activities when you in turn achieve power."[2] Public administration theory, in all its variations, revolves around the strategies for structuring and exercising political power.

Public administrationists have long celebrated the field's diversity in analyzing questions of political power. In the leading textbook of the mid-twentieth century, *Introduction to the Study of Public Administration,* Leonard D. White wrote, "There are many ways to study the phenomenon of public administration. . . . All of these approaches are relevant and from all of them come wisdom and understanding."[3] For public administration's critics, however, that is precisely the problem—a "complacent, undiscriminating eclecticism," as Herbert Storing put it, which frustrated the search for enduring theory.[4] If any approach could be useful, then no approach could be central. If the field could not focus on a central theory, then critics wondered if there was really any intellectual center to the field. Public administration's eclecticism, especially in the middle of the twentieth century, undermined its theory and its reputation in the social sciences. It was little wonder that Leonard D. White, perhaps the leading student of administration from the 1920s to the 1950s, ended his career not with grand theories but with administrative histories.[5] It was almost as if he felt compelled to begin again at the beginning, to rebuild the field on a new foundation with fresh interpretations.

Public administration, as well as the competing approaches to administrative theory, all must grapple with the application of power. They must do so in the setting of political institutions and in the crossfire of political conflicts. By necessity, that means that they must wrestle with the enduring administrative traditions of American democracy and how they combine. The big issues of administrative theory constantly present themselves in new ways, but they inevitably must deal with the big puzzles:

— How strong should the executive function be?
— Should the executive exercise its influence from the top down or the bottom up?
— Should administrative theory focus on hierarchical relationships within the bureaucracy?
— How should the executive connect with the other political institutions in the American balance-of-powers system?

These questions play out in different combinations of the four basic traditions: Hamiltonian, Jeffersonian, Wilsonian, and Madisonian. Scholarship on public organizations sorts itself out into the combinations these traditions define.

The Hamiltonian-Wilsonian Connection

The Hamiltonian and Wilsonian traditions combine to frame the classic approach to strong administration. The Hamiltonian tradition presents the executive as a strong leader who works from the top down to ensure efficiency and control. The Wilsonian tradition explains *how* managers can do so, especially within the constraints of American constitutionalism. Together, they frame the classical approach to public administration. They have also framed many of the principal administrative reforms that practitioners developed toward the end of the twentieth century.

"Traditional" Public Administration

The modern study of public administration dates from the Progressive era. Modern theorists traced the launch of traditional public administration from the publication of Wilson's "The Study of Administration" in 1887, although as noted in chapter 2, his article did not achieve "classic" status until the 1950s. Frank J. Goodnow and other prominent political scientists championed the same cause, however, drawing a clear line between administration and politics. They argued that administration matters; that by intruding into the practice of administration, politics had undermined the efficient and effective pursuit of government policy; that insulating administrative practice from political influence could significantly improve the results of government programs; and that this separation would improve democratic accountability. Indeed, they were not so much interested in taking administration out of politics as in taking politics out of administration. Wilson, Goodnow, and others argued that this would improve administration by allowing administrators to focus more on efficiency. This, in turn, would improve democracy by clarifying the relationship between policy decisions and administrative results.

By the end of the nineteenth century, theorists were in a bind. The industrialization of the economy and the rise of corporate trusts had brought the need for stronger government regulation, but the federal government that emerged from the Civil War was not remotely up to the task. Reformers faced a knotty problem—creating a stronger administrative system to tackle the problems of industrialization and the trusts without courting tyranny and threatening democratic accountability. The Wilson/Goodnow solution was simple and elegant. Separating policy administration from policymaking provided a way to hold administrators ultimately accountable to policymakers. If administrators could be held accountable, then their power could grow without sacrificing accountability. For Wilson, the task was strengthening government so it could properly do its job. Government might be a "necessary evil," but "it is no more an evil than is society itself." In fact, Wilson argued following an extensive study of governments throughout history and around the world, "It is the organic body of society: without it society would be hardly more than a mere abstraction." In fact, "government is the indispensable organ of society." Government's crucial role is "to assist in accomplishing the objects of organized society."[6] Wilson's view was of a strong society. A strong society needed a strong government. His argument for a separation of politics from administration grew directly out of his long-term research and his belief that the Progressives' approach to administration was critical for taking the United States into the twentieth century.

The decades that followed showed how hard it was in practice to pursue these theoretical ideas. Not everyone agreed on the need for a strong public administration, and certainly not everyone agreed on giving administrators their head. Nevertheless, traditional public administration provided a neat, elegant approach to the problem of government. It provided the intellectual foundation for the stronger administration that inevitably accompanied the Progressives' views of a vigorous government.

This theoretical solution proved short-lived. Soon after the public administrationists helped found the American Political Science Association, some pragmatists tried to split off in a separate movement to train public managers. That effort failed, but not before planting the seeds of ongoing theoretical strife that was to plague public administration for the next century. Practitioners wanted to develop programs to teach future administrators. Public administration theorists wanted a secure seat in budding academic departments. As the decades wore on, though, the policy-administration dichotomy troubled more of their political science colleagues. To many political scientists, public administration seemed a peculiarly apolitical theory of politics. Public administration, however, had no other intellectual base, and at least in the American Political Science Association's early years, the considerable strength of public administration nurtured the new field. For better or worse, political science became the theoretical home for the study of public administration.[7]

These strains worsened as public administration developed. Frederick W. Taylor led the movement toward management efficiency. He devoted himself to "scientific management" and his famous search for the "one best way" to perform work.[8] Taylor helped popularize time-and-motion studies, in which researchers carefully studied the motions of workers, examined alternative ways of performing the same task, and recommended techniques that could do the work most quickly, easily, and cheaply. The scientific management movement revolutionized assembly lines and clerical work alike. Critics complained that Taylorism reduced workers to mere cogs in huge machines, an image Charlie Chaplin made memorable in his classic 1936 film, *Modern Times*. Defenders countered that Taylorism improved the lives of workers by reducing physical strain and increasing output, which in turn increased wages.

Traditional public administration thus inevitably posed problems as it grew and developed. It sought to resolve a fundamentally irresolvable problem—creating an administration strong enough to be effective but not so strong as to endanger accountability. It sought to do so by creating a theory of public administration insulated from the pressures of politics. As Roscoe Martin explained in 1952, " 'Politics' was anathema—not the politics practiced by administrators, but the politics of the 'politicians.' " The rise of Wilson's approach to public administration in the early twentieth century was also a triumph of Hamiltonianism. Hamilton would have recognized, and perhaps applauded, the approach of traditional public administration—"not only impatience but also profound distrust" about the politics of legislation, as Martin put it.[9] Proponents of the scientific management school built on the Wilsonian and Hamiltonian traditions. They saw virtually no barrier to the ability of public administration to improve government—if only government administrators could be protected from political meddling.

By the time Franklin Roosevelt appointed the Brownlow Committee in 1937 to help him reorganize the Office of the President, traditional public administration was triumphant. The committee's three members—Louis Brownlow, Charles Merriam, and Luther Gulick—were in the pantheon of public administrationists.[10] Brownlow had helped establish the city manager movement, whose efforts to create a cadre of professional, nonpartisan, local administrators grew directly out of the Wilsonian approach. Merriam vigorously supported scientific management, and Gulick's "Notes on the Theory of Organization" was perhaps the field's definitive catechism. The young scholars who staffed the committee in turn became the field's next generation of intellectual leaders. Future stars like James W. Fesler, Arthur W. Macmahon, Schuyler C. Wallace, Harvey Mansfield, Paul T. David, and Robert H. Connery staffed the commission.[11]

The field's growing practical influence, however, did nothing to soothe the intellectual tensions. Within the American Political Science Association, scholars squabbled about whether public administration was a science, process, or art—indeed, about whether public administration even belonged within political science. Several political scientists led another breakout effort in 1939 by forming a new association, the American Society for Public Administration (ASPA). A new institutional home, they concluded, was needed to train new public servants better. They embraced all of the competing perspectives by committing the ASPA to the "science, process, and art of public administration." Even if its seat within political science was an uncomfortable one, traditional public administration demonstrated its strength by helping craft the management strategies for winning World War II. The field continued to enroll large numbers of students in the nation's universities.

The war brought two big problems to the field, however. On one hand, as the social sciences attempted to become more scientific, traditional public administration lagged far behind. Some public administrationists focused on improving practice and simply rejected the effort. Their approach to "science" was scientific management—the pursuit of efficient administration, not scientific theory—the search for more rigorous models. The social scientists struggling to bring more rigor to the field found that the new statistical techniques worked far better for studying voting behavior and polling, where they could collect large quantities of data, than for studying public programs and government agencies, which resisted the application of statistical techniques. *How* scholars studied political behavior increasingly defined *what* they studied. The rise of these new research techniques squeezed public administration off the lists of top-rank social science issues and high-profile social science fields.

Meanwhile, traditional public administration began losing ground on its own soon after World War II. Public administration became more fundamentally power-related and less executive-centered. David Rosenbloom, for example, argues that the passage of the Administrative Procedure Act in 1948 marked the rise of a legislative-centered public administration, with Congress shaping the structure, process, and behavior of administration.[12] Norton Long's argument that administration was about the exercise of power reshaped the theoretical foundation of the field.[13] Public administrationists took a more compelling view of their field by recognizing that attempting to separate politics and policy from administration was a fool's errand. They attempted to rebuild theory that explicitly recognized the link between politics and administration.[14]

If traditional public administration became more politically aware during the 1950s, the erosion of the politics-administration dichotomy threatened the field's intellectual foundation.[15] With the downfall of traditional administrative theories and the rise of a new political science, Allen Schick concluded, "Public administration had come apart and could not be put back together."[16] While many within public administration vigorously fought separatist tendencies, public administration and political science moved apart.[17] Many public administrationists sought refuge from political science, especially in the American Society for Public Administration and in schools of public administration separate from political science departments. For their part, many political scientists saw little merit in studying administrative institutions in their search for a new theory of politics. In 1904, public administration had been a critical pillar in Goodnow's vision of political science, and the field had been central in defining and leading the association itself. By 1962, when the American Political Science Association issued "Political Science as a Discipline," a special report on instruction in the discipline, public administration was mentioned only in passing as a subfield of American government.[18]

Allen Schick forcefully argued that "public administration can no more escape political science than it can escape politics." He concluded, "Until it makes peace with politics, public administration will wander in quest of purpose and cohesion."[19] Public administrationists have disagreed among themselves about the prospects for resolving this crisis, especially within the discipline of political science. Dwight Waldo's John M. Gaus Lecture before the American Political Science Association contended, "*Estrangement* is perhaps too mild to character-

ize the relationship of public administration to other fields of political science."
Waldo suggested that for most political scientists, "public administration concerns the lower things of government, details for lesser minds."[20] Herbert
Kaufman, in his Gaus Lecture, worried that public administration and political
science were reaching "the end of alliance."[21] To solve the problem, James W.
Fesler concluded in a third Gaus Lecture that the worlds of governance and of
political science "should not be far apart."[22]

Despite these admonitions, traditional public administration continued to
struggle for acceptance within other social science disciplines. It did not develop
the rigor that economics, sociology, and political science expected. It continued
to search for a way to bridge the gulf between the administrative power embodied in the Hamiltonian and Wilsonian approaches and the political accountability required by American democracy. Much of the instruction in public administration remained remarkably similar to that in the salad days of the 1940s and
early 1950s. Courses continued to focus on issues like personnel, budgeting, and
organizational structure. These issues undoubtedly remain important. In fact,
neglect of these important issues has seriously weakened other approaches to
administrative theory. But traditional public administration suffered serious blows
in the 1950s and 1960s, most notably in the intellectual rigor of its theory and in
its difficulty in grappling with the connection between politics and administration. In the next half century it showed only halting signs of recovery.

FORMAL THEORIES

Despite its manifest problems, traditional administration's solution to the dilemma of empowering bureaucrats without creating an unresponsive bureaucracy
proved remarkably long-lasting. By the 1960s, however, political science had grown
markedly impatient with its intellectual problems. Traditional public administration gradually was squeezed out of the field's mainstream and its premier
journal, the *American Political Science Review*. Bureaucracy was an institution of
unquestioned power. How could this power be reconciled with accountability—
and how could the inquiry regarding it be made more scientific?

Some political scientists responded by borrowing heavily from the formal
theories that had transformed microeconomics. The formal theories focused primarily on individuals, what motivates them, and how those motivations shape
their behavior when they join in organizations. The theory started by asking:
Why do employees of complex organizations behave as they do? Traditional public
administration tended to assume that authority relationships between superiors

and subordinates provided at least part of the answer. Individuals did what they did because superiors asked them to do it. The formal approach, by contrast, applied economics principles. Microeconomics assumes that individuals seek their self-interest—to maximize their utility. Workers agree to work because the work provides them rewards, such as pay and fulfillment. Employers agree to pay workers to get the job done. The market determines how much employers must pay and what employees agree to accept. These basic assumptions led to theories that saw bureaucracies as networks of contracts rather than systems of hierarchies and authority.[23]

Such contracts, theorists argued, identified the key relationships in bureaucracy and key problems that officials had to solve. In particular, Nobel laureate Ronald Coase argued in 1937, such relationships created "transaction costs" for supervisors in managing these contracts, and Oliver Williamson further advanced that work during the 1970s.[24] Their work suggested that theory builders not only needed to focus on contracts, written and implicit, between superiors and subordinates, but they needed as well to understand what incentives best shaped the behavior that supervisors wanted to shape.

Closely related to this work was principal-agent theory. This approach developed models for describing the contracts between superiors and subordinates. A top-down alternative to hierarchical authority, the approach stipulated that higher-level officials—principals—initiated the contracts and that they then hired subordinates—agents—to implement them. It also provided an alternative theory of accountability. Workers (agents) would be responsible to top-level officials (principals) not because they were ordered to do so but because they negotiated contracts in which they agreed to pursue specific actions in exchange for specific rewards. Principal-agent theory thus provided a more elegant and theoretically powerful solution to the problems with which traditional public administration had been struggling for nearly a century. The task of devising the most efficient organizational structure and the best operating processes became a matter of constructing the best contracts. In both cases, the measure of "best" was the same—the ability of the organization to produce the most efficient and responsive goods and services possible.

Because principals and agents operate through contracts, results will be only as good as the contracts. Theorists contended that predictable problems grow out of any contractual relationship. To write a good contract requires good information. But principals can never know enough about their agents to make sure they have selected the best ones. That can produce "adverse selection" problems, in which ill-chosen agents cannot or choose not to do what their principals want. Moreover, principals can never observe their agents' behavior closely enough to be sure that their performance matches the terms of the contract. That can produce "moral hazard" problems, in which agents perform differently than the principals had in mind.

Agency theory thus focuses on information and the incentives for using that information as the critical problems of public administration. Principals need to learn the right things about their agents before hiring them. They can improve their monitoring of agents' behavior to learn what results they produce. They can use this improved knowledge to adjust agents' incentives and to redesign organizations to reduce the risks from adverse selection and moral hazard. And because conventional wisdom and formal theory alike predict that bureaucrats resist change, principals can use this analysis to improve performance and oversight. For public administration, this produces a straightforward theory: Institutions headed by elected officials, such as the presidency and Congress, create bureaucracies; that is, bureaucracies can be viewed as agents for the principals' (elected officials') wishes. The principals design bureaucracies' incentives and sanctions to enhance their own control. When the principals detect bureaucratic behavior that does not match their policy preferences, they use these incentives and sanctions to change that behavior. Among the important sanctions are the president's appointment power and the budgetary leverage that the branches share.[25]

Not only did principal-agent theory introduce a more theoretically elegant solution to the enduring puzzle, but with the theory of contracts, it also provided important insight into the linkage between organizations and their results. Moreover, principal-agent analysis provided an inductive approach to theory-building. Starting with a simple assumption—that individuals seek their self-interest—the theorists built propositions about why individuals join organizations, how organizations structure their work, and what problems can emerge from such relationships. Those propositions, in turn, produced hypotheses—for example, that rational bureaucrats seek to maximize their budgets—that seemed to explain much commonly observed administrative behavior. Principal-agent theory not only helped develop an alternative explanation of bureaucratic behavior in the Hamiltonian-Wilsonian tradition, but it also identified the pathologies that, especially by the late 1970s, seemed so often to afflict bureaucratic behavior.

Political science seized on it as an answer to the theoretical problems that had long plagued the field. It provided both clear analysis and strong predictions that could be empirically tested. It coupled important political institutions with an approach that enjoyed a strong theoretical base. For public administration, this spelled trouble. Increasingly estranged from the association they had helped found, public administrationists found it difficult to counter either the mathematical rigor of the principal-agent approach or the zeal with which its proponents espoused it. The schism grew greater because few public administrationists were trained in applied calculus and formal models, so they were unprepared to fight back. The principal-agent challenge drove some public administrationists out of political science into public policy and public administration schools. A considerable number of public administrationists remained in their traditional home, but by the 1980s, they found themselves scraping for intellectual traction and struggling for acceptance. The formal approach has had tremendous intellectual appeal and great influence within political science. For a field seeking to keep up with the theoretical advances in economics, the combination of economic, transaction-cost, principal-agent, and related theories led to formal approaches to the field. Its supporters claimed that these approaches, in turn, established a strong movement that would soon become the dominant method for studying public administration.[26]

Its very popularity, however, also stirred heavy criticism, especially from theorists who contend that the search for rationality robs the study of organizations of their very life. Economic theories of organization, Charles Perrow contends, represent "a challenge that resembles the theme of the novel and movie *The Invasion of the Body-Snatchers*, where human forms are retained but all that we value about human influence and resentment of domination has disappeared."[27] Even one of formal theory's strongest voices, Terry M. Moe, agrees. He argues that the inner workings of bureaucracies tend to evaporate from most of these models. Instead, they appear "as black boxes that mysteriously mediate between interests and outcomes. The implicit claim is that institutions do not matter much."[28] Traditional public administrationists often add that the same goes for the people inside these institutions.

A more serious dispute arose within political science. Donald P. Green and Ian Shapiro charged that "rational choice scholarship has yet to get off the ground as a rigorous empirical enterprise." Indeed, they argue, "many of the objections that rational choice theorists characteristically advance against rival modes of social science turn out to be applicable to their own empirical work."[29] Kenneth A. Shepsle and Mark S. Bonchek counterattacked by admitting that "political science isn't rocket science." However, they argued, the formal models provide "purposely stripped-down versions of the real thing." These models, they wrote, provide greater rigor than the storytelling approach that characterized much of the post–World War II literature in political science.[30] They contended that solid study of bureaucracy requires embedding it in larger political systems; therefore, any effort to separate politics from administration is folly.

They argued that the relationships between bureaucrats and the rest of the system can be modeled as a bargaining process. From this work they spin three different (and conflicting) alternatives to explain bureaucratic behavior. First, because the bureaucracy has huge information advantages over elected officials, they exploit their knowledge to produce budgets that are too big, bureaucracies that are too numerous, and results that are inadequate. This approach builds on William A. Niskanen's 1971 work that argues politicians have insufficient information and incentives to provide better oversight.[31] Second, because politicians can be proactive and well informed, they can use their information to bargain effectively with bureaucrats over results. Improved information can reduce moral hazard.[32] Finally, they review the argument that information asymmetries might actually favor politicians. Elected officials can know more about key assets, especially the dynamics of political support, and can use their advantages to control effectively the behavior of bureaucrats.[33]

These conflicting propositions lead to several important conclusions about the formal approaches to bureaucracy. First, although they are intriguing, they are not theoretically mature. Their proponents frankly acknowledge that large holes remain in their arguments and that far more work needs to be done. In particular, even though the approach builds from models of individual behavior, many of the models are peculiarly people-free. Public administration, at the least, demonstrated that bureaucratic behavior matters, and if theory-builders are to be successful, the approach will need to become more sophisticated about modeling that behavior. Second, the approach leads in different, even contradictory, directions. The theorists have engaged in lively, even heated, arguments among themselves about which formal approach is most useful, and the battles are nowhere close to being over. Third, the theoretical propositions are far more elegant than their empirical tests. The behaviors they seek to model are extremely complex and not easily reducible to equations and statistics. To conduct empirical tests, the formalists must impose large constraints and look only at pieces of the puzzle. That, they contend, is a natural part of theory-building.

Traditional public administrationists have found the assumptions and models arbitrary and unrealistic. Especially for practically inclined researchers and practitioners, the formal models have proven unpersuasive. The formal approaches provide little guidance to administration-in-action. They also provide scant guidance, at best, about what they ought to do about it. In a previous research project, I interviewed one of the governors on the Federal Reserve Board. He laughed hard when talking about efforts by formal analysts to model his decision making. Those models, he said, bore little resemblance to what he actually did on the job.

The formal approaches thus have become far more advanced and sophisticated, but they have not yet won the day within political science. Nor have they bridged the gap between administrative theory and practice. Despite these criticisms, the theories introduced new approaches and developed new explanations that had largely escaped traditional public administration in the past. They provided, in particular, a far richer explanation of the linkages between bureaucrats and bureaucracies, on the one hand, and the larger political system on the other. They advanced the debate by framing some central questions far more sharply. In particular, formal theory provided an especially imaginative approach to resolving the Hamiltonian-Wilsonian dilemma. It is an approach that did not resort to artificial distinctions between politics and administration and that did produce a more scientific approach to the field. Public administration has learned it cannot ignore formal theory's significant contributions—even if it does not completely accept its approaches.

REINVENTING GOVERNMENT

In the 1980s, a very different front opened in the effort to solve the Hamiltonian-Wilsonian dilemma. Unlike traditional public administration and formal theory, which academics launched, the new strategy emerged from pragmatic tactics government officials developed to cope with budgetary stress and complaints about public performance. In fact, theorists struggled to keep up with a blizzard of reforms in the United States and around the world: to sort the efforts into analytical categories, to gauge their results, and to assess their implications for administrative theory and practice. Unlike the Progressive reforms of a century before, the American "reinventing government" effort grew from the experiments of front-line administrators, popularized by journalists who covered them. For example, in 1988, journalist David Osborne celebrated a new breed of American governors, including a then little-known Arkansas chief executive, Bill Clinton.[34] His next book, in 1992, written with former city manager Ted Gaebler, fueled a broad-scale movement. They embraced "a new form of governance" created by "public entrepreneurs" around the country. These entrepreneurs, Osborne and Gaebler concluded, were reinventing government using ten strategies, ranging from "steering rather than rowing" to "meeting the needs of the customer, not the bureaucracy."[35]

The book described what some managers had been doing for years. In part, it was a critique of existing administrative practice. Traditional public administration, Osborne and Gaebler argued, hamstrung government managers because it did not allow them the flexibility to do their jobs. As a result, the performance of government suffered. In part, the book was also a polemic that made the case for a fundamentally reinvented government. In the best of the Hamiltonian-Wilsonian tradition, it argued that reinventing government required giving government managers, especially on the front lines, more responsibility for managing their programs. It was a claim that these managers knew best how to do their jobs—and that they would do those jobs well if they were given flexibility and were motivated.

Their work caught the eye of the 1992 Democratic candidates, Bill Clinton and Al Gore, who made Osborne and Gaebler's argument the government management theme of their campaign. Soon after Clinton's inauguration, he named Gore to head a "National Performance Review" (NPR) to apply Osborne and Gaebler's model to reinventing the federal government. Their book quickly moved from being a bestseller to a how-to guide for the new administration's program. The NPR pursued hundreds of recommendations and an aggressive downsizing of the federal bureaucracy. The Clinton administration did indeed produce substantial accomplishments, and it shrank the federal workforce by more than 350,000 positions. Some parts of the federal government were largely unaffected by the reinvention effort, and some federal employees criticized the effort as not so much a positive effort to improve the federal government and motivate as a negative strategy to reduce the number of government employees.[36]

Some of "reinventing government's" reforms were Jeffersonian-style bottom-up initiatives, like "empowering" lower-level employees and pursuing a major customer-service initiative to make government programs more responsive to citizens' needs. For the most part, however, reinventing government was a Wilsonian-Hamiltonian initiative that sought to strengthen bureaucracy and reduce the number of levels to strengthen the hierarchy. The reinventing government model replaced the traditional administrative model, but it was more a rebuff to the rigidity it had spawned than a revolt against its principles. Indeed, the movement grew directly out of Wilson's argument to separate politics and administration. Osborne and Gaebler made a strong case for administrative competence and discretion.

It was scarcely surprising, therefore, that modern Madisonians roundly attacked the NPR as they had attacked other variations of the Hamiltonian tradition. As editor of public administration's leading journal, *Public Administration Review*, David Rosenbloom warned reformers, "Don't forget the politics!"[37] Congressional Research Service analyst Ronald C. Moe contended that the NPR threatened serious damage to democracy by seeking to uproot public administration's roots in administrative law and constitutional practice.[38] Frustrated with the drumbeat of private-sector models, H. George Frederickson argued strongly that public administration is *public* and ought not be confused with private-sector strategies.[39] Indeed, the NPR's arguments for "customer service" and "entrepreneurial government" enraged Madisonians. Not only did they see the public and private sectors as so different that private reforms simply were not transferable to government, they also believed that private-sector approaches threatened democratic accountability.

The conflicts were deeply rooted. Madisonians have scrapped with Hamiltonians for generations over where the balance of power in the American political system ought to lie. Moreover, the Hamiltonian and Jeffersonian forces within the NPR led to a constant tug-of-war among its elements: Should the reinventers stress downsizing or customer service, performance-driven control or employee empowerment? Administrative reform movements are hard-wired into the national political culture. Indeed, perhaps no other nation has so consistently pursued such reform, especially during the twentieth century. The NPR was very different, compared with the others. Its intellectual provenance came from a bestseller produced from outside academe, not from its theoretical leaders. Its instincts, however, contained internal contradictions. Its Hamiltonian and Jeffersonian features ensured both internal conflict and attack from academics, who had been marginalized in the debate and who often found themselves opposed to at least some of the NPR's tactics.

THE NEW PUBLIC MANAGEMENT

America's NPR was but part of a broader, global management reform movement christened "the new public management."[40] The movement grew out of a strategy devised by a liberal New Zealand government and a conservative British government to shrink government's size and improve its performance. These governments self-consciously sought to drive government administration by models of market-like, self-interested behavior. In fact, the reformers borrowed heavily from principal-agent theory, to the point that phrases like "moral hazard" and "adverse selection" regularly popped up in conversations among government officials. Together, these reforms—and others occurring in a surprising array of nations around the world—comprised "the new public management."[41]

While scholars debated whether it, in fact, represented a new paradigm or part of a continual battle to reconcile old ideas, there was little doubt that it represented an approach substantially different from public administration.[42] It focused on management rather than social values; on efficiency rather than equity; on mid-level managers instead of elites; on generic approaches rather than tactics tailored to specifically *public* issues; on organizations rather than processes and institutions; and on management rather than political science or sociology.[43] It also provoked a substantial new literature with a strong comparative focus.[44]

The New Zealand reforms became the very center of the new public management. In the early 1980s, the country faced staggering economic problems. The economy stagnated, inflation soared, the currency was in crisis, and the nation could not afford its expansive welfare state. The nation's leaders launched perhaps the world's most aggressive management reforms. Policymakers would clearly define the outputs they wanted to buy and sign contracts with managers to deliver them. The managers would have great flexibility in deciding how to do so. They would receive financial rewards for meeting the targets, and their jobs would be in jeopardy if they did not. The government also privatized many formerly government-owned enterprises and deregulated many industries.[45]

Thus, the reformers quite explicitly borrowed from the formal models of bureaucracy. The New Zealand reformers attempted to substitute markets for traditional governmental mechanisms, and contracts for authority. The reformers not only followed the formal model, they embraced its theoretical propositions. Even in casual conversations, New Zealand Treasury officials spoke easily about principal-agent problems and moral hazard. Indeed, in explaining the reforms, two former government officials wrote, "The goal for designers of public sector institutions and processes is to avoid public choice problems and minimize agency costs."[46] In fact, New Zealand officials sometimes joked about how closely they followed the principal-agent model. They told stories about American public choice economists who visited to study their experiences. "We developed this model," they quoted the economists as joking, "but we never expected anyone to follow it."[47]

These changes dramatically transformed New Zealand's government. For reformers, the New Zealand experiment was a beacon of change—privatizing public assets, substituting markets for governments, giving managers more flexibility but holding them accountable for results.[48] Careful and balanced assessments have found that the reforms in fact produced substantial improvements. The market strategy encountered some problems, especially because some public services had no private markets to use for comparison, because managers tended to rely on a "checklist" mentality of meeting narrow output goals without necessarily fulfilling the broader public purpose, and because the new competition model imposed its own compliance costs. As Allen Schick pointed out in his definitive analysis of the New Zealand reforms, "No other country has accomplished what New Zealand has in building accountability into the framework of government." Indeed, Schick finds, "it is a singular accomplishment in the development of modern public administration." Moreover, "taking accountability seriously is a genuine triumph of New Zealand public management."[49]

Despite New Zealand's substantial progress, however, Schick found that the process-based accountability, which in turn was based on defining each manager's responsibility for outputs, created substantial gaps in performance. The problem became especially serious "when unspecified matters escape accountability," especially issues not anticipated in management contracts, for which clear responsibilities cannot be defined in advance or for which outputs cannot clearly be measured after the fact. Greater efforts to write contracts in more detail, Schick worried, might "split government into seemingly airtight compartments" that would leave important issues out. The problem, Schick explained, is that "in practice, the boundaries between . . . accountabilities are somewhat fuzzy." Focusing more on specific outputs, Schick also worried, might undermine a government's ability to build "the capacity to achieve its larger political and strategic objectives."[50]

The Hamiltonian-Wilsonian approach produced tremendous results. Indeed, it is perhaps most responsible for the energy and accomplishments of American government, as well as some of its most significant reform ideas. But it has long proven unsatisfying to theorists because of the messy intellectual problems it leaves behind, and it has never resolved the fuzzy-boundary dilemma of how to create enough capacity in bureaucracy to do the job without so strengthening it that its power threatens democracy.

From Wilson to the new public management, practitioners and analysts alike have struggled to reconcile these competing aims. At both the beginning and the end of this period, as well as much of the time between, academics provided the intellectual foundation for many of the reforms. The Progressives built on the orthodox view of public administration that Wilson, Goodnow, and Taylor helped create. The modern executive branch then built on their efforts, through the Brownlow Committee and World War II. As that orthodoxy came under increasing attack, practitioners looked for other solutions. The search for a new pragmatism ironically relied on the more abstract view of public administration embodied in formal theory. That theory provided a critique of traditional public administration. It also provided straightforward remedies—understanding decisions as the central administrative act, information as the central element in decisions, and information pathologies as the central administrative problem. Finally, it prescribed how to improve administrative practice—substitute markets and competition for authority and hierarchy.

The new public management and reinventing government grew directly from these roots. They were very different reform movements than those that previously had emerged in the twentieth century, which had built exclusively on the orthodox approach spun out by Wilson, Goodnow, Taylor, and others. They were scarcely atheoretical. But they grew from roots grafted onto practice from microeconomics, not political science. Especially in the United States, they tended to grow more from ad hoc experimentation than from the more coherent philosophy that shaped the Progressive influence. Both forces crippled traditional public administration's ability to grapple with the big ideas of the new public management and reinventing government. Because they grew out of a fundamentally different discipline, public administrationists had a difficult time defending their ideas. And because practitioners pursued their reforms in such an ad hoc fashion, inspired in part by formal theory but often not fully informed by it, analysts often lacked clear categories into which to sort the efforts, let alone to examine them carefully. Traditional public administration, formal theory, and reinventing government efforts thus found themselves strange bedfellows, often without realizing that they even shared the same bed.

Assessing the Hamiltonian-Wilsonian Connection

Beyond those tensions lay the basic problem with the Hamiltonian-Wilsonian approaches, which Schick's argument revealed. The approaches all relied on being able to draw clear boundaries. The increasing fuzziness of those boundaries, however, undermined the effort. How can administrators build sufficient administrative capacity to make government effective without making it so strong that it threatens democratic accountability? The variations on the Hamiltonian-Wilsonian approach, from separating politics from administration through the variations of reinventing government and, ultimately, to New Zealand's creation of a contract-driven model of management, share the same problem—attempts to protect democracy by carefully circumscribing the discretion of bureaucrats ultimately fail. Many theorists have tried to strengthen administrative theory by drawing clearer boundaries, but these efforts have come at precisely the time that policy strategies have made boundaries ever fuzzier.

In contrast, traditional public administration has a long and noble tradition of research on the fuzzy boundaries of discretion. Woodrow Wilson's work focused fundamentally on that problem—how to strengthen administrators without risking an administration going out of political control. By World War II, traditional public administration had developed two standard but conflicting perspectives on accountability. One perspective, following Carl J. Friedrich, contended that accountability had to come from an administrator's own integrity and thus was largely a product of professional training and experience.[51] Herman Finer strongly disagreed and argued that accountability essentially had to flow from control by outside forces with legal oversight powers, such as Congress, the president, and the courts.[52] This debate has never been, and indeed never can be, resolved. Both personal qualities and legal prescriptions inevitably are part of the accountability process, and the balance between them can never be finally fixed.

The policy problems that emerged at the end of the twentieth century, however, illustrated that even seeking an equilibrium between checks internal and external to the administrator is insufficient. As policy problems have become more complex, as divided party government has become a fixture in American politics, as the role of interest groups has increased, as policy administration has become more interconnected with the private sector, as bureaucratic politics has become more complex and less formalized, as organizational networks have departed more from standard chains of command, as bureaucratic structures have simultaneously become more centralized and decentralized, and as politics generally has become more volatile, accountability has become more elusive.[53] Control can come from within an agency or from the outside. The kind and context of the policy, furthermore, can make the degree of control relatively high or low. Accountability can therefore flow through different channels: bureaucratic control by supervisors; legal control by formal overseers, such as Congress or the president; control through the norms of professional groups; and political control through democratic pressures imposed on administrators.[54] In American democracy, no concept is more central to the role of bureaucracy than accountability. As the conduct and context of policy has become more complex, however, ensuring accountability has likewise become more difficult.[55]

This tradition grows from public administration's firm foundation in public law, which seeks to guide administrative discretion without a strong reliance on constitutional government.[56] When tough policy problems challenge public law, public administration reformers have long suggested broadening public participation in the administrative and political processes. When process becomes hard to manage, reformers have tended to focus more on results, especially equity in public policy decisions.[57] Other approaches, including many of the public management and reinvention perspectives, have tended toward silence on these issues. They have focused little on public law and concentrated more on empowering administrators. But with administrators increasingly charged with bridging fuzzy boundaries, the puzzle of how to structure and manage discretion has become even more difficult, and the need to respond has grown markedly.

Theorists therefore built alternatives that focused on a more self-consciously political approach to government management. These alternatives often conflicted, but they shared one central premise—that effective study and practice of administration had to begin on the outside, unlike the inside-out approach of the Hamiltonians and Wilsonians. Moreover, they put politics, not administration, at the center of things. Administration was not so much the fulcrum from which politics swung, as sometimes seemed the case for the Hamiltonians and Wilsonians. Rather, administration was but one aspect of American politics. If some theories painted a richer, more textured picture of administration's role, the alternatives struggled far more with the challenge of devising a prescriptive model of administration. Given the realities of politics, what should administrators do? And given the imperatives of democratic government, how can administrative power be held accountable?

Chapter Five

Boundaries outside the Bureaucracy

The issue of administrative accountability—the challenge of controlling bureaucratic power in a democratic republic—depends most on managing the boundaries between bureaucracy and the political institutions beyond it. Each of the four administrative traditions has developed its own approach, and policymakers have struggled constantly to balance the competing instincts of the different traditions. Moreover, the basic problem has itself grown as the boundaries have become fuzzier. All of the traditions have increasingly focused on the importance of building politics into the model, but the enormous uncertainties and variations in politics have taken them into an increasingly tumultuous analytical and pragmatic world.

The Hamiltonian-Madisonian Connection

Some scholars have sought to marry Hamilton's strong-executive model to Madison's distinctively political approach to government. However, instead of following Wilson's strategy of making bureaucracy the center of the analysis, they have built an approach focused fundamentally on America's constitutional balance-of-power system. In the Hamiltonian-Wilsonian approach, what was important was what bureaucracies did. The Hamiltonian-Madisonians, by contrast, rejected the politics-administration dichotomy in favor of an explicitly political model. Because their approach grew so strongly from political reality, they produced richly detailed analyses of how things actually work. The very richness of the analyses, however, made it hard for them to produce normative recommendations or sharp theoretical propositions. The political instinct to probe the system's vast complexities ran headlong into the administrative imperative for clear guidance.

American political thought has a rich Madisonian tradition built on two elements. First, politics depends on compromise, political compromise flows from power, and the power of political institutions depends on balance. Madison worried about balancing executive power with Congress and the courts to shrink the risk of tyranny. Second, administration is secondary to politics. Madison wrote little about administration, but he implicitly made the case for subordinating administration to politics. The great struggles to balance political power came first, and administrative issues followed later. That differed sharply from the Hamiltonian-Wilsonian approach, which made administration central to the analysis.

BUREAUCRATIC POLITICS AND IMPLEMENTATION

In the 1970s and 1980s, some American political scientists used the Hamilton-Madisonian model to develop a new "bureaucratic politics" approach to administration. They saw administrative behavior in largely pathological terms, the product of tensions in the administrative process as it implemented public programs. In particular, they reacted to the perceived failures of so many of the Johnson administration's Great Society programs—suggesting that they seemed to have so little to show for themselves. In the extended subtitle to their classic, *Implementation*, Jeffrey L. Pressman and Aaron B. Wildavsky frame the problem: "How Great Expectations in Washington Are Dashed in Oakland; Or, Why It's Amazing that Federal Programs Work at All, This Being a Saga of the Economic Development Administration as Told by Two Sympathetic Observers Who Seek to Build Morals on a Foundation of Ruined Hopes."[1]

Indeed, the subtitle captured the major themes of the bureaucratic politics literature. Bureaucratic politics sought to explain why public programs so often produce disappointing results. That often gave the literature a distinctly pathological touch, since much of it focused on case studies explaining policy failures.[2] Indeed, Brian W. Hogwood and B. Guy Peters explicitly borrowed the pathology metaphor from medicine to create a typology of why programs get sick and die.[3] The roots of failure, the analysts argued, lie in the complexity of the system. Federalism and a flood of interest-group cross-pressures, coupled with balance-of-powers politics, made it hard to build a consensus in favor of doing anything. These forces, in turn, made it easy to derail ambitious policy proposals. As Pressman and Wildavsky explained, if a policy process required seventy different approvals and the chance of a successful agreement at each step was very high at 99 percent, there was nevertheless less than a fifty-fifty chance of success.[4] It was little wonder, they concluded, that so many governmental programs failed so often.

Bureaucratic politics did not focus exclusively on postmortem research. Although complexity was endemic and failure common, the scholars who framed the bureaucratic politics movement believed that a richer understanding of the administrative system's politics could improve its results. For Morton H. Halperin, for example, improving the management of the State Department required understanding first the cross pressures operating on it.[5] All this assumed that administrators actually wanted to pursue the program's goals. The implementation game was so complex that they enjoyed many chances to scuttle it.[6]

Thus, the implementation researchers believed that the disappointing results of Johnson's Great Society's programs demanded a fresh interpretation that went beyond traditional public administration. The study of implementation provided the "missing link," as Erwin C. Hargrove put it, which helped connect ambitious ideas and effective results.[7] The approach's insight was positively anti-Wilsonian. "No one is clearly in charge of implementation," Randall B. Ripley and Grace Franklin concluded. Therefore, they said, "domestic programs virtually never achieve all that is expected of them."[8] The work created a depressing forecast of the prospects for success.

Like newspaper reporters, analysts tended to be drawn to interesting stories. As in journalism, the most intriguing stories were programs that seemed not to work well. This approach produced an elaborate inventory of the causes of failures, but they did not yield a very sharp sense of what separated failures from successes. In fact, from air-traffic control to delivering Social Security checks, many programs do work very well, but this approach did not help explain why.

Moreover, much of this literature focused heavily on intergovernmental programs that involved state and local implementation of federal programs. In fact, nearly 80 percent of all of the entries for programs and organizations in one standard implementation textbook were for programs and organizations that have an important intergovernmental dimension.[9] That focus is scarcely surprising, given the predominantly intergovernmental nature of the strategies the federal government used in launching the Great Society programs of the 1960s. The literature did not capture the rich range of other policy strategies. Neither did it fully depict the sharing of power that was central to intergovernmental programs, in which state and local governments adapt federal money and programs to their local needs. Indeed, funding state and local experimentation, adaptation, and variation was precisely the object of many of these programs. Any attempt to build local discretion and a shift of power into federal programs was bound to produce conflict—and it did. By contrast, much of this literature took the top-down, goal-driven approach characteristic of Hamiltonian analysis. From that perspective, conflicts over program goals seemed chaotic. The Hamiltonian approach, moreover, has no room for dynamic change as different players in the system tinker with program goals along the extended implementation chain. Much of the implementation literature combined a Hamiltonian approach with Jeffersonian cases. It succeeded far better in capturing the enduring conflicts between these traditions than in advancing new ideas about how to resolve them.

By the mid-1980s, a new stage of implementation research emerged, as scholars searched for the systematic variations that separated success from failure.[10] They contended that public programs could in fact succeed. The conditions that produced success and failure varied over time and across levels of government. Implementation, therefore, depended on its political context. Critics pointed out that this second phase of implementation illustrated but could not prove their propositions. The literature remained grounded in case studies of individual programs, but the propositions they developed remained invalidated by comparison.[11] That led to a third stage of implementation research, led by scholars like Laurence J. O'Toole Jr., which sought a more systematic investigation of implementation and a better sense of what conditions produced which results.[12] This shift helped implementation advance past the presumption of failure that dominated the first stage and the broad synthetic work of the second stage. It also focused on what administrators do—manage programs—instead of how they do it. That, in turn, separated implementation from traditional public administration.

By the 1990s, the implementation approach helped frame a distinctly Madisonian alternative. It also undermined traditional public administration. In pointing to manifest failures, it armed an attack on traditional administrative approaches. If so many programs worked so badly, could the underlying theory survive? It also argued that any attempt at theory-building had to build on very different intellectual and political traditions. Implementation established that government programs were hard to manage and that the political setting of these programs helped explain why. However, with the notable exception of so-phisticated analysis by scholars like O'Toole, much of the literature did not pro-vide very clear guidance about what either analysts or managers could do about it.[13] The rise of the reinventing government movement made managers less pa-tient for analysis that focused on complexity. They searched for a sharp sword with which to cut the Gordian knot, not a thicker knot that resisted assault.

PUBLIC MANAGEMENT

Within the rise of public policy schools in the 1970s, a new "public manage-ment" approach emerged. Public management sought to understand what administrators—especially top-level executives—could do to make programs work. Unlike implementation, it focused less on programs than on managers. Unlike public administration, it focused on decision-making more than on or-ganizational processes and structures. And unlike formal theory, it reveled in the complexity of the management process instead of seeking to impose order upon it. In fact, as Laurence E. Lynn Jr. contends, "there is no intellectual alter-native to regarding the experience of each public executive as a unique case." Since managers always find themselves in different positions, generalizable prin-ciples are impossible.[14] The search for teachable truths therefore leads to broad propositions, guideposts for public managers to check. Public management used case studies to understand the behavior of top administrators, typically political appointees such as cabinet secretaries and agency administrators, and to under-stand how best to craft management strategies.[15]

For public management scholars, "leadership counts," as Robert Behn put it.[16] Solving problems depends on "managerial craftsmanship" to "break through bureaucracy."[17] Its proponents self-consciously distinguished public management from public administration.[18] Public management teaches that managers must develop strategies and that their strategies must solve three problems. First, they must devise a strategy for overseeing their programs and for the administrators who manage them. Second, since in the Madisonian tradition managers find themselves in conflict about what they should do and how, they must build po-litical support—within and outside their agency—for their strategy. Finally, they must maintain their agency's health—its credibility and capacity—and obtain the resources they need to do their job—especially legislation, funding, and skilled personnel.[19] The public management movement developed along three fronts. Its researchers focused first on building the leadership skills of top managers.[20] In looking to the outside world, its researchers then examined relations between top executives and other political forces, especially the president, Congress, and interest groups.[21] In looking within public agencies, they finally built on the pathological approach of implementation to chart the games that bureaucrats play in frustrating the strategies of top officials.[22]

Public management, often implicitly, sometimes explicitly, rejected public administration and related Hamiltonian-Wilsonian approaches. Public management scholars, in fact, typically referred to "traditional public administration," with "traditional" as a pejorative term. Instead, these scholars focused heavily on the Madisonian and political dimensions of administrative behavior. For example, two public management experts from Harvard's Kennedy School pointedly argue, "Public managers are negotiators," and "public managers are leaders." By contrast, "Public administrators are experts."[23] Traditional administration has a place in the management of public programs, but the public management movement holds that it is subordinate to the leadership of top managers. There is rich irony in public management's rejection of public administration, for most of the public policy programs grew from the foundations of earlier public administration programs. For example, the premier public management program, at Harvard's Kennedy School, came from the Graduate School of Public Administration, originally established in 1936 as part of the field's training movement. Public administration scholars like Francis E. Rourke had for decades championed the importance of a political understanding of public administration, but the public management programs sought to replace the old traditions with a new approach.[24]

The public-management movement has made useful contributions to the study of public policy and administration. Far more than implementation, it celebrates the art of the possible. Far more than traditional public administration, it focuses on the unique role played by top-level administrators and on the special problems they face. Perhaps most important, it builds on its Madisonian roots to describe, in top-down Hamiltonian fashion, how managers can simultaneously be powerful and politically shrewd. Public management helped solve some of the knottiest problems of the Hamiltonian-Wilsonian approach to government management. It did so, however, by minimizing the role of organizational structure and administrative processes, which lay at the core of the Wilsonian approach. It also replicated, without building the linkages, the arguments that scholars like Rourke had made within public administration for a generation. As a result, faculty members at public policy programs often pointedly wondered what theoretical structure public management brought to policy debates.

Institutional Choice

Meanwhile, a variant of the formal modeling approach developed within political science. Christened the "institutional-choice approach," it introduced a more Madisonian perspective to the microeconomic models by incorporating the influence of political players outside of the bureaucracy. It examined the basic interactions among bureaucracies, politicians, and interest groups, and it postulated bureaucracy as an agent of political forces.[25] The institutional approach thus fundamentally changed the role that bureaucracy plays in the analysis. Bureaucracy was no longer central. Nor did it play the primary role in others. It is one player among others and an instrument others within the political system create with which to pursue their own political ends. The formal approach eliminates the policy-administration dichotomy by placing bureaucracy squarely in the middle of its political environment. Institutional-choice theory thus completes the steps, in rigorous form, first made by bureaucratic politics. It replaces the traditional public administration view of bureaucracy-as-actor, as independent variable, with a new view of bureaucracy-as-acted-upon, as dependent variable. Organizations are not designed to promote efficiency but, rather, to reflect the power of political interests.

Institutional-choice analysts conclude that the power of bureaucracies is the result of an equilibrium that contending political forces produce. Different organizational strategies produce different configurations of political forces and different kinds of uncertainty. Therefore, policymakers can shift policy results by making the institutional choices most likely to produce the results they seek.[26] Thus, it is scarcely surprising that bureaucracies so often seem to be inefficient. Institutional-choice theory contends that they are not fundamentally designed to be efficient. They are not so much policy instruments as the product of rules, implicit and explicit, shaped by political forces. These rules can be discovered, influenced, and changed. Any attempt to reform bureaucracy thus must take account of, not just efficiency (which might not even be accounted for at all), but also the political forces that will create the rules under which the bureaucracy must operate.

Some research in this tradition, such as John E. Chubb and Terry M. Moe's controversial study on reform of local schools, builds on economic theories to recommend more choice as a way to make bureaucracies more responsive.[27] Other analyses have become even more sophisticated both in modeling bureaucratic behavior and in specifying outcomes. Morris's examination of the Federal Reserve, for example, carefully assesses the "independence" of Fed policymaking. He compares the Fed's decisions with presidential and congressional policy preferences to conclude that monetary policy results from a highly interactive system.[28]

By changing focus from bureaucracy-as-actor to bureaucracy-as-acted-upon, institutional-choice analysis fundamentally shifts the inquiry. It seeks not so much to understand bureaucracies in order to improve their efficiency and results but, rather, to understand how the power of political interests shapes bureaucratic behavior. By extension, improving government performance thus is a matter of making the right institutional choices to produce the most productive bureaucratic incentives (hence the label "institutional choice"). Moreover, the theory suggested that the key to holding bureaucracies politically accountable lies in strong administrative oversight by elected officials. Why does bureaucracy so often seem unaccountable? Formal theorists had a ready explanation. As David Mayhew concluded, members of Congress engage in little oversight because they have few incentives for doing so. Their constituents care much less about overseeing government bureaucracies than they do constituency casework and policymaking.[29] Thus, the theory of incentives not only determines how bureaucrats-as-agents behave, it shapes the behavior of elected-officials-as-principals as well.[30]

Institutional choice thus provides a mechanism for asking—and answering— whether elected officials can change bureaucratic results. Is the bureaucracy so intransigent that bureaucrats resist efforts by presidents and Congress to shift policy? Or can elected officials find the right incentives to shift bureaucratic behavior? Several scholars have found that elected officials can actually shift bureaucratic outcomes.[31] In fact, B. Dan Wood and Richard W. Waterman conclude, "elected leaders can and do shape bureaucratic behavior in systematic ways."[32] This analysis has tended to focus on the process, rather than the outcome, of bureaucratic behavior. For example, analysts tend to study the number of seizures by drug enforcement agencies or the level of enforcement activity by regulatory agencies. Those numbers are easier to gather, and they fit more neatly into the models' predictions. The analysis tends not to focus, however, on the results the activity produces.

Of course, this is an old problem—one that traditional public administration did not deal with any better. In drug enforcement, for example, thousands of small dealers can be put out of business without affecting the large suppliers; a large number of seizures can produce high levels of activity without demonstrating effectiveness. Likewise, hundreds of small antitrust cases can pale by comparison with the implications of a single case, such as the divestiture of AT&T or the breakup of Microsoft. Thus, statistical links between independent variables, such as changes in presidential administrations, and dependent process measures, such as the number of seizures or inspections, may in fact say very little about bureaucratic outcomes. That weakens the argument for a clear principal-agent connection between the preferences of elected officials and the activities of government bureaucracies. It undermines the power of the formal approach. It also underlines the critical information problems that afflict inferences about the whole process. But it does little to sap the great intellectual appeal and power of the straightforward formal model, which derives clear, testable propositions from simple, clear assumptions.

That is why, in the view of institutional choice scholars, bureaucratic structures often do not promote efficiency and too often produce ineffective results. Poor performance comes from poor design. Bureaucracies are the result of rules, implicit and explicit, that are, in turn, the result of political forces. These rules can be discovered, influenced, and changed. Any attempt to reform bureaucracy thus must take account not just (and perhaps not even) of efficiency but, rather, of the constellation of political forces that will create the rules under which the bureaucracy must operate. That has enhanced the appeal of the institutional-choice model within political science.

Assessing the Hamiltonian-Madisonian Connection

Hamilton long ago made the case for a strong and effective public administration. For analysts, the question has always been whether to start building from the inside out or the outside in. Orthodox public administration and its Wilsonian alternatives took the former approach. They tended to view political pressures from outside the bureaucracy as a problem to be dealt with—as a possible drag on efficiency but as a necessary element of democratic accountability. Students of implementation and its variants took precisely the opposite approach. They began by recognizing the reality of crosscutting political forces and the American separation-of-powers system for balancing them. Bureaucracy tended to be more the source of pathologies that frustrated the accomplishment of public purpose than a tool for executing the public will. Reconciling administration with the inevitable power of politics was the central problem for the Wilsonian variants. The Madisonians, on the other hand, struggled to devise strategies to make bureaucracy effective within the constraints of political reality.

Both of these Hamiltonian approaches, however, shared a fundamentally top-down view of bureaucracy. For Wilsonians, this was a natural product of their focus on hierarchy. For Madisonians, it flowed from a model of political accountability that held administrators responsible to elected officials. The long Jeffersonian tradition, however, spun out two alternatives that built bureaucracy instead from the bottom up.

The Jeffersonian-Wilsonian Connection

Jeffersonian dimension to public administration has not developed with nearly the richness of the Hamiltonian variants. In large part, this is because the Jeffersonian influence in American politics has been more religion than reality, more ideology than practice. Indeed, as chapter 2 pointed out, as president, even Jefferson himself was more a Hamiltonian. Moreover, the American administrative tradition has been most strongly dominated by the two top-down variants of Hamiltonianism: working from the inside to make bureaucracies strong and effective; or working from the outside to hold them accountable. The bottom-up approach has historically carried little influence. Top administrators have found little to tell them how to manage their agencies better; elected officials have found little to help them hold administrators more accountable; and the top-down approach has most captured scholars' attention. Thus, despite the reverence for the Jeffersonian tradition, there has been relatively little work, by either practitioners or academics, to develop it.

Street-Level Bureaucrats and Customer Service

One notable effort by Michael Lipsky focused on the role and behavior of "street-level bureaucrats." Lipsky built an elegant analysis of administrative behavior by focusing on how police officers, social workers, legal aid lawyers, and other front-line workers translate governmental policy into action. Like other Wilsonians, he focused on the bureaucratic context—the pressures that street-level bureaucrats face in trying to manage complicated services while coping with insatiable demands. Lipsky found that ambiguous expectations and enormous caseloads pose huge challenges for these government officials. They cope by rationing services and struggling to match expectations with demands. They thus exercise genuine discretion and enjoy substantial autonomy from the organization's authority. Agency "policy" becomes defined by how their individual decisions add up. For Lipsky, politics and policy become joined in the behavior of these front-line managers. Both policy and behavior build at least as much from the bottom up as from the top down.[33]

That recognition of the importance of front-line workers spilled over into the government reform movement of the 1990s, especially into one part of the Clinton administration's "reinventing government" campaign. The administration's efforts to improve customer service and "empower" lower-level administrators, in particular, followed the bottom-up philosophy. These initiatives elaborated on David Osborne and Ted Gaebler's proposal that government meet "the needs of the customer, not the bureaucracy." They argued, "The greatest irritant most people experience in their dealings with government is the arrogance of the bureaucracy." Private companies were investing more energy in trying to satisfy their customers, and government, they concluded, had no alternative but to do the same. For government, that required "turning agency-driven government on its head," by putting the needs of citizens first—over the convenience of government administrators. Customer-driven systems, they contended, make governments more accountable, stimulate more innovation, and improve efficiency. Government officials often have to change their behavior to make this happen—to make government officials more entrepreneurial and to empower lower-level administrators.[34]

The federal government launched a major customer-service initiative to improve government's relations with citizens. In the last year of the Clinton administration, the government applied the American Customer Satisfaction Index, a joint product of University of Michigan Business School, Arthur Andersen, and the American Society for Quality, to federal programs. The survey found that customer satisfaction with many government services compares favorably with the private sector and that the range of satisfaction scores was roughly similar in the public and private sectors.[35] While some critics objected to the "customer" metaphor, there was little doubt that focusing more attention on how well the government performed was helping to improve government's service.

Focusing on service, however, required reengineering government's service systems from the bottom up instead of from the top down. For example, the efforts of several states to improve their drivers' license bureaus led them to study patterns in the demand for help, to cross-train workers so they could meet variations in those demands, and in some cases even to relocate license offices to shopping malls and to expand their hours. That further underlined the service function and gave front-line operators more discretion in solving problems.

Assessing the Jeffersonian-Wilsonian Connection

Although Americans have celebrated the Jeffersonian ideal of local self-government for centuries, in the bureaucratic tradition it has been honored far more in the abstract than in practice. The Wilsonian approach, which has long focused on the role and behavior of bureaucracies, contains a natural bias toward top-down analysis. Lipsky's book proved a major breakthrough by turning bureaucratic behavior on its head and looking at administrative functions from the outside in and from the bottom up. With few exceptions, like Richard Elmore's analysis of implementation as "backward mapping," from the desired result to the process that produced it, the Hamiltonian top-down analysis has proven far more powerful than the Jeffersonian bottom-up variant.[36]

The Jeffersonian-Madisonian Connection

Other theorists have understood that authority and hierarchy have traditionally rested at the very core of traditional organizational theory. They also have recognized, however, that many of government's most important strategies, especially since World War II, have involved more partnerships between governments, more government contracting with nongovernmental organizations, and more multiorganizational partnerships within government. These partnerships grew not so much because of an explicit policy choice but from pragmatic strategies devised to help government cope with the growing complexity of public programs.[37] Public managers built these partnerships to assemble those who had a piece of the policy action, to incorporate expertise that the government lacked, and to avoid growing the government bureaucracy as government programs expanded. The government's pragmatic responses developed first; analysts' efforts to describe and categorize them followed, especially in network theory and a more advanced approach to devolution. These new approaches emerged as government's behavior traveled further from its traditional roots in hierarchical authority and, thus, posed growing problems for describing how public administration worked—and how it ought to work.

Networks and Governance

Analysts, for example, discovered that government relied more on a wide variety of partnerships with nonprofit and voluntary organizations.[38] The result, H. Brinton Milward and others argued, was a trend toward a "hollow state," with government organizations providing essential services but with most of the production taking place outside the bureaucracy's walls, through relationships with nongovernmental partners.[39] These increasing connections among public, private, and nonprofit organizations profoundly disrupt traditional notions of administration. In fact, such interorganizational relationships epitomize the ultimate "fuzzyboundary" problem. Successfully bridging the boundaries requires different strategies and fresh tactics to ensure effective and responsive programs.[40]

Public administrationists responded by developing new ideas founded on networks and informal relationships instead of hierarchy and authority. Its contributors have disagreed about whether "networks" constitute an approach, a theory, or a loose construct. What they did share is a focus on the relationships among the players in the network.[41] Those players focus not on the network's structure, as in traditional bureaucracy, but on the purposes they share. Moreover, these networks are not fixed with unchanging players. Different relationships spring up around different programs. Grants, contracts, and money tie the players together. The partners in each network might well find themselves working with each other often on different projects, but perhaps never in the same network configuration twice. The network approach, in fact, represents the virtual bridge from traditional hierarchy to the knowledge-driven information society. Some government agencies, like the Occupational Safety and Health Administration, have restructured themselves to make their organization more "horizontal" than "vertical."[42]

This work has made several important contributions. First, it helped public administration escape the pathologies of theory deeply rooted in hierarchical authority. Second, the reality-driven features of the network approach presented a theoretical structure that far better matched developing administrative practice. Third, the network approach has led to intriguing new methods for coordination that do not rely solely on authority.[43] The primary force behind authority had always been its power to secure coordination. Networks presented a genuine alternative for both theory and practice. Fourth and most important, it linked the notion of *governance* with an understanding of the workings of *government*. This last contribution is the most important because, as H. George Frederickson argues, this provides the critical connection "to the big issues of democratic government. It is in governance theory that public administration wrestles with problems of representation, political control of bureaucracy, and the democratic legitimacy of institutions and networks in the time of the fragmented and disarticulated state."[44] For Laurence E. Lynn Jr., Carolyn J. Heinrich, and Carolyn Hill, "governance" consists of "regimes of laws, administrative rules, judicial rulings, and practices that constrain, prescribe, and enable governmental activity."[45] This approach, coupled with careful investigation of the web of relationships within government, provides a strong foundation on which to build future theoretical advances.

The terrorist attacks in September 2001 underlined the importance of the network approach. The attacks themselves emerged out of a closely coordinated network of terrorist cells that were supported, in turn, by a loose network of terrorist organizations. In the first minutes following the attacks, emergency forces in both New York and Washington used long-developed network-based approaches to forge a response pulling together firefighters, police officers, emergency medical technicians, hospital workers, doctors, and nurses into a vast network of help. Part of the Bush administration's response to the attacks was to devise a new cabinet-level Office of Homeland Security. President Bush named Pennsylvania Governor Tom Ridge to coordinate the office's activity—as, essentially, a czar to bring together the diverse elements of the domestic antiterrorist network. Meanwhile, the president's foreign policy team built a coordinated effort to undermine the terrorists' financial, military, and diplomatic support. In short, what emerged from the terrorist attacks was a front-line network to cope with the attacks' immediate aftermath, a high-level domestic network to reduce the risk of future attacks, and an international network to undermine the terrorists— who themselves operated through a network. In the aftermath of that sad day, reports identified numerous problems in the short- and long-term response. But it is impossible to escape the fact that the network approach proved far better than competing administrative theories in charting the major issues and in taking the first steps in framing a response. Indeed, a careful empirical study by Thad E. Hall and Laurence J. O'Toole Jr. demonstrates that public programs have been consistently and unambiguously network-based, with heavy reliance on networks since at least the 1960s.[46]

Thus, networks have provided a framework for understanding the growing connections between varied organizations that find themselves working together to implement public policy. They have also helped public administration gain fresh purchase on the question that has occupied it since its founding—and, indeed, the nation since its creation: how best to understand the connections between political power and representative democracy. Network-based analysis has not yet approached the status of theory. But it does provide a framework for defining a central problem, understanding how organizations operate with each other across the boundaries they share. It has framed the first steps toward providing effective tools for managing networks, which could significantly improve public policy. Achieving the approach's promise, however, awaits further work to develop and confirm theoretical propositions about the way networks behave.

Complexity

Beginning in the mid-1980s, political scientist Robert Axelrod used game theory to advance a formal model of how individuals and organizations cooperate. It brought together formal models, governmental institutions, evolutionary biology, computer science, and social interactions. Important, complex relationships change over time because those involved in them learn. Following the lead of Darwinian evolution, he argued that "whatever is successful is likely to appear more often in the future."[47] Evolution is most successful when many new things are tried and when feedback provides good evidence of what works. In time, everyone involved would learn what works best for them and settle on a "collective stability" that makes everyone better off.[48] Axelrod took this simple concept and applied it to how individuals cooperate—and how cooperation can thrive. That, in turn, led him to speculate that his approach could be used for everything from designing institutions to shaping leadership. If individuals can speed up evolution—the interplay of trial and error—they can speed up the development of cooperation.[49]

Axelrod built his insight into a considerable movement, christened "complexity" theory.[50] He designed it to prescribe how many players, working from different perspectives, could collaborate. That then led him to identify a dozen concepts, ranging from strategies to performance measures, from which managers could work in building cooperation in complex systems. The hope, he and coauthor Michael D. Cohen explained, was "to contribute a coherent approach to designing interventions in a complex world."[51] Some critics countered that the approach, while intriguing, was simply a reframed view of outdated systems thinking, a translation of inputs into outputs. With the growth of the knowledge economy, the critics contend, information—getting it and managing it—has become more important.[52]

This debate has joined some of the more abstract foundations of formal theory with clear and lively recommendations for improving administration, among many other forms of complex human interactions. It has not yet produced prescriptions as sharply focused on practicing managers as public management, the reinventers, or mainstream public administration, and many theorists in the field have not thoroughly explored its theoretical insights. Complexity theory, however, provides a formal framework that complements the network approach. Indeed, they are different lines of argument flying in close formation. As theorists and practitioners alike seek new ways to understand how multiple players sharing the same mission can interact and collaborate, the two approaches offer great potential.

DEVOLUTION

The network approach built on America's rich tradition of intergovernmental relations. Like most of the richly textured elements of the American constitutional system, it has undergone constant change and reform. In 1938, Jane Perry

Clark Carey noted "the rise of a new federalism" with Roosevelt's New Deal programs.[53] Since then "new" new federalisms have reappeared periodically and predictably, with the Eisenhower administration's foray into interstate highways and urban renewal; the Johnson administration's Great Society; the Nixon administration's block grants; the Carter administration's strategy to restructure federal grants; the Reagan administration's rollback of federal aid to state and local governments; and the Clinton administration's devolutionary welfare reform.[54]

American federalism combines the Jeffersonian and Madisonian traditions—Jefferson's commitment to pushing government to the lowest possible level and Madison's careful balance of competing forces. Indeed, since the days of the Articles of Confederation, American federalism has teetered back and forth between an emphasis on state control and national power. From the Civil War to the Great Society, to rollback in federal aid and devolution of welfare, American government has never constructed a stable balance of power. Federalism is, of course, a political, not an administrative theory. State and local governments have been participants in the service delivery network, but they have been much more. As American opinion has swung from an emphasis on local autonomy to an insistence on national uniformity, federalism has been the battleground. But the administrative implications of federalism—especially the recurring call for devolution matched by repeated efforts to pull power back to Washington—have long been the arena for playing out the Jeffersonian-Madisonian administrative themes.

Assessing the Jeffersonian-Madisonian Connection

Of all the administrative approaches in the American administrative tradition, the Jeffersonian-Madisonian approach is at once the most deeply rooted and the least prescriptive. The long tug-of-war over federalism has provided less a clear answer to the problems of American administration than it has touchstones for the struggle. The network approach to governance has not built a new theory as much as it has suggested problems with the dominant authority-driven model and provided a new framework for understanding the central problems. Both network and federalism approaches provide more a road map for understanding the complex crosscurrents in the American political system than an administrative guide.

Thus, it is scarcely surprising that neither networks nor federalism produce strong normative models for either theory or practice. In the case of federalism, it is because the approach depends ultimately on balancing federal and state power. The beauty of the American political system is not setting that balance but creating a mechanism for resetting it often without fundamentally disrupting the system. The network approach offers considerable potential. Developed toward the end of the twentieth century, it provided a way to understand the nonhierarchical forces that increasingly were responsible for service delivery. The approach promised to develop both theoretical and practical alternatives to the limits and pathologies of authority and hierarchy.

Competing Solutions for the Central Problems

Public administration's biggest challenge at the beginning of the twenty-first century was to resolve the fuzzy-boundary problem—to develop new theoretical and practical tools for understanding the boundary-spanning issues that have become the field's knottiest and most important problems. The fuzzy-boundary problem had not replaced earlier administrative dilemmas. Rather, it became a new one layered on top of the enduring issues that had shaped debate in American public administration for more than two decades. The four basic traditions had not evaporated. Their primary instincts remained key themes: whether to manage from the bottom up or from the top down; to have a strong or a weak executive branch; to view the executive branch as the center of the analysis or as a political player in the constitutional balance-of-power system; and whether to make authority or market mechanisms the building block of bureaucratic analysis. Moreover, as table 5.1 shows, they produced a rich—if often competing—set of arguments about how to proceed.

In the twentieth century, both practitioners and academics developed even more intricately textured approaches, from the Progressive movement through reinventing government and from scientific management through formal economically driven models. As befits a field struggling to provide descriptive and normative analysis of the way government works, public administration at the start of the twenty-first century was vastly more complex than at the end of the nineteenth century. Moreover, the level of conflict within the field remained high as the level of outside support for its work fell. It was scarcely the case that public administration had become less important, but confidence in its ability to speak truth to power had unquestionably fallen.

Moreover, as Lynn pointed out, the field lost its moorings. It "seems to have let lapse the moral and intellectual authority conferred by its own recognition that enacting democracy in our constitutional order requires us to confront the dilemmas of reconciling capacity with control."[55] Lynn sadly concluded, "As a

Table 5.1 Public Administration Theory and the American Administrative Traditions

	Wilsonian Hierarchical	*Madisonian* Balance of power
Hamiltonian Strong executive/ Top down	"Traditional" public administration Principal-agent theory New public management Reinventing government (procedural reforms)	Bureaucratic politics Implementation Public management Formal theory
Jeffersonian Weak executive/ Bottom up	Reinventing government (employee empowerment and customer service)	"New" federalism Network theory

result, the profession mounts an unduly weak challenge to various revisionists and to the superficial thinking and easy answers of the policy schools and the ubiquitous management consultants." The problem, he wrote, was that the battles missed a "recognition that reformers of institutions and civic philosophies must show how the capacity to effect public purposes and accountability to the polity will be enhanced in a manner that comports with our Constitution and our republican institutions."[56] Thus, not only had public administration theory and practice become more conflict-ridden and less clear in its voice, but, Lynn argued, many of the competing theories had been less true to important theoretical traditions and less sound a guide. In short, Lynn believed, the new ideas had failed to serve America's political traditions and constitutional expectations. For its part, public administration had lost its compass. Many analysts would contest Lynn's arguments, especially about reinventing government and the public policy approaches. Indeed, these approaches gained ground because they offered fresh insight into problems where orthodox public administration had seemed to run dry.

But beyond these disputes are three larger themes that frame the basic challenge of this book. First, public administration faced important unresolved issues that it had to tackle. Second, the field has diverged widely, both on theoretical approaches and on practical solutions. Given the competing cross-pressures of complex public policies, there is little prospect that a consensus, in theory or practice, will soon emerge. Third, any approach must at least confront, if not resolve, the basic administrative traditions embodied in Hamiltonian, Jeffersonian, Wilsonian, and Madisonian ideas. The challenge is how to pursue these themes to resolve the field's basic dilemmas—and to produce fresh insight for tackling the fuzzy-boundary problem. Compounding that challenge was a fundamental change in the strategies and tactics of government that vastly multiplied the boundaries, made them even fuzzier, and posed profound new challenges for democratic government.

Chapter Six

Administration and Governance

All four administrative traditions seek a solution to the enduring problem of bureaucratic power in a democratic republic. How can government—especially its administrative arm—be made strong enough to do the job without threatening individual liberty? Hamiltonians believed that a strong executive would promote commerce. Jeffersonians struggled to limit government's power. Madisonians worried about balancing political power while Wilsonians sought a powerful administration balanced by political accountability. For more than two hundred years, Americans worked to balance competing ideas about how best to solve the enduring problem. If they never came to a solution that remained stable for long, they came at least to agree, at least implicitly, on where the battle lines lay.

Toward the end of the twentieth century, those battle lines began to erode. The processes of government spilled out into strategies of governance. In doing their work, American governments at all levels became increasingly interconnected with private corporations and nongovernmental organizations (NGOs) that share in the task of delivering public services. Government policy thus became the product of how government managed its relationships with an increasingly devolved system. In framing its role, the national government became intertwined with broad global forces, including multinational organizations, corporations and NGOs with global reach, and other sources of multinational influence. Theorists once built their views about government's role on a foundation of national sovereignty, but the rise of globalization in its numerous forms has, at least, transformed the meaning of national sovereignty and, at most, substantially eroded it.

The rising importance of these twin forces—devolution and globalization—has fundamentally altered the foundation on which the four dominant traditions were based. No longer was it possible to frame the big questions in terms of how to structure administration's internal relationships or its linkages with the rest of government. The four traditions concentrated on administration's relationship with government. The transformations of governance that emerged toward the end of the twentieth century focused on government's relationship with the rest of American society—indeed, with the rest of the world. In 1950, John Gaus argued, "A theory of public administration means in our time a theory of politics also."[1] To that we can add: A theory of public administration means in our time a theory of governance as well.

"Governance" is a way of describing the links between government and its broader environment—political, social, administrative. It is also a way of capturing the initiatives that governments around the world have deployed to shrink their size while struggling to meet their citizens' demands. As Jon Pierre and B. Guy Peters have put it, governance is about government's "changing role in society and its changing capacity to pursue collective interests under severe external and internal constraints."[2] For Robert O. Keohane and Joseph Nye, governance is "the processes and institutions, both formal and informal, that guide and restrain the collective activities of a group."[3] "Government," they explain, is the portion of the activity that "acts with authority and creates formal obligations." "Governance" describes the processes and institutions through which social action occurs, which might or might not be governmental.[4]

The concept is slippery indeed. It is not new—the French have been using the term *gouvernance* since the fourteenth century.[5] Toward the end of the twentieth century, however, governments and scholars have used it to capture the stress on governmental institutions: the inescapable pressures on government to do more with less; the increasingly complex partnerships governments have been building to do their work; and the search for intellectual guidance through these extremely difficult practical problems. Not only did government officials feel the heat from the growing burdens they faced, but they struggled for guidance on how best to deal with them. Western Europeans more directly confronted the theoretical implications of the transformation. Americans, by contrast, proved more energetic in devising new strategies. In both cases, governments are struggling for the insights and practical steps to cope with the challenges they face. "Because societies are ever more complex the analytical tools currently used to tackle problems of governance are outmoded," Robert Cameiro wrote in 2001. Moreover, he argued, "it is hard to believe that improved government performance in the next [twenty-first] century will be compatible with the government models of the 19th century."[6]

This transformation has strained the traditional roles of all the players. For decades, the United States has debated privatizing and shrinking government. While the debate raged, however, the nation incrementally made important policy decisions that have rendered much of the debate moot. Government has come to rely heavily on for-profit and nonprofit organizations for delivering goods and services ranging from antimissile systems to welfare reform. These changes have scarcely obliterated the roles of Congress, the president, and the courts. State and local governments have become even livelier. Rather, these changes have layered new challenges on top of the old ones, under which the system already mightily struggled.

New process-based problems have emerged as well: How can hierarchical bureaucracies, created with the presumption that they directly deliver services, cope with services increasingly delivered through multiple (often nongovernmental) partners? Budgetary control processes that work well for traditional bureaucracies often prove less effective in gathering information from nongovernmental partners or in shaping their incentives. Personnel systems designed to insulate government from political interference have proven less adaptive to these new challenges, especially in creating a cohort of executives skilled in managing indirect government. Public administration orthodoxy simply is a poor match for these problems.

Consequently, government at all levels has found itself with new responsibilities but without the capacity to meet them effectively. The same is true of its nongovernmental partners, which now find themselves under heavy public scrutiny as they implement public policy through their older organizational cultures. Moreover, despite these transformations, the expectations placed on government—by citizens and often by government officials—remain rooted in a past that no longer is relevant. Citizens simply expect that their problems will be solved; they care little about who solves them. Indeed, nothing more frustrates most citizens than to complain about a problem and be told, "Sorry, that isn't my job." Elected officials tend to take a similar view: They create programs and appropriate money. They expect government agencies to deliver the goods and services. When problems emerge, their first instinct is to reorganize agencies or to impose new procedures.

That, they hope, will streamline administration and clarify responsibility. The problem is that this instinct no longer fits reality. As management responsibilities have become more broadly shared, it has become harder to define clearly who is in charge of what, as the StarLink corn case makes clear. The performance of American government—its effectiveness, efficiency, responsiveness, and accountability—depends on devising new solutions to this problem.

Consider the case of Wen Ho Lee, arrested in December 1999 and charged with mishandling classified nuclear secrets on his computer. For two decades, Lee had been a researcher at the Department of Energy's (DOE) Los Alamos National Laboratory. As an analyst in the secret "X Division," he had access to the secrets and had moved massive amounts of data—806 megabytes—to unsecured computers. Intelligence analysts believed that the Chinese government had captured the secrets of the W-88 warhead, America's most advanced nuclear device, and they searched for how it had done so. The analysts concluded that Lee, either by intentionally spying or making the information accessible through sloppy handling of secret data on his computer, had provided some of the nation's most valuable secrets to the Chinese.

Federal agents could not prove that Lee had leaked the data. In fact, they could not even demonstrate that data had leaked—or whether the Chinese had somehow managed to replicate the design on their own. The investigation itself had been sloppy. It had focused prematurely on Lee, and that precluded a close look at other possible suspects. At the very least, however, the agents believed that the Chinese had obtained the information, and they concluded that Lee, one way or another, had made the system vulnerable to Chinese spying.[7]

Congress responded in typical fashion. In a series of hearings, members of Congress expressed outrage at the problem and resolved to take firm action. They concluded that the DOE could not be trusted to plug the leaks on its own. Members asked pointedly, "What can we do to solve this problem?" Congress's answer: Split off the security issues into a new, quasi-independent National Nuclear Security Administration. If the DOE could not ensure the security of nuclear secrets, Congress resolved to create a new agency that could. Congress responded with a strategy steeped in tradition: in response to a separation-of-powers problem, it sought to restructure the function to improve accountability.

This instinct, however, did not match the challenge. It was not clear that there even was a problem, or that if there was a problem it was with Lee, or that if the problem was Lee's whether restructuring the DOE would fix it. In fact, Lee was not even a federal employee. He worked for the Los Alamos National Laboratory, which was a subcontractor to the University of California, Berkeley. Nuclear research had been conducted there since World War II. To the degree there was a problem with Lee, it lay in the DOE's ability (or inability) to manage its contractor—the University of California—and the contractor's ability (or inability) to manage its subcontractor, the Los Alamos National Laboratory. The DOE's contractor employee list is vast. Paul Light, for example, has estimated that there are thirty-five contractor employees for every DOE worker.[8]

The DOE's management of its contractors depends not on traditional hierarchy but on a hybrid marketplace built on two generations of contracting. Transforming the organizational structure would not necessarily give top DOE officials any greater leverage over the contractor network. Given the inevitable disruptions that always accompany restructuring, such a move could even make it worse. But Congress had responded in reflexive fashion to the appearance of administrative problems. It misidentified the problem: it saw it as a structural problem within the DOE instead of the department's management of its nongovernmental partners. It solved the problem poorly—by reorganizing instead of strengthening the department's leverage over its partners. Suggestions that the solution failed to fit the problem were ignored. Congress did what it was used to doing. What it was used to doing, however, failed to match how the rest of the federal government was doing its work.

On one hand, more responsibility for both making and implementing policy has flowed to state and local governments and to for-profit and nonprofit service partners. In many communities, small-scale, quasi-governments are managing everything from education to arts districts. Some governance mechanisms have become computer-based, neighborhood-based, or both. In many communities, the welfare reform initiative of the late 1990s sought to use new computer technologies to integrate a large, disparate collection of services. To deliver those services, governments relied increasingly on nongovernmental agents, including for-profit contractors and social-service-based nonprofits. In the course of three decades, from the mid-1960s through the late 1990s, the entire fabric of the American administrative state had been substantially transformed.

On the other hand, the global linkages affecting American governance had multiplied dramatically. State and local governments had, in many cases, developed their own foreign policies through strategies to promote trade and attract foreign investment. Organizations like the World Trade Organization (WTO), World Bank, and the International Monetary Fund (IMF) have taken a strong hand in shaping international relations. Ad hoc international structures have managed the world's response to recent ethnic conflicts, from the Kosovo peacekeeping operation to the intense bombing campaign in Serbia. Foreign—or shared—command of American troops proved a hot domestic issue, but it has become increasingly common in the deployment of military forces. Other policy arenas that used to be domestic, from telecommunications to the environment, now have major international components. More decisions have flowed from the national to the international levels—and at the international level to both ad hoc and multinational organizations. Permanent organizations like the State Department have struggled to build the capacity to cope with these changes, while ad hoc ones never institutionalize. Maintaining national sovereignty while effectively pursuing international policy has become an increasingly difficult challenge.

In short, America's preeminent policy strategies have tended to grow beyond the nation-state, to linkages with international organizations, and to focus below it, on partnerships with subnational, for-profit, and nonprofit organizations. Supranational organizations have grown to take on new but poorly understood functions. Subnational partnerships have transformed the role of state and local governments. As we have debated "privatizing" government, we have paradoxically also governmentalized a substantial part of the for-profit and nonprofit sectors. The federal government's institutions, political and administrative, find themselves with yet more challenges, from orchestrating these partnerships to shaping the national interest. The roles of all of these players have changed dramatically.

Managing these roles requires capacity that lies far beyond the standard responses, structures, and processes that have gradually accumulated within American government. It requires, in particular, devising new strategies to deal with four basic transformations of governance: the devolutionary and globalizing forces that grew out of the changing world scene; the merger of function and place as administrators struggled to deal with the consequences of fuzzy boundaries; and a hyperpluralism in politics and administration that shaped the changing politics of a transformed government. The challenges are substantial, for both theory and practice. But to a surprising degree, governmental institutions have shown remarkable resilience in adapting. In this chapter and the next, I explore the challenges and chart some of the most promising solutions.

Devolution

As I noted in chapter 2, devolution has dominated the practice of American public management since World War II. The federal government has managed every major policy initiative through grants, contracts, and other indirect tools.

H. Ross Perot, who gained national attention as a maverick presidential candidate in 1992, became a millionaire by running a company that helped develop computer systems that, in turn, helped manage Medicare and Medicaid. These programs rank as some of the most complex the federal government has ever created. A small federal agency with just over 4,000 employees, the Department of Health and Human Service's Centers for Medicare and Medicaid Services, runs both programs. Together, they are budgetary giants—$221 billion for Medicare and $108 billion for Medicaid (in fiscal year 2001).

For example, a senior citizen might receive treatment from a local doctor or hospital. The health care provider submits the bill to a private company, which manages reimbursement procedures on behalf of the government. Computer links, typically provided by another private company, transfer the information. The private management companies collect payments from the federal government and distribute them to the health care providers. The federal government neither provides care nor manages the providers. Rather, it manages the managers and attempts to oversee the system. For low-income individuals who receive care through Medicaid, the process is similar. The federal government sets basic standards and monitors the programs. State governments tailor Medicaid to local tastes—and contribute about 43 percent of total Medicaid spending. The states have followed the federal government's course in contracting with financial intermediaries, often the same ones used in the Medicare program, to manage the reimbursements. The government has thus built an extensive publicly funded health care system without making it publicly run.

The system has grown rapidly and it works remarkably well. But as in welfare, responsibility is broadly shared while no one is fully in charge. And as the General Accounting Office has noted, the complex management strategy poses huge challenges. In analyzing Medicare, the GAO concluded:

> Even though Medicare is a complicated program for the agency to administer through its more than 50 contractors, HCFA [the Health Care Financing Administration, the predecessor agency charged with managing the programs] cannot devote all its attention to Medicare because it is also responsible for administering Medicaid and other state-centered programs. In addition, frequent changes in HCFA leadership make it difficult for the agency to develop and implement a consistent long-term vision. Finally, constraints on HCFA's ability to acquire human capital expertise and shortcomings due to its aged

information systems limit the agency's capacity to modernize Medicare's existing operations and carry out the program's growing responsibilities.[9]

The combination, the GAO concluded, makes Medicare vulnerable to waste, fraud, and abuse—to the point that, by one 1999 estimate, one in twelve dollars spent on the program's fee-for-service payments was improper.[10] The point is not so much that the government has mismanaged the program but that the government has chosen to manage the program through a vast network of private contractors so as to avoid creating a huge expansion of the government bureaucracy.

This complexity increases the difficulty of managing the program. Moreover, the program does not fit the strategies and tactics of twentieth century administrative orthodoxy. Although the HCFA operates through hierarchical authority, its relationships with state governments, private contractors, and health care providers are neither hierarchical nor authority-driven. The HCFA has had to devise different strategies for those who deliver the services, and Congress has had to develop new ways for overseeing the HCFA.

Devolving Welfare

The same is true of the radical transformation of the nation's welfare program in 1996, through the Personal Responsibility and Work Opportunity Reconciliation Act. President Clinton celebrated the change as an "end to welfare as we know it." But "welfare as we knew it" ended largely by passing the administrative burdens to the states, after they had complained for years about federal constraints and some states had advanced new strategies. The act built especially on Wisconsin's experience in the "Wisconsin Works" program—W-2—widely hailed for its dramatic reduction in the welfare rolls. The reforms depended on state, local, and nonprofit partnerships. Wisconsin's state government, for example, divided the state into eighty W-2 areas. County governments administered the program in most areas; in eleven areas, for-profit or nonprofit organizations ran the program. Native American tribes managed the program in three areas. Many county governments subcontracted the program to other private and nonprofit organizations. The program's administrative chain, from Washington to the front lines, where officials worked to get welfare recipients off welfare and into jobs, built a complex network of governmental and nongovernmental partners.

Nowhere was this truer than in the state's largest city, Milwaukee. Officials divided Milwaukee County (with roughly the same boundaries as the city) into six regions and collected bids for the work. In four regions, nonprofit organizations won the job. For-profit organizations—one based in Virginia—won two of the contracts. In all six regions, community steering committees, designed to link private employers and others in the network of services such as transportation, provided advice on how best to manage the transition from welfare to work. The government had to determine which contractors were equipped to do the job. It had to maintain competition among them to prevent the criticisms of government monopoly, which plagued traditional welfare programs. It had to devise new systems of oversight, especially of auditing the contractors' financial records. It had to determine what level of profit was acceptable. Reports of excessive profits produced criticisms that the contractors were squeezing the poor. The effort enjoyed remarkable success in its first years, with far more welfare recipients moving to jobs than the program's advocates had dared hope. That, in turn, led to questions about appropriate benchmarks: What level of performance was expected and desirable in welfare reform?

Welfare reform surely ranks as one of the most complex policy initiatives American government has ever attempted. It sought nothing less than ending generations-long cycles of poverty and dependence on government programs by moving welfare recipients to long-term employment. That, in turn, required an uncommon coordination of services, from screening welfare recipients for job skills to helping them find good jobs. It often also required coordinating a broad array of support, from health care and transportation to day care for children and social services to help address family problems. For the effort to succeed, the network had to perform without allowing serious problems to slip through unaddressed. The government's nongovernmental partners had to synchronize their own missions to the program's goals. The government's federal, state, and local partners had to align their different perspectives. And government had to transform its role from service provider to service arranger and coordinator. Government faced the challenge of allowing partners enough flexibility to do the job, on the one hand, while holding them accountable for federal goals, on the other.[11]

The result was an extended chain of implementation. A vastly complex network produces the program; no one is in charge of everything. In Milwaukee, the typical welfare recipient does not even encounter a government employee—federal, state, or local—in the journey from welfare to work, except for workers who qualify as recipients for Medicaid and Food Stamp programs. In a subtle, unplanned way, W-2 became the model for welfare reform, and welfare reform was but part of a broader transformation of governance in the United States.

In short, welfare reform turned the existing system on its head. Government workers found themselves managing contractors instead of delivering services. Contractors, many of whom had substantial experience managing social services but did not have a track record running such a broad or ambitious effort, had to find employees and develop mechanisms for the new program. The success driven by a rapidly growing economy with low unemployment helped disguise the underlying management issues that Milwaukee and the state struggled to resolve. Other local governments hired private companies to serve as general contractors to manage the entire program. These contractors, in turn, hired subcontractors to conduct front-line operations. Understanding welfare reform required an understanding of the networked programs that supported it. Understanding what helped make welfare reform work required building a theory to explain the administration of this network.

Devolutionary Strategies

Contracting out for urban social services, of course, is nothing new. The practice dates from the 1960s, when Model Cities and other antipoverty programs supported neighborhood organizations—even religious organizations—around the country. Federal government officials worried that cities were unresponsive to the needs of their citizens—and especially of their poor. They gave local governments grants with the expectation that the communities, in turn, would develop service-delivery partnerships with neighborhood groups. The funding helped institutionalize these groups, as well as the pattern of service partnerships. Nongovernmental organizations have become partners with local governments in managing federal- and state-funded programs.

Welfare reform marks the maturing of a generation-long trend that fundamentally transformed community governance. It is a trend with great political attraction: It wires local nongovernmental groups directly into the service system, and it allows government to increase its reach without increasing its size. It spreads administrative responsibility and, hence, political risk. It provides a way to tailor broad programs to community needs. Having forged partnerships that serve so many inter-locking purposes, it would be hard for governments to undo them.

At the state and local levels, more partnerships have developed. Mayor Steve Goldsmith launched major reforms of Indianapolis's government through his "Yellow Pages" test. If the local Yellow Pages contained at least three entries for a service the city provided, the city would contract it out.[12] Phoenix won an award as one of the world's best-run cities by pursuing an aggressive contracting-out approach.[13] Driven by the legacies of the federal Model Cities, Comprehensive Employment and Training Act, Community Development Block Grant, and Title XX block grant programs, state and local governments have contracted out most of their social service programs. Local "smart growth" initiatives have led to new partnerships among local governments. And state governments also have tended to manage their highway construction programs through contracts.

In general, the lower the level of government in the United States, the more the government is engaged in direct service delivery. At every level, however, partnerships with both other governmental and nongovernmental units have proliferated at an accelerating rate. That has made government both *horizontal*—in search of service coordination and integration with nongovernmental partners in service provision—and *vertical*—through both traditional, hierarchical bureaucracies and multilayered federalism. It is not so much that the horizontal relationships have supplanted the vertical ones, but rather that the horizontal links have been added to the vertical ones. That, in fact, was one of the implicit precepts of the reinventing government movement of the 1990s.

After a decade-long emphasis on strengthening performance within the United Kingdom, the Blair government moved to a greater emphasis on "joined-up government." British officials discovered that the "new public management"–style reforms had in fact produced efficiency gains, but they also created new problems. Managers focused narrowly on the specific outputs they were charged with producing. They tended to do well on the outputs that political officials explicitly identified. Problems that didn't fit neatly into such output-based structures, however, tended to be managed poorly if at all. A series of serious train accidents, for example, revealed that strong pressures for on-time performance led to a neglect of safety and maintenance. A 1999 white paper committed the government to integrated policy—to "tackle the issues facing society—like crime, drugs, housing and the environment—in a joined up way, regardless of the organisational structure of government."[14] The new strategies focused more on service delivery to meet the needs of citizens, not on the narrow functions that preoccupy bureaucrats.

Over the last several decades, the federal government's work has increasingly been carried out through an elaborate network of contracting, intergovernmental grants, loans and loan guarantees, regulations, and other indirect administrative approaches. As the case of W-2 shows, the same is true of state and local governments, especially in human services.[15] The federal government manages most of its domestic programs through such indirect partnerships. It mails entitlement checks directly, handles air-traffic control, and runs the national parks. From Medicare to Medicaid, and environmental to transportation policy, the federal government shares responsibility with state and local governments and with for-profit and nonprofit organizations.[16] Indirect tools have gradually and subtly risen in prominence. In part, this represents a conscious strategy to avoid increasing the size of the federal government while expanding its programs. In part, it represents an unconscious strategy to wire civil society ever more directly into public programs. As Light has shown, the federal government's "shadow" employees, in the state and local governments as well as in the for-profit and nonprofit sectors, outnumber federal workers by nine to one.[17]

The Challenge of Devolution

Therein lies a central challenge for domestic governance. Reformers have focused on reorganizing administrative structure and reshaping organizational processes (especially budgeting and personnel). Elected policymakers have seen in these vertical relationships the cornerstone of bureaucratic responsibility—delegation of authority to administrators in exchange for accountability for results. They have tried to strengthen the hierarchical chain, driven by authority, to provide the critical linkage between front-line workers and policymakers. But the pragmatic realities of public policy innovation have not mirrored these approaches. For public administration, the challenge is reconciling the management and accountability challenges of these networks with the bedrock ideas that hierarchical authority has long provided. How can government ensure accountability in extended service networks where administrative responsibility is widely shared and where no one is truly in charge? How can government, structured and staffed for an era when vertical relationships dominated, build the capacity to manage horizontal partnerships effectively?

The devolution movement has not been just an American phenomenon. At the end of the twentieth century, the United Kingdom's government gave in to growing demands for devolution of power to Scotland and Wales. As Eastern European nations struggled to regain their footing after two generations of communist rule, they sought to push power down to local governments. Japan committed itself to delivering more services through NGOs.[18] Around the world, more governments have contracted out service delivery. In sum, as the Organization for Economic Cooperation and Development (OECD) pointed out, "Government has become just one player among many seeking to represent and serve the public."[19] The United States might well have devolved more programs faster than other countries, but nations around the world have quickly followed the same trail, for both pragmatic and ideological reasons.

Globalization

The United States and the European Union (EU) brought in the new millennium with an ongoing banana battle. The row did not involve bananas grown in either place. The EU had created rules that favored growers in territories of EU countries, including the Caribbean. Those rules, the United States charged, discriminated against bananas grown in Latin America by American companies, like Chiquita Brands International. The United States won its case before the WTO and imposed sanctions on imports from the EU. The EU revised its import license procedures, but American trade representatives complained that would in fact change nothing. In retaliation, the Bush administration signaled it was ready to impose a 100 percent import duty on EU imports to the United States—doubling their price—and shift to a different product every six months. The sanctions would begin with products including lead-acid batteries and cardboard packaging and would rotate in carousel fashion to other products, the administration warned. The threat infuriated EU officials, who promised to take their case to the WTO. They threatened to retaliate with their own sanctions if they were unsuccessful before the WTO.[20] Although the dispute was resolved early in 2001 by creating a new import license system, other issues, including an EU ban on hormone-treated beef, continued to fester.

It was a prototypical twenty-first century globalization policy puzzle. It involved two multinational organizations—the EU and the WTO. It involved governmental policy over trade relations and mainstream products. In this case, the product had not even originated from within the two warring bodies. Like the Aventis case, it involved products that ordinary citizens used all the time. It defied any effort to draw clear boundaries.

Debates about globalization have ranged from French complaints about McDonald's "burger imperialism" to American worries about StarLink corn. International disputes over imports, quotas, and tariffs, of course, are nothing new. American colonists protested against Britain's long colonial reach by tossing tea into Boston Harbor. What changed was the rapid spread of globalizing forces at the end of the twentieth century and the widespread recognition, by both public officials and citizens, of the trend. London School of Economics Director Anthony Giddens noted that globalization "has come from nowhere to be almost everywhere." In the early 1990s, the term was little used. By the turn of the millennium, no speech was complete without it—even if those who used the term agreed on little more than the fact "that we now all live in one world."[21]

GLOBALIZATION AS MOVEMENT, MARKET, AND IDEOLOGY

"Globalization" is poorly defined. Most often, the term is synonymous with the galloping expansion of the worldwide marketplace. But it is much more. It includes political, technological, and cultural forces. It is an ideology that defines basic expectations about the roles and behaviors of individuals and institutions. Giddens suggests, in fact, that globalization is about "action at a distance"—the increasing "interpenetration" of individual lives and global futures.[22] For some, it is an ideology of hope and potential—a belief that the global marketplace can improve the living conditions and economic well-being of all.[23] For others, it is an ideology that warns of the threat unrestrained megacompanies can pose for individual welfare. As the UN report on the 2000 Millennium Summit succinctly put it, "The benefits of globalization are obvious—faster growth, higher living standards, new opportunities. Yet a backlash has begun, because these benefits are so unequally distributed, and because the global market is not yet underpinned by rules based on shared social objectives."[24]

These issues quickly sprang from widely disparate roots.[25] The sudden end of the Cold War left the United States as the world's remaining superpower. By uprooting a generation of ideologies and power relationships, that change also scrambled relationships among all the world's nations. The major conflicts since the end of the Cold War have been not international but rather subnational and ethnic ones. These conflicts have posed tough dilemmas: How much do internal conflicts threaten international stability? How can—and should—the world's nations respond to such conflicts? These nations have delicately picked their way through the battles. When they have responded, they have tended to do so by forging multinational alliances. In the 1999 bombing campaign against Serbia, for example, nearly 30 nations negotiated which targets to bomb and when to bomb them. American pilots found themselves under the de facto command of a loose, ad hoc multinational coalition. The coalition shored up international support but made it far harder to fight the war. Other multinational peacekeeping operations have struggled to reduce conflict in places as different as Somalia and Bosnia. In each case, the essential war-fighting strategy was surrender of national autonomy in exchange for (more or less) international unity. Nations acted awkwardly together because no nation could—or desired to—act alone.

Behind these military actions, however, lies the accelerating globalization of world markets. Manufacturers debate "global sourcing," where manufacturing and marketing know no national boundaries. Indeed, Nike manufactures and markets its shoes around the world. The company has reduced its market presence to a single, universally known symbol—its unique swish. Hungry travelers can enjoy Burger King in Australia or Pepsi in Moscow. The French resent the spread of Disney and McDonald's but visit both anyway. Street corner cafes in Berlin advertise "genuine American pizza" from Pizza Hut. Global trade, of course, does not flow one way. Corporate mergers have sometimes become mania, especially in consolidation of communications industries across national borders. Scandinavian companies distribute two of the fastest-selling cellular phones in the United States—Nokia (from Finland) and Ericsson (from Sweden). No American television factories exist any longer. Classic American clothing from the Lands' End catalog might come from North Carolina, Scotland, or Thailand—and be sold through the Internet from Wisconsin to Tokyo. Some analysts have gone so far as to suggest that globalization "is increasingly forcing us to live in an economy rather than a society"—with shrinking national political power and "with government's role in economic affairs now deemed obsolete."[26]

While that might be going a bit far, it is impossible to ignore the fact that it is at least a debatable proposition. With on-line stock, futures, options, and commodity trading, along with the world's rotating time zones, the markets never close, and no nation can insulate its finances in the world economy. Capital markets are global, and hiccups in one region can quickly spread to everyone else, as the "Asian flu" in 1997 and 1998 painfully proved. The Clinton and Bush campaigns to wipe out the national debt produced surprising spillovers. The U.S. Treasury's thirty-year bond has long been the world's interest-rate benchmark. International investors have worried that if the national debt declines sharply—or even disappears—so too will the bedrock of investor security. While it surely is better to develop a new touchstone than to lean too heavily on an expansive old one, the worldwide ripples flowing from the treasury's decision showed how tightly linked the world's economic finances have become.

The markets have become more important than national governments in setting the economic rules. Nations can choose to go their own way, but the markets exact retribution for policies that run afoul of the global marketplace. No country is exempt. It was a U.S. policy decision to rescue the Mexican peso in 1995, for example. But once the United States made the decision, it lost control about *how* to do so. The bond markets, not national governments, ultimately set the terms for the rescue.[27] Corporations are outgrowing the world's governments, some observers suggest.[28]

GLOBAL COMMUNICATION

At the core of the globalization movement are the lightning-fast communication systems—especially the Internet—that have developed over the last decade. The communications revolution has made it possible to spread information around the world quickly and easily and cheaply. It has not only fueled the twenty-four-hour financial markets, it has also transformed governance. For the price of a local telephone call to connect to the Internet, organizations around the world can instantly exchange information. As Jessica Mathews argued in *Foreign Affairs*, "Widely accessible and affordable technology has broken governments' monopoly on the collection and management of large amounts of information and deprived governments of the deference they enjoyed because of it. In every sphere of activity, instantaneous access to information and the ability to put it to use multiplies the number of players who matter and reduces the number who command great authority. The effect on the loudest voice—which has been government's—has been greatest."[29] The result—so far, at least—has been rampant fragmentation of norms, ideologies, values, and institutions. "We are at the beginning of a fundamental shake-out of world society," Giddens bluntly suggests, "and we really do not know where it is going to lead us."[30]

GLOBALIZATION AND NONGOVERNMENTAL ORGANIZATIONS

Instantaneous communication has already fueled an important transformation. Nongovernmental organizations have quickly acquired great influence, in the United States and around the world. (In the United States, they are better known as nonprofit organizations, for their tax-exempt status.) When nations debated trade liberalization in the 1986 Uruguay round of talks, twelve NGOs registered to follow the proceedings. Seattle's 1999 WTO meeting drew so many NGO representatives that they crammed the city's symphony hall to plot strategy. About 1,500 NGOs signed an anti-WTO protest declaration created online by Public Citizen. The Internet allowed organizers to share ideas and tactics instantly. They overwhelmed the Seattle police who found themselves using 1970s-era crowd-control strategies in trying to tame twenty-first century organizers.[31]

These nongovernmental organizations are powerful engines for organizing and driving policy change. Their influence has been impressive. At the 1992 Earth Summit in Rio de Janeiro, they exerted public pressure for governments to commit to reducing greenhouse gases. In 1994, they dominated the World Bank's fiftieth anniversary meeting and forced the bank to rethink its goals and techniques. In 1998, a coalition of environmentalist consumer rights activists pressed for the end of the Multilateral Agreement on Investment, a draft treaty under the auspices of the OECD meant to improve foreign investment rules. In the late 1990s, Princess Diana's much-publicized campaign to outlaw land mines was part of a broader movement, which, in just that year, led to substantial success. The Jubilee 2000 campaign elevated the push to forgive the debts of the world's poorest countries. The number of international NGOs behind these and other movements grew from 6,000 in 1990 to more than 26,000 at the end of the decade. The total number of NGOs around the world, from neighborhood-based groups to large international organizations, surely is in the millions.[32] Moreover, not only have these NGOs been important in political organizing, they have in many countries (including the United States) become important as well in delivering public services.

INTERNATIONAL ORGANIZATIONS

Add to this the widely recognized and growing power of formal, quasi-governmental, international organizations like the World Bank, IMF, WTO, and the EU. The IMF played a powerful (and much-criticized) role in steering Asian nations through their brutal but short-lived economic storms. In Seattle, the WTO stumbled into a vicious political battle as it attempted to transform international trade. The UN has had intermittent success in launching peacekeeping missions. The EU has reshaped everything from environmental policy and drug manufacturing to agricultural policy and transportation in Europe. Its policies are coming in America's back door through the international companies that do business in both places.

RISK

As the terrorist assault on America on September 11, 2001, showed, globalization has a dark and dangerous side. The terrorists did more than demonstrate the nation's—indeed, the world's—vulnerability to an exquisitely planned attack. It confirmed as well that globalization brings great risk as well as opportunity. The more interconnected social and economic forces are, the more easily disruptions in any part of the global network can reverberate throughout it. Indeed, the 2001 attack echoed other risks that worked through the global system. The United Kingdom's 2001 struggles with mad-cow disease not only closed down much of its animal export market. It also mobilized worldwide forces to prevent the disease's spread. Genetically modified crops, like the Aventis bio-corn that created the American agricultural crisis, have likewise created policy issues that have spread throughout the world.

Globalization has provided great opportunity for businesses, governments, and citizens. But it has also brought new, and often unexpected, risks that in turn have challenged governments' abilities to respond.[33] The challenges have not only been substantive—fending off terrorism or preventing the spread of disease, but they have also cut to the heart of the role and sovereignty of government. They have, moreover, introduced new uncertainties into public affairs. Many of these problems have emerged from channels outside the usual course of public policy. They can, in turn, be solved only by adopting new, collaborative strategies that draw together governmental and nongovernmental partners alike.

Globalization thus has transformed government not only by posing new administrative challenges but also by introducing new risks and uncertainties in solving these challenges. Public administration has always been about far more than managing public programs. The cross-pressures of globalization have multiplied the challenges for success and magnified the costs of failure.

Governance and Government

Amid galloping globalization, the United States has found itself squarely in the middle of an international paradox: It has become the world's only superpower but has found itself unable, for political and pragmatic reasons, to act alone. It has struggled to craft a policy to accommodate these new realities, to organize its governmental apparatus to cope with them, and to help lead the redefinition of the international community.

To deal with this paradox, American government has sought to answer two questions. First, what is the role of the American national government at a time when international organizations—formal organizations like the WTO and the UN, informal organizations like the NGOs, and multinational corporations—have become so strong? The rise of these organizations has limited policymakers' discretion about both what to do and how to do it. National sovereignty, even for the world's remaining superpower, has eroded. At least in relative terms, the federal government has become more marginalized in the international debate. It has found itself drawn into the debate, which first bubbled up from the governments comprising the EU, about what role nation-states will play in the globalized world.

Second, what capacity does the federal government need to play this emerging role? Following a forty-two-year career in the State Department, outgoing Assistant Secretary of State Phyllis Oakley worried in 1999 that America's ability to conduct foreign policy had become "threadbare." The State Department itself lacked people skilled in dealing with the issues of globalization. Its budget stagnated while the CIA and Pentagon budgets grew. Special envoys took important jobs that previously would have gone to senior career foreign service officers. "The only thing we have left is the military," she complained, "so we use it in Iraq and Kosovo." Consequently, the nation tends toward "using military means for diplomatic purposes."[34]

Some critics might dismiss Oakley's comments as the parochial complaints of a long-term State Department official bruised by too many budget wars. Her worries about the nation's capacity to cope with new issues, however, took on new and pressing meaning following the 2001 terrorist attack. Former Clinton administration reinventing government official Elaine Kamarck pointed out, for example, that homeland defense requires careful coordination between the Immigration and Naturalization Service (INS) and the Customs Service, as well as with the Coast Guard, FBI, and CIA. She pointed to longstanding tensions between the INS and Customs: "They took lunch breaks at different times; they didn't share information; even their dogs hated each other."[35] Globalization, as Oakley and Kamarck both pointed out, is not the province of any cabinet department. Indeed, in addition to the usual suspects in the State, Defense, and Treasury Departments, no cabinet department is untouched by globalization. Its implications strike at issues ranging from the Department of Health and Human Service's health care programs to the Environmental Protection Agency's (EPA) clean air standards, from the Labor Department's job security programs to the Commerce Department's efforts to help American businesses compete. Ad hoc White House and interagency teams have sprung up to deal with crises, but they have failed to build long-term capacity to anticipate and cope with tough problems. Executive-branch political leadership has often been lacking. Congress, for its part, has scarcely proven equal to the task of framing policies to cope with this trend.

Globalization has helped homogenize cultures. The phenomenon is far broader than the spread of American fast food and movies. The Internet has helped establish English as the global language and has fueled rapid communication. Because these forces are so decentralized, from information to markets, governments cannot hope to control this trend. At best, they can learn to cope and take advantage of the synergism it offers. They can also work to shape the process and redress some of its risks. For example, governments can devise policies to ensure that the rampant spread of electronic communications technology does not create an underclass without a knowledge of or access to communication systems.

In many ways, however, globalization has sparked an emerging system of governance without government, management, or control. Shared values that shaped governmental policies in the past have yet to emerge. National sovereignty has shrunk along with government's capacity to understand and shape the emerging issues and the conflicts that underlie them. European concerns about American "Franken-foods," products incorporating genetically modified organisms, have shaped a new generation of public policy problems. So, too, has the rise of global warming, ethnic conflict, international currency flows, and multinational business mergers. The puzzle is how to build the administrative capacity, in sustained rather than ad hoc fashion, for tackling these problems. Equally difficult is how to strengthen the ability of our political institutions, especially Congress, to frame the policies the nation will need for negotiating the problems and utilizing the potential of globalization.

Function and Place

A final transformation epitomizes how government administration is organized. For deeply historic and practical reasons, most of American government is organized by function, with separate bureaucracies for jobs such as health, environment, defense, and transportation. As policy problems have become more complex and interrelated, government has needed to frame policy solutions that likewise are more interconnected. Citizens expect that government will solve their problems, and they think about how problems affect their neighborhoods. They want the road department to work with the sewer and water departments to avoid repeatedly digging up and repaving the same highway. When cars collide at the border between two communities, they expect that the right mix of emergency units will promptly arrive. In short, citizens expect that a government organized primarily by *function* will be well coordinated in each *place*. Such coordination tasks have always been important. The spread of globalization, devolution, hyperpluralism, and ever more-complex problems have made it both more important and harder to accomplish.

COORDINATING ADMINISTRATIVE ACTION

At first blush, this kind of coordination might not seem any different from any of the other coordination problems that government must address. As Luther Gulick argued, however, in his classic 1937 paper, "Notes on the Theory of Administration," the problem cuts to the core of public administration.[36] Franklin D. Roosevelt appointed Gulick as a member of the famous Brownlow Committee, charged with reorganizing the executive branch. Gulick asked: Is there an ideal form of organization? He concluded that, in fact, there were four basic alternatives in organizing government bureaucracies: organization by process (such as engineering or medicine); by clientele (the people served, such as veterans or children); by place (such as region of the country); or by major purpose (such as water supply or crime control).

Gulick contended that policymakers could not simply pick bits of each approach. The task of management inevitably required top officials to emphasize one approach over the others. They were conflicting, indeed contradictory, strategies, moreover, and each one had its own advantages and disadvantages. For example, focusing on process could bring all the accountants into one office and put all the scientists into another office. That would make supporting their operations much easier and cheaper, since the government could create a single accounting computer center and just one scientific laboratory. The purpose of both accounting and science, however, is to support the government's policy decisions, not to make life easier for the accountants and scientists. Governments therefore have tended to focus more on function, like environmental policy or job training, than on process. That has required more investment in process and has, perhaps, led to process-based support that is less useful than might otherwise be the case. But the functions receive far stronger support, and that, in turn, has improved governments' pursuit of their basic goals.

Policymakers have had to choose which organizational advantages to pursue and which disadvantages to tolerate. That, Gulick observed, was more a matter of value choice than of scientific management. Policymakers simply had to choose what balance of costs and benefits they could accept. However, Gulick concluded, researchers could not predict very accurately which combination of costs and benefits any particular administrative strategy would produce. As a result, he said, "we must rest our discussion primarily on limited observation and common sense, because little scientific research has been carried on in this field of administration."[37]

That sets up tough dilemmas. Policymakers want to pursue certain goals, but there are different strategies for achieving them. Choosing one option forecloses others. Every strategic choice has advantages and disadvantages, but it is impossible to know all implications in advance. Public administration thus inevitably is doomed to suboptimization. Some alternatives surely will prove better than others, but it is hard to predict in advance which alternatives will produce the best results. These basic principles have not changed since Gulick's time, and they set up a recurring pattern. The administrative pursuit of public policies leaves some groups unsatisfied because they disagree with the administrative balance of benefits and costs—or unanticipated problems arise and they object. Reformers reform by selecting a different administrative strategy, which in turn creates new problems. Cynics suggest that it is simply a case of bureaucracy gone bad again; realists recognize that public administration is the pursuit of political aims through political choices, and such choices inevitably create friction. As a result, few administrative patterns remain stable.

In the last decades of the twentieth century, however, new organizational problems became layered on top of these traditional ones. With more policy problems crossing bureaucratic boundaries, it has become harder for any government bureaucracy to own or control administrative solutions. With more policy problems involving collaboration among federal, state, and local governments, as well as among governmental organizations and NGOs, it has become more important for these partners to coordinate their efforts. And with more policy problems stretching across both functions and places, it has become more important for government managers to develop strategies that enhance both functional specialization and place-based effectiveness.

Managing Environmental Policy

In environmental policy, for example, the EPA has traditionally been organized by function, with separate pollution-control offices for water, air, solid waste, and toxic chemicals. These functional offices enabled the EPA's staff to build the considerable scientific expertise needed to regulate the different sources of pollution. As a result, the EPA made substantial progress in reducing pollution. In focusing on the individual "media," or sources, however, the EPA was less effective in reducing pollution that crossed media lines. Substantial water pollution, for example, comes as rain falls through contaminated air, and streams collect contaminated runoff from farms. Media-based efforts risk missing pollution problems that cross these organizational boundaries, as well as "nonpoint-source" pollution like contaminated storm water runoff from parking lots and urban streets where a specific pollution source cannot be identified.

After its considerable success in its first generation, the EPA faced a "second generation" of environmental problems, such as nonpoint-source pollution, global warming, and cross-media challenges. As the EPA has waded into these "second-generation" problems, its "first-generation" tactics, including inspections and litigation, proved less effective. The agency found it had to rely far more extensively on innovative strategies implemented through partnerships with other players.[38]

Since the EPA manages many of its programs through partnerships with state governments, it faced further coordination problems. Statehouses were not subsidiary field offices of the EPA but, rather, quasi-independent entities with their own environmental programs and policies. At the same time, through incentives and requirements of the EPA's programs, the states took on legal responsibility for enforcing the EPA's standards. For the state agencies, the job was melding the EPA objectives and requirements with their own programs and goals. For the EPA, the job was ensuring that the states enforced policies set in federal law, that the states uniformly enforced standards intended by Congress to be uniform, and that the EPA allowed the states flexibility where pursuit of national goals made that possible. Those problems multiplied as environmental agencies began shifting more emphasis to nonpoint-source and other pollution problems, problems that earlier strategies left relatively untouched.

Put bluntly, citizens wanted their neighborhoods—the air they breathed, the water they drank, the ground on which they walked—to be free from pollution. For the EPA, this meant crafting a way to make a functionally based agency work effectively on problems that increasingly were place-based. The EPA had tried a host of reorganization strategies only to discover what Gulick had predicted: a new strategy could help solve the problems of the past effort, but it created new ones in turn. "We've tried almost everything," one senior EPA official said, "and we still haven't been able to solve this problem."[39] At its most basic level, organizing the EPA's efforts by place—for example, focusing on a state-by-state approach— risked undermining the agency's functional expertise. Continuing the EPA's organization by function had already weakened its ability to coordinate disparate programs as they affected individual communities. The agency continued to experiment with new organizational strategies, but frustrated managers concluded that they were unlikely ever to crack the problem fully.

This is not just a problem for the EPA. As globalization and devolution have become more widespread, the boundaries that once constrained problems and shaped solutions have become less useful. On the other hand, the boundaries created long ago for political and administrative convenience can get in the way of solving problems. Wallace Stegner's intriguing biography of geologist John Wesley Powell, for example, compellingly explains why managing the American

West has long proven so difficult. The state boundaries were drawn from long distance by people who did not understand the land, its strengths, and its problems. When they sketched out the states, they did so in ways that separated responsibility over the region's most valuable resource—water—into many jurisdictions. Governments in the area have struggled ever since to coordinate their policies for controlling the flow and managing the use of water.[40]

Public managers face the challenge of improving coordination among agencies within their own level of government, since fewer public problems fit neatly within any one agency's jurisdiction. They face the challenge of strengthening ties to governments at other levels with which they share responsibility for solving problems. They must improve their relations with their nongovernmental partners in administering public programs. They need to devise tactics for linking functionally organized programs with place-based impacts—for connecting air, water, and soil programs, for example, to create clean and livable communities. As a result, the strain between the vertical processes of government (represented in function-based departments) and its horizontal processes, however, has been growing. The problem, recognized ages ago by public administration's best scholars, has emerged as one of the field's most pressing ones.

Hyperpluralism

Madison long ago recognized the importance and proliferation of political interests. As the country grew older, his warning about the "mischiefs of faction" in *Federalist* 10 proved even truer. And as the nation entered its third century, the factions of its founding had grown into hyperpluralism. The number of political interests multiplied. More of the interests became better organized, with full-time lobbyists and extensive staffs. More of the interests also became partners with the government in delivering public services.

In fact, the rise of globalization and devolution elevated the issue. With more responsibility for public programs shared more broadly, no one was fully responsible for anything, and many more players became responsible for everything. Moreover, the technological revolution has further decentralized information, lowered the cost of access to political debate, and accelerated hyperpluralism. The federal government could not frame international policy except by consulting with other nations and by working through international organizations. It could not implement domestic policy except in concert with state and local governments and with its for-profit and nonprofit contractors. At the state and local level, the same held true. Of course, uncertain responsibility has always been one of the guiding principles (and enduring frustrations) of American democracy in general and American federalism in particular. What happened toward the end of the twentieth century, however, was a quantum increase in the scale and scope of the sharing of responsibility—and of its advantages and pathologies. Moreover, this sharing occurred not only within the constitutional framework of American federalism but, increasingly, through an extraconstitutional skeleton that provided limited, often underdeveloped mechanisms for ensuring accountability.

As American governments pursued more public policy through nongovernmental partners, public policy increasingly became entangled in private goals and norms. Government, for example, relied more on private and nonprofit contractors to train welfare recipients for new jobs. But those contractors were not solely governmental agents. They each had their own missions, operating procedures, and other projects—frequently nongovernmental ones—that they pursued as well. It was hard enough for government to manage nongovernmental contracts to administer governmental programs well. It was far harder ensuring that their parallel private missions did not distort their pursuit of public goals.

HYPERPLURALISM AND ENVIRONMENTAL PROTECTION

Nowhere was this truer than in environmental protection. Since its creation in 1970, the EPA has faced an ongoing dilemma. Although it was nominally in charge of framing, coordinating, and enforcing the nation's environmental standards, it did very little of the work itself, and it did not have a strong hand on the steering wheel. In fact, a National Academy of Public Administration (NAPA) panel found that "the nation's environmental 'system' is so rich and complex that no one institution—not Congress, not EPA, not the states or Wall Street, or even the myriad NGOs and private companies—controls the system."[41] The Justice Department litigates on its behalf. Private contractors clean toxic-waste sites in the Superfund program. State governments do much of the enforcement. Congress mandates the EPA to set national environmental standards, and the EPA conducts some enforcement activity. Despite its image in the popular (and sometimes congressional) mind, the EPA does most of what it does by working with partners elsewhere in the federal government, in the states, and among private contractors.

To some degree, of course, the EPA has relied on such partnerships since its creation. The states asked for more flexibility in fulfilling their responsibilities under federal laws. They worked to integrate federal requirements with their own policy goals and to tailor environmental approaches that matched the needs of individual communities. In concert with the EPA, they created the National Environmental Performance Partnership System, which set measurable goals in exchange for granting the states more operating freedom. American multinational companies, driven to compete with EU companies, have sought uniform environmental standards so they did not have to face widely differing rules in different countries. They were especially eager to import the ISO 14001 approach from Europe, which gives companies greater flexibility to create environmental management systems in exchange for agreements to meet environmental standards. The EPA has thus found itself pulled toward more devolution while its policy strategies have faced increasingly global pressures.[42]

Environmental problems piled up quickly and demanded quick reaction from EPA administrators, but any effective action required linking a host of different organizations both within and outside government. The NAPA panel bluntly argued that these problems were extremely serious:

> The nation's current environmental protection system cannot deliver the healthy and sustaining world that Americans want. Absent significant changes in America's environmental governance, the accumulation of greenhouse gases will continue to threaten the stability of the global climate and all the systems that depend on it; the uncontrolled runoff of fertilizers and other pollutants will continue to choke rivers, lakes, and estuaries with oxygen-depleting algae; smog will continue to degrade the health of millions of Americans. The regulatory programs in place in this country simply cannot address those problems at a price America can afford.

Instead, the panel concluded, what is needed is a "transformation of the nation's environmental governance. From the EPA through states and communities, from regulatory agencies to businesses, individuals and organizations with an impact on the environment need to adopt new roles and accept new responsibilities."[43]

The panel recommended a multipart strategy. The EPA, the panel said, should focus on a handful of the most strategically important issues, invest in the information required to understand the issues, and chart policy and build partnerships with the states that hold them accountable for results. But beyond these steps, NAPA also found that the EPA needed to work aggressively to revamp its management culture and rely more on regional offices as the crucial bridge between functionally organized national policy and place-based integration of environmental results. Indeed, the panel found, "the challenge is not merely technological." It is also "organizational: EPA will have to change, as will state environmental agencies, businesses, and the many other organizations that comprise the nation's system of environmental governance." The panel argued, in short, that linking vertical functions with horizontal coordination was central to environmental policy, and that successfully pursuing that policy depended on the government's building strong partnerships with its partners in governance.[44] The EPA has enjoyed considerable success in the past, but existing strategies were unlikely to allow the agency to satisfy those who expected an effective and coordinated future attack. Moreover, as the EPA gradually moved past the early environmental goals into second-generation problems, the fit of its organizational strategy to its policy goals became far worse. It not only faced harder problems but growing difficulty in structuring itself to solve them.

MAINTAINING GOVERNMENTAL SOVEREIGNTY

The EPA and many other government agencies share the problem of encouraging other governmental organizations as well as private and nonprofit organizations to become productive partners in delivering public services. That means setting government's goals clearly enough so that others can pursue them. It means finding incentives attractive enough to redirect the attention of the partners. Those incentives must be large enough to cement the partnership without being so large as to create inefficiency. It means giving government's partners enough operating flexibility to do the job well without the government's surrendering control over policy and process to the partners.

Formal organizational theory recognizes these issues clearly: it is the "moral hazard" problem, the risk that the goals of principals and agents will not coincide and that, therefore, agents' work might distort the goals of the principals. Hyperpluralism incorporates that issue as well as the deeper challenge that springs from the distinctly *public* nature of public services. Government's foremost job is to focus society on achieving the public interest. To do so requires enough leverage to maintain its sovereignty over its partners without exercising so much leverage that it crushes individual liberty. As the number and importance of government's partners has grown, so too has the challenge of finding that balance between sovereignty and threats to liberty. American government, especially in the Madisonian tradition, has always celebrated political interests. With growing devolution, however, government has sliced its programs ever more thinly. With globalization, multinational corporations have become even more powerful, and international organizations have taken on more responsibility for framing public policy. The movement toward more contracting out has further accelerated this trend. As governments have, for good and pragmatic reasons, relied more on partners to deliver public services, they have increasingly had less autonomy in managing their policies. To manage these partnerships, they have increasingly relied more on market-like controls through contracts and performance agreements.

Although the evidence is only suggestive, the New Zealand experience raises cautions about the implications of slicing government into smaller slivers and relying on market-based controls for accountability. The reforms separated public services into more discrete packages managed through performance contracts. These changes unquestionably produced substantial gains in efficiency, but some New Zealand analysts have worried that this approach also reduced the "social capital"—the civic engagement, mutual trust, and opportunities for debate about community concerns required for a healthy community. Such output-based contracts might well lead to less broad sharing of information, greater difficulty in translating narrow outputs to the broader outcomes that are the focus of public concerns, and less ability to manage the broader networks on which successful public programs and vital communities depend.[45]

Although the answers are far from clear, these reforms do define a critical problem. Government strategies to increase control and sovereignty over public programs might in fact increase leverage over outputs, but they risk weakening government's ability to manage the networks on which effective implementation of public programs depend. They also risk eroding the already weak base of social capital. This does not mean governments should abandon the reforms that helped strengthen public management in the 1990s. It does suggest, however, that the reforms are at best only partial remedies for the complex problems of managing hyperpluralism in both politics and administration.

Implications for Governance

Government must not only devise new strategies for managing public programs effectively in a globalized and devolved policy world, but it must also build the capacity for pursuing these strategies. This is the first and most central challenge for governance in the twenty-first century. Most government bureaucracies remain structured and staffed to manage traditional direct programs through traditionally structured and staffed bureaucracies. As the government's strategies and tactics have changed, however, its structures and process—especially its personnel systems—have not. Governance of twenty-first century

American government is more likely to resemble the complex partnerships of W-2 in Milwaukee and of the Medicare and Medicaid programs than traditional administrative orthodoxy.

If government must devise new strategies for working effectively in this world, public administration must devise new theories to explain and guide it. Public managers worked with little theoretical guidance to cope with the twin challenges of devolution and globalization. That has hurt both the practice and the study of government. It is the central challenge to which twenty-first century public administration must rise. This certainly does not mean abandoning the traditional public administration model. As chapter 2 showed, the model builds on centuries-old principles of separation of powers and democratic accountability. It *does* mean updating it to deal effectively with the horizontal networks that have been layered on top of the traditional system. Thus, the first governance problem is *adaptation*: fitting traditional vertical systems to the new challenges of globalization and devolution; and integrating new horizontal systems into the traditional vertical ones.

The second governance problem is *capacity*—enhancing government's ability to govern and manage effectively in this transformed environment. Devolution and globalization have undermined the traditional foundations of administration, especially delegating power to the bureaucracy in exchange for accountability through the hierarchy. Government faces the challenge of building new strategies for effective management and accountability. The federal civil service system, for example, is built on the assumption of direct service delivery. It performs more poorly in developing and rewarding a cadre of skilled contract managers.[46] The federal budget system simply does not track well the number and dollar volume of contracts awarded. The data that are available are rudimentary and require great interpolation. How can government strengthen its ability to govern and manage while maintaining democratic accountability?

This is also a problem of education. Many, perhaps most, of the nation's schools of public affairs, public administration, and public policy have not adjusted themselves to cope with the challenges well under way in public institutions. Consequently, future public servants, who will pursue the public interest both within and outside the government, might well fail to receive the education they need. Increasingly, the pursuit of public value occurs in the nongovernmental institutions that manage many of government's programs. It is also increasingly the case that the careers of many public affairs' program graduates take them, at least for part of their professional life, into NGOs. Public affairs education needs to broaden its perspective to the emerging tools of government action—and to the transforming environment in which managers use them.

Closely related is a third governance problem, *scale*—sorting out the functions of different levels of governance and, in particular, redefining the role of the federal government. As Daniel Bell argued in his prescient 1988 forecast, "Previewing Planet Earth in 2013":

> The common problem, I believe, is this: the nation-state is becoming too small for the big problems of life, and too big for the small problems of life. It is too small for the big problems because there are no effective international mechanisms to deal with such things as capital flows, commodity imbalances, the loss of jobs, and the several demographic tidal waves that will be developing in the next twenty years. It is too big for the small problems because the flow of power to a national political center means that the center becomes increasingly unresponsive to the variety and diversity of local needs. In short, there is a mismatch of scale.[47]

Some problems, like welfare reform, are better suited to devolved systems. Other problems, like international capital flows and regional security policy, might best fit globalized systems. The federal government, like other national governments, risks finding itself in a squeeze for relevance. The rise of global pressures in international (and even domestic) policies, coupled with the increasing importance of state-local governments and nongovernmental partners in implementing domestic programs, raises sharp questions about what role the federal government should play.

The problem, as World Bank Vice President Jean-Francois Rischard pointed out, is that "inherently global issues," from global warming and water problems to education and disease, are becoming increasingly important. The problems are serious, solutions are urgent, and actions inevitably are slow. Moreover, Rischard worries that "there's no pilot in the cockpit" for most of these issues. Governmental institutions have not risen to their challenges. Indeed, he argued, the lack of boundaries and the "urgency" of inherently global issues conflict with the "territorial and hierarchical nature of the traditional institutions that are supposed to solve them, that is, the nation-states." As a result, he continued, "current ways of handling IGIs [inherently global issues] are essentially bankrupt, if they ever worked at all."[48]

Washington politics already shows the strain of trying to cope with these questions. The executive establishment has increasingly relied on "ad hocracy," especially in the Executive Office of the President. Decisions have leaked from the executive departments. That has made it harder for the vast reservoir of the executive branch's policy expertise to find its way into major decisions. As a result, the executive's machinery for coping with cutting-edge issues risks atrophy. Whatever capacity accumulates in the ad hoc machinery can quickly leak away when crises end. Most major policy issues cannot be the province of any single agency or department, so ad hoc mechanisms tailored to important problems are inevitable. To improve public performance, government agencies must strengthen their capacity to manage such ad hoc tactics. Meanwhile, Congress too often finds itself trapped in gridlock, unable to take more than symbolic stands on a host of important issues. Some of this undoubtedly flows from the bitter politics of divided party government and, in particular, the fallout from the Clinton impeachment battle. The tensions and inaction on Capitol Hill are a sign of the mismatch of congressional behavior and the mission that is expected of it in the twenty-first century. There is indeed a mismatch of scale. Its symptoms show up regularly enwrapped in Washington's dysfunctional politics.

The United States is scarcely alone in facing this problem. A worldwide survey by the OECD in 1998 found that there is "more interdependence between levels of government as the problems to be addressed become more complex and difficult to resolve unilaterally. Divisions of responsibility for the design, implementation and evaluation of programmes are changing; and the distinction between who finances, delivers, and administers is increasingly unclear in many programmes. The search for greater flexibility in managing public programmes can blur lines of accountability."[49] These changes, the OECD concluded, produced three dichotomies:

— encouraging more *autonomy* at lower levels of government, while providing overall *direction*;
— allowing for *differentiation* through flexibility, yet ensuring some minimum degree of *uniformity*; and
— providing for more *responsiveness* to local needs, but not to the detriment of *efficiency* and *economy*.

The OECD's analysis surely applies to the United States as much as to any of the world's nations. The United States has become increasingly intertwined in the world's governance, and global governance problems increasingly apply to the United States as well. The federal government shares domestic policy with state and local governments and with NGOs—and state and local governments do the same. These changes are not the result of an explicit policy decision; rather, they grew gradually and imperceptibly from hundreds of tactics decisions over two generations of public policy. They have accumulated, however, into a fundamental transformation of governance—a transformation that poses substantial challenges for public institutions, how we manage them, how we study them, and how we prepare the nation's future public servants.

Chapter Seven

Who Governs—and How?

Since the dawn of the human race, administration has been about building expertise to accomplish complex tasks. *Public* administration has been about building expertise to accomplish tasks defined by government on behalf of the people. Within democracies, the challenge has been to translate public wants and needs into policy, to marshal expertise to answer the wants and provide for the needs, but then to limit that expertise so the very power required for effective administration does not threaten individual liberty. That frames a basic paradox for public administration in a democracy. It is a discipline focused constantly on a search for strong and stable tools, but the more successful it is the more it potentially threatens the democratic forces charged with controlling it.

This paradox has frustrated public officials and scholars alike. Harry S. Truman famously once called for a one-armed economist. He was tired, he said, of constantly getting the "on the one hand" but "on the other hand" advice. This has been even more true of public administration. When public officials have wanted clear advice, they have tended to receive warnings about complexity. When they get strong recommendations, equally compelling arguments on the other side invariably emerge. The field's traditional roots in America, in fact, have long been framed by the eternal conundrums—centralization versus decentralization, efficiency versus responsiveness. Public administration and its related disciplines have struggled for greater precision, and some approaches have indeed produced sharper theoretical focus. The various economics-based formal approaches, in particular, have struggled to push aside the field's traditional tradeoffs for clear and replicable propositions. But the field has never been able to move far from the basic, irresolvable tradeoffs, and that has frustrated managers and theorists alike.

The problem flows in part from issues inherent in public administration. When problems fall through the cracks—when fire companies cannot agree on whose jurisdiction is responsible for fighting a fire, or when intelligence agencies fail to share information adequately—calls for better coordination arise. Coordination is hard to achieve, however, because it is hard to get different agencies with different missions and different organizational cultures to work together.[1] Moreover, agencies cannot simultaneously coordinate all activities at all times. They have to concentrate on something in order to build the capacity to do anything. In addition, coordination is expensive: it requires substantial investment by supervisors and public officials to build and nurture the required links. Coordination on some missions risks weakening capacity to achieve others. Strengthening coordination between and among agencies also is difficult to achieve without undermining the very strengths within each organization that policymakers hope to capitalize on.

The problem also flows in part from issues inherent in American democracy. Public administration is not a freestanding entity; it is the creature of a political system and is designed to accomplish its ends. All of the tradeoffs that are endemic to American republicanism occur throughout public administration also. Public administration seeks to accomplish public goals, but American democracy is exquisitely designed to ensure that policy goals are neither defined in detail nor fixed for long. Furthermore, Americans have never been consistent in their eagerness for a strong government. The Bush administration in early 2001 had sought to pick up the Reagan administration's downsizing-government banner. Soon after the September 11 terrorist attacks, however, presidential spokesman Ari Fleischer told reporters, "People need help, and in a time of war, it is principally the government that is the best instrument to help people."[2] The United States does not have just one rich tradition shaping the relationships between public administration, American democratic institutions, and the public. It has four, and the balance among them has constantly shifted.

American public administration, in theory and practice, thus, is not so much a matter of finding stable models but in adapting its various tools to fit shifting political and administrative goals. It never has and never will be a field of study that systematically builds clear, replicable propositions. In practice, it inevitably will produce ammunition for critics who will point to problems and breakdowns. Public administration is a complex business and problems constantly occur. Efforts to redress past problems plant the seeds for future ones. The emphasis on some values de-emphasizes others, and that spurs complaints. It is little wonder that Pressman and Wildavsky plaintively noted that "it's amazing that federal programs work at all."[3] The constant tradeoffs and recurring complaints often seem to make public administration just as depressing as Thomas Carlyle's "dismal science" characterization of political economy.

The tradeoffs and complaints, rooted in the very business of public administration and in the political forces shaping it, have become magnified by the increasingly fuzzy boundaries shaping the field. Administration draws its strength from boundaries: defining functions, building capacity, focusing narrowly on the job to be done, and getting it accomplished. Fuzzy boundaries challenge public administration. The forces of fuzziness have multiplied, both within the bureaucracy, between bureaucracies, and between the administrative system and democratic institutions. Devolution and globalization have tugged bureaucratic theory in opposite directions. The old tradeoffs between function and place have become sharper. Efforts to resolve the tradeoffs have become vastly more complex because of the hyperpluralism in the political system.

On one level, these are issues facing public administration around the world. The special traditions and forces within American democracy, however, pose special problems for American public administration. In considering these traditions and forces, it is impossible to escape one profoundly important conclusion: *At the dawn of the twenty-first century, neither the theory nor the practice of American public administration proved sufficient for the problems it has to solve.* The same was true at the dawn of the twentieth century, and public administration underwent a major transformation, driven by the Wilsonian tradition, to catch up. The field needs to transform itself again, just as completely. Less clear is how it ought to do so.

Front-line pragmatists have been cobbling together new tactics on top of old ones. In the 1996 welfare reform, for example, neither the federal nor the state governments decided as a matter of policy that they would rely on nongovernmental organizations (NGOs) to manage the program. Faced with tough challenges, tight budgets, and a public not eager to expand public bureaucracies, the quasi-privatized approach was simply a pragmatic response to a pressing problem. In areas as far-ranging as environmental policy and local land use, ad hocracy trumped strategic thinking. Unlike reformers in New Zealand and the

United Kingdom, who drafted white papers to chart a revolution, American officials avoided writing a master plan. They worried less about plans than solving problems, less about theory than balancing challenging cross-pressures.

Even at their most tumultuous, however, the struggles of American public administration have built on powerful foundations. The strong guiding power of the great administrative traditions meant that the revolutions were merely evolutionary and that no new idea was ever fully new. When Lyndon Johnson launched his "Great Society," public administrators saw a theoretical foundation in ageless Jeffersonian debates about decentralization. When Ronald Reagan proposed to downsize government by privatizing key programs, they recognized the old Hamiltonian debates about the balance of public and private power. Richard Nixon's failed plan to restructure the executive departments built on the Wilsonian traditions of government efficiency, while Bill Clinton's reinventing government swirled around the old Madisonian balance-of-power battles. Public administrationists often contended that nothing was really new; they were not so much cynics as intellectual historians. Indeed, much of recorded history—from Moses' struggle to organize the children of Israel in their flight from Egypt and Roman emperors' efforts to conquer and organize the world—is a story of recurring themes about organization and administration.

In its relatively short life, American public administration has added two important elements to these ageless debates about administration. First, Americans introduced a self-conscious tension between individual liberty and government power. All basic values in the American republic, including the role of public administration, rest in intricate balance. Second, the American Constitution mirrored this tension by balancing political power among governmental institutions. The genius of politicians was to find everything a lasting strategy to capture different political values and to manage conflict among them. Public administration grew as endless twists on old ideas.

Nevertheless, with the start of the twenty-first century, it was clear indeed that this time-proven approach to public administration had developed large fissures. In their efforts to become more scientific, the social sciences rejected the old approach as too relativistic and directionless for the social sciences. One could always find some combination of old themes that fit new situations, but the theory could not predict what approaches would produce which results. Meanwhile, when practitioners faced increasingly complex problems, they looked to public administration theory for answers. It was scarcely the case that public administration had nothing to offer. The field had deep roots in the nation's great political traditions. But practitioners who faced tough new problems found little there that appealed to them. Instead, they turned to journalists and other practitioners who told them how to "reinvent" their activities. Some sought the counsel of consultants grounded in private-sector management practice. Theorists, however, worried that reinvention pushed public administration off its constitutional foundations and risked surrendering public power to private interests.

The great insight of the founders was to discover that they could not control or end such conflict, but they could channel and manage it. As historian Joseph J. Ellis argues in *Founding Brothers,* the American republic that emerged "was really an improvisational affair in which sheer chance, pure luck—both good and bad—and specific decisions made in the crucible of specific military and political crises determined the outcome."[4] The genius of the American revolutionaries was that they "found a way to contain the explosive energies of the debate in the form of an ongoing argument or dialogue that was eventually institutionalized and rendered safe by the creation of political parties." The political history that followed became "an oscillation between new versions of the old tension." As a result, "the debate was not resolved so much as built into the fabric of our national identity." Indeed, Ellis argues, "we are really founded on an argument" about what Jefferson's Declaration of Independence really means.[5]

By the end of the twentieth century, the arguments had become more pointed and the oscillations more rapid. Moreover, the Constitution and the politico-administrative system it generated had become less useful in capturing and channeling the conflict. In 1999, protesters in Seattle trashed much of the downtown to argue that the World Trade Organization was undemocratic. The world's governments, they said, were surrendering their sovereignty to large businesses. Globalization, in short, had created new policy venues over which the Constitution held less sway and in which important new decisions were being made. American governments devolved more decisions to state and local governments and, in many cases, they spun more programs out to NGOs. At the same time, however, these governments had not sufficiently strengthened their capacity to manage the devolution they created. In welfare reform, many program recipients and managers complained that devolution of welfare reform to the states and the states' privatization of welfare management to NGOs had wrung the public interest from publicly funded programs. Far too much money went into profits for NGOs, they charged, and far too little into public services.

Functionally organized governments—by health, environment, labor, and commerce, for example—strained to cope with the coordination demands of a world with fuzzy boundaries, in which no important problem would agree to stay within the lines of any governmental agency. Coordination among government agencies has always been both important and difficult, but by the end of the twentieth century the problem had increased substantially. Cross-agency task forces and coordination teams became more important. At the same time, local officials and citizens worried as much as ever about how decisions made in far-off government agencies would affect them and where they lived. Matching functional expertise with place-based impact is one of public administration's eternal challenges, but increasingly fuzzy boundaries enormously complicated that problem.

As American governments struggled to manage these forces, they fractionated their management approaches. They sliced programs more thinly to increase management control. They experimented with performance-based management as a substitute for traditional hierarchical authority. They privatized and contracted out. Ever-thinner slices, however, presented the grave difficulty of reassembling them into a coherent whole. Perhaps even more important, they created new arenas for conflict and action that lie at—or beyond—the fringes of the American constitutional system, like devolution and globalization. American government often had neither the administrative capacity nor the political institutions for channeling conflict and ensuring democratic accountability. That is why twentieth-century governance increasingly grew out of sync with administrative practice and theory.

Periodically throughout American history, and especially in times of great economic transformation, governance problems and public administration theory have become mismatched. That was the case at the end of the nineteenth century, when the rise of business monopolies concentrated political power just as the people's expectations for more public functions grew. Government risked being captured by narrow interests and becoming less accountable even as its role grew more important. The Progressives charted a strategy for government to be more capable while becoming more accountable. Their approach—advanced hierarchy with authority-based control—fed a theory that increased administration's power while holding it more responsible to policymakers. Through two world wars, the Great Depression, and the rise of the nation's global power, that approach proved remarkably resilient.

By the end of the twentieth century, however, the transformation of governance had rendered that approach obsolete. New economic forces—this time, global ones—threatened to capture public power. Government struggled to build the capacity to manage transformed strategies. Americans showed no eagerness to abandon the traditions that had guided political and administrative practice for more than two centuries. Less clear, however, was how those traditions ought to guide political and administrative practice for the future. As boundaries became fuzzier, how could government effectively coordinate public programs? As NGOs became increasingly important in governmental service delivery, how could government hold them accountable? How could the living Constitution adapt to manage and channel conflicts that strained existing institutions?

Among these questions, one is most important. As responsibility for public programs becomes more broadly shared—where no one is fully responsible for anything and many players are responsible for everything—how can American government pursue the timeless values that have guided the nation since its founding? This is an echo of the question Robert A. Dahl posed plainly in his classic 1961 book, *Who Governs?*: "In a political system where nearly every adult may vote but where knowledge, wealth, social position, access to officials, and other resources are unequally distributed, who actually governs?" For Dahl, political power was pluralist, with power distributed among a wide range of interests, and dynamic, with patterns of power shifting over time.[6] Dahl's argument helped move political science from an institutional approach to politics—one that built theories of political power on the formal organizations empowered by law and the Constitution to make decisions—to a process-driven approach—one that analyzed political power by who exercised it and how. That approach helps frame the answer to how American government can best cope with the transformation of governance.

In many ways, Dahl anticipated by a generation a similar transformation of the study of public administration. During the twentieth century, public administration prospered with a theory built on organizational structure. Clearly framing administration's role and function—and defining what its role was not—helped make government larger and more effective without sacrificing the pursuit of democratic accountability. John Gaus's 1950 article in *Public Administration Review* argued, "A theory of public administration means in our time a theory of politics also."[7] To that we can add, "No theory of politics is complete without a theory of administration." Building a theory of public administration that is true to the realities of politics has become both more critical and more difficult because constraints on and expectations of public administration grew significantly in the last half of the twentieth century. Citizens and elected officials expected administrators to eradicate poverty, manage rapid transportation systems, provide high-quality, low-cost health care, and clean up the environment. On the other hand, building a theory of politics that embraces the central role of administration has become far more critical, because turning policy aspirations into reality has, by any measure, become more difficult. Indeed, more than ever before, administration has become the essence of political reality. On many fronts, politics has become less a battle over what government ought to do and more a battle over how it can do it better and cheaper.

The Rise of a New Governance

If the problems of public administration seem daunting and the prospects for resolving them seem small, it is important to remember two things. One is that while many of the cross-pressures are new, the inescapable reality of making tradeoffs is not. The great strength of American democracy and public administration is its almost infinite ability to flex, transform, and adapt to new realities—and to do so in ways consistent with the nation's enduring values and traditions. Indeed, American public administration has been remarkable in its intellectual and pragmatic elasticity, to stretch its approaches without losing its basic norms.

The other is that, despite the manifest problems, most of government works pretty well most of the time. The news media focus on news, and success stories rarely make the headlines. The Social Security Administration, for example, correctly posts 99 percent of wage earners' contributions, and 82 percent of citizens rate the SSA's service as "good" or "very good."[8] The U.S. Department of Transportation's regulatory and grant programs have brought down the number of gas pipeline explosions.[9] New York City's performance system has reduced crime and improved the productivity of city agencies.[10] Problems dominate the news, not the system's overall high level of performance, and that can make discussion of the transformation of governance seem a rather gloomy affair.

Thus, the basic issue is not to rue government's failures. Rather, given the constant and inevitable swings among traditions and strategies in American government, which approaches are most likely to help government cope with the transformation of governance? What new approaches must public administration forge to cope better with the inescapable challenges facing government and governance?

Americans have never been fully satisfied with the performance of their governments. Of course, performance can always be improved. Higher performance can always produce lower taxes or more service for the same level of taxes. Moreover, what Americans want often changes. At the core, Americans have always wanted more government services without having to pay higher taxes. But just *how* best to deliver those services and *which* problems government needs to solve have changed constantly.

If the nineteenth-century challenge was the rise of corporate power that threatened to swamp the public interest, the challenge at the beginning of the twenty-first century was the diffusion of administrative action, the multiplication of administrative partners, and the proliferation of political influence outside government's circles. American politics has always been famous—or notorious—for the multiple channels it provides citizens to participate in the process and for the intricate balance the constitutional framework provides. Citizens can seek redress from their local, state, or national governments. They can press their views in the legislative, executive, and judicial branches. It is a rare policy decision in the American system that is ever truly final. The American political tradition, however, made government the arbiter of policy. Americans have always debated just how far government ought to reach into their lives, but those battles were fought with the ground rules the constitutional system established.

These puzzles multiply Dahl's basic question: Who governs—and how? How can we make effective public policy? How can we implement it well? And how, in the course of administration, can we pursue the goals of American democracy that have for centuries been the bedrock of the political system? The questions certainly are not new. Neither is conflict in how best to answer them. As Ellis pointed out in his study of America's "founding brothers," new oscillations in the old patterns develop. Each new oscillation presents new challenges of finding an equilibrium among the old cross-pressures. With the transformation of governance at the end of the twentieth century, these challenges had grown. Meanwhile, the ability of America's political institutions to find that new equilibrium—to channel and to manage conflict—had shrunk.

Government thus finds itself with several complex, interwoven problems. It faces new service demands from citizens, but citizens usually show little enthusiasm for paying higher taxes. It is deploying increasingly complex public programs, but no one really wants to increase the size of government bureaucracies. To solve these problems, it has devised new management strategies, but it is struggling to build the capacity to manage the strategies and to cope with unexpected side effects, such as a possible reduction in social capital. Practitioners have struggled to cobble together new solutions to these problems—and to speed the learning curve so that they could quickly appropriate successful strategies from other practitioners. However, unlike during the Progressive movement, when Wilson, Goodnow, and other thinkers helped lead the effort, theorists at the end of the twentieth century lagged behind the transformation of governance. Together, they struggled to devise new strategies for the new governance: to develop an effective government without sacrificing accountability, to pursue efficiency without sacrificing the public good. The transformation of governance thus frames five big issues:

1. *Challenges.* American government is stretching to perform tasks that no government has attempted before. Terrorist attacks demand new strategies for safeguarding travel, work, home, and play. New health threats, like mad-cow disease, easily cross international borders, while bioengineered food presents unprecedented regulatory demands. The Internet and other tools for instantaneous communication and networking provide great opportunities but also new challenges. None of these problems easily fits within the province of existing bureaucracies, and it would be hard to imagine how to create a bureaucracy that could encompass them. The challenges require new administrative strategies and tactics.

2. *Capacity.* Many of these challenges require government to develop and deploy new skills as well as to expand existing ones significantly. The capacity problem not only involves finding and hiring smart people but also means devising effective strategies to tackle the new problems of governance. As government relies more on nongovernmental partners to deliver services, it increases its own need to define sharply what it is trying to accomplish. It also increases its need for tools to supervise grantees, contractors, and other third parties who work on its behalf. Finally, government must be able to gauge the success of its complex chain of action. Because much of government remains deeply rooted in traditional command-and-control techniques and direct-service strategies, it faces the twin task of escaping the bounds of its existing culture and building capacity to meet its emerging challenges.

3. *Legitimacy.* American government's increasing dependence on nongovernmental partners—and their increasing dependence on government programs and cash—highlight important problems for the legitimacy of public power. As Fritz W. Scharpf argues, the more government and its partners become interdependent, the more its policy options are constrained and the more previous policies "become less effective, more costly, or downright unfeasible—which must be counted as a loss of democratic self-determination even if new options are added to the policy repertoire."[11] Political interests help frame governmental policy but then also become important in administering it. That shifts the balance of political forces, because some interests become far more tightly wired

into both the making and the administration of governmental policy. It makes it harder for those outside this network to oversee that policy. And it changes government's role from one of hierarchical supremacy to that of one player in a broader network. This disrupts the age-old notions of government's role and of the workings of democratic accountability. How does influence over public policy work? Are all voices equal? What should government do when a place within the administrative network privileges some political voices over others?

4. *Sovereignty.* Government also needs to devise new strategies to ensure that its voice is not just one among many in the network. Especially with the simultaneous rise of devolution and globalization, the federal government's role has become far less clear. To rule effectively, government must first attain and then exercise sovereignty. It must be able to chart its course and ensure that that course is followed. Hyperpluralism, policy networks, devolution, and globalization have all greatly diffused power. Government might retain its legal position, but exercising practical sovereignty amid such diffused power presents a major challenge to twenty-first century government. It requires government both to know what it wants to accomplish and to devise strategies for doing so. Government is not just one participant in policy networks, working on the same level as others. It has a responsibility to the law and to the public interest and must, therefore, ensure it has the capacity to steer the behavior of the policy systems that produce public programs.

5. *The public interest.* Perhaps the strongest argument of traditional public administration is its particular focus on the public interest—the use of administration to pursue programs to advance the interests and to solve the problems of citizens. The Hamiltonian and Wilsonian traditions, in particular, have always carried a heavy public-interest argument. Administration needed to be strong enough to allow government to do what citizens wanted done. Of course, defining "the public interest" has always been the most daunting of practical and theoretical problems. The diffusion of sovereignty has made the tough job even tougher. Nevertheless, public administration—in all its competing theories and traditions—remains single-mindedly committed to what Waldo calls "the good life."[12] Indeed, White believed that "in its broader context, the ends of administration are the ultimate ends of the state itself—the maintenance of peace and order, instruction of the young, equalization of opportunity, protection against disease and insecurity, adjustment and compromise of conflicting groups and interests, in short, the achievement of the good life."[13] The Brownlow Committee in 1937 echoed that argument by concluding, "By democracy, we mean getting

things done that we, the American people, want done in the general interest."[14] Public administration thus stands among the highest traditions of American government—and squarely in the middle of its biggest tests. Its task is to rise to the challenge of the transformation of governance.

Strategies for Transforming Governance

What would strategies for twenty-first century governance look like? American governments face three capacity problems: fine-tuning their traditional, hierarchical systems to work more productively in managing direct service systems; creating new nonhierarchical approaches for managing indirect service systems; and, perhaps most daunting, configuring those systems to operate effectively side by side, without the authority-based system disrupting the network and without the network disrupting the authority-based system. In particular, the expansion of both contracting out and federalism as administrative strategies brings new burdens.

Capacity

Government strategies, especially grants and contracts, do not manage themselves. Rather, they require the cultivation of new skills to specify program goals, negotiate good contracts, and oversee the results. Moreover, the contract system requires the development of markets that could supply the goods and services the government wanted to buy; replacing a public monopoly with a private monopoly scarcely could increase the efficiency of service delivery.[15] In assessing the government's "high-risk programs," the U.S. General Accounting Office identified contract management as one of its most difficult problems.[16] The rise of this contractor workforce raises important challenges to the federal workforce and fuels its "human capital" problem. Comptroller General Walker argued, "The problem is not federal employees, it's the policies, procedures and legislative framework that guide federal human capital actions."[17]

The rise of intergovernmental relations as both a political and an administrative system has complicated this problem. The federal government has long managed many of its operations through direct systems, such as Social Security and air-traffic control. As the scope of its activities expanded through the last decades of the twentieth century, the federal government began relying more on state and local governments as front-line field agents to deliver federal programs, from interstate highways and antipoverty programs to Medicaid and environmental programs. The federal government relied on state and local governments in part because they provided useful administrative intermediaries. The federal government also, however, relied on subnational governments to share decision-making and make government programs more responsive. The history of American federalism has always rendered the federal-state-local administrative relationship complex. Federalism has long sought to define uniform national policies and to give state and local government responsibility to tailor those policies to local conditions. Determining where federal goals leave off and local policy discretion picks up has long been a difficult puzzle.

The rise of these strategies—contracting and intergovernmental relations—requires the federal government to shape policy and measure results without intruding on administrative flexibility. These activities require greater skill in negotiation and information management than does direct service delivery. The federal government must develop these skills—enhancing its "human capital"—without undermining its ability to manage direct programs, which continue to rely on hierarchy and authority. When a department uses both strategies, such as the U.S. Department of Transportation's air-traffic control and highway grant systems and the EPA's enforcement and Superfund cleanup systems, it faces the task of constructing parallel administrative systems. These systems have vastly different organizational cultures but must be cultivated by the same senior management team. Building the skills to manage these strategies is a substantial challenge. Leading them in parallel is an even bigger one.

Add to that an additional challenge: America's local governments have maintained more direct service delivery than the federal government. So not only must America's administrative system develop parallel direct and indirect management systems. It must also accommodate the different rules of different levels of government, an issue as much political as administrative.

COORDINATION

No problem is more central to administration than coordination. Hierarchy and authority have long offered two great advantages in solving this problem. They allow top managers to break complex jobs into smaller, manageable pieces. They also allow top managers to assign precise responsibilities to each administrator and thereby hold them accountable for results. With the transformation of governance, these approaches had scarcely become less widespread or useful. Rather, they solved a smaller share of government's management problems. As more organizations shared responsibility for producing results, American government at all levels sought additional strategies and tactics to supplement hierarchy and authority—to solve the problems that the traditional approaches left unresolved.

For example, the path-breaking welfare reform strategy Wisconsin Works (W-2) taught an important lesson about helping welfare recipients get off welfare and into productive long-term employment. In three years ending in September 2000, the number of people on cash assistance had dropped by half. Most of the front-line work was done by for-profit and nonprofit organizations and, in fact, the typical welfare recipient never saw a government employee in the journey from welfare to work. In the program that became the model for the 1996 federal welfare reform legislation, devolution was the driving strategy.

Reducing the welfare rolls was one thing. Getting welfare recipients into good jobs and keeping them there was quite another. As a 2001 Wisconsin state legislative audit report showed, one-third of the 2,129 individuals who left the W-2 program in the first three months of 1998 did not file a 1999 income tax return.[18] Experts suspected that they were not earning enough money to file. Another third had incomes below the poverty level, while one-third had incomes above the poverty level when benefits from the earned income tax credit were included. Many participants cycled into and out of the program. A little more than one-fourth of those who left the program returned by July 2000. In Milwaukee, which had the lion's share of Wisconsin's case load as well as many of its most difficult cases, 42 percent of W-2 clients were back in the program because work had not worked out.

What strategies proved most successful in getting people off welfare, keeping them off, and helping them climb above the poverty level? The W-2 alumni with the highest incomes were those who had received extensive job training and other support services and then moved on to un-subsidized private-sector jobs. Those who went into subsidized jobs did not fare nearly as well. Those with the greatest success benefited from "case management," in which service coordinators working for one of the NGOs pulled together job training, child care, housing and food support, health care, and the other services that families need to make the jump from welfare to work.

Service delivery has become less a process by which government agencies convert inputs (including money, people, and expertise) into outputs and more a process by which many agencies, in government and outside, share responsibility for producing services. To the traditional command-and-control functions of management have been added new functions of building and managing partnerships. Although the job varies tremendously by level of government—direct service delivery continues to predominate in local governments while the government by proxy dominates federal programs—the functions of public management have subtly but dramatically changed since the Progressive era. In dealing with citizens, effective government managers are increasingly case managers; in coordinating different agencies and programs, government managers are increasingly service integrators.

This heightens the value of the network approach that emerged in public management research during the 1990s. If it has not yet become a fully developed theory, it has at least provided an important step toward understanding the complexity of the service system and charting strategies for operating effectively within it. Moreover, the coordination imperative increased the importance of information technology and electronic government.[19] Information strategies and tactics that move seamlessly across those boundaries offer great potential.[20]

CONTROL

When demonstrators swarmed Seattle in 1999 to protest the meeting of the World Trade Organization, they joined the issues of globalization and democratic accountability. Amid the tear gas and broken glass, they argued that large multinational corporations and organizations like the WTO were taking power away from citizens. If the proposition was debatable, it was surely true that the rise of global trade and multinational organizations stretched the boundaries of constitutional government. Behind the headlines, the demonstrations focused attention on big issues: assessing the power of groups like the WTO; determining how to hold it accountable to democratic governments and their people; and structuring patterns of popular participation in critical decisions such organizations make. It was an important case of how constitutional democracy had lagged behind the forces shaping critical decisions.

Within devolved systems, similar issues surfaced without the glass-shattering impact of the Seattle demonstrators. As NGOs took on greater responsibility for service delivery, critics worried about how to hold them accountable. Government reformers countered that market-style contracts and incentives were the key. But when large declines in the Wisconsin welfare rolls produced big profits for the contractors, interest groups representing the poor complained that the money should have gone instead to provide better services to more welfare recipients. Since Dwight D. Eisenhower's warning about the military-industrial complex—indeed, since George Washington warned the Continental Congress that military contractors were stealing desperately needed provisions from his troops—thoughtful observers have worried about the leakage of public power and money into private hands.

In the American administrative traditions, the dominant approach to this problem has always rested in the delegation doctrine: voters elect public officials; they make policy; they delegate the management of complex issues to administrators; and the administrators are accountable through the chain of command to elected officials. In fact, the doctrine of delegation tightly controls administrative behavior. In the private sector, managers may do anything not prohibited by law. In the public sector, managers may do only what the law allows. Responsiveness to the public occurs from the top down through the electoral process. Elected officials have not always been eager to exercise their responsibility, but the fabric of bureaucratic power in the American republic depends on this relationship.

The transformation of governance has unraveled that fabric, however. Elected officials might delegate power to administer programs, but the real task of administration is coordination—weaving together separate programs into a sensible policy. That coordination results in responsibility shared among administrators at different agencies, at multiple levels of government, and among nongovernmental partners. Hyperpluralism means that no one is fully in charge of anything and that nearly everyone ultimately shares responsibility for results. That does not mean that accountability through the delegation process has evaporated. It does mean that it is less effective, both in drawing a clear link between policy decisions and the ultimate results and in ensuring that the administration of individual programs meshes to produce sensible policy. As in bureaucratic organizations that use hierarchy and control through authority, the traditional approaches have not disappeared. But the transformation of governance has created a powerful need to layer new systems on top of the old to ensure democratic accountability.

In the best Jeffersonian tradition, moreover, citizens expect to have direct influence on public administrative decisions. Citizens would quickly reject a theory that worked only from the top down and through elected officials. From decisions about local zoning to disposal of nuclear waste, citizens expect to be able to speak and to have their words heard. With so many front-line decisions made by NGOs and with supranational organizations making other decisions, the process for incorporating citizen involvement is anything but clear. It was this worry that drove frustrated demonstrators to violence in Seattle and at subsequent meetings of international bodies in Washington and Quebec City.

The problems, at their most basic level, involve how to apportion responsibilities among the elements of complex policy networks; how to hold individual members of the networks responsible for their contributions; and how to ensure that these contributions combine into prudent policy. Reformers in nations like the United Kingdom and New Zealand have experimented with market-based accountability mechanisms, by transforming public programs into competitive arrangements and relying on competition and self-interest to promote the public interest. In the United States, advocates of the reinventing government movement have argued similar approaches. More broadly, reformers have argued the value of a performance-based approach, in which elected officials would manage accountability by judging results instead of the process that produced them.

In global networks, there is an additional concern—how to ensure adequate participation in and accountability for decisions shaped by multinational organizations—some public, some private—over which the different constitutional systems of individual nation-states have limited leverage. Nation-states have structured the ground rules for these organizations, and they have voting rights for their policies and chief officials. The effectiveness of such accountability mechanisms, especially in the face of the rising power of global corporations, however, is anything but clear.

Complex public-private networks raise vastly different accountability questions than programs managed directly through government bureaucracies. They require creative strategies that build on the strengths of time-honored traditions while incorporating new tactics that work effectively to shape the behavior and results of the networks. Perhaps more than any other element of the transformation of governance, the control issue raises most sharply the tough problem of who governs—and how.

Governance for the Public Interest

American public administration has never had—and it never will have—a steady state. The field, in its study and practice, is the product of an uneasy and dynamic balance between four very different and competing administrative traditions. Americans have never embraced any of them for long. Meanwhile, competing economic, political, and social forces have constantly presented new challenges that require new—and always uneasy—fits between management tools and political goals, between administrative organizations and political institutions. To explore public administration in either theory or practice is to make oneself a captain of a ship on a sea where the waves never settle. But as anyone who has devoted hours of serious research to studying the patterns of tides and waves on a beach can testify, the same patterns never recur in precisely the same ways. The administrative process is always undergoing change.

Every once in a while, however, storms churn up the waves and dramatically rearrange the shoreline. Engineers once built a bridge on North Carolina's Outer Banks to connect two barrier islands. Within a decade, a large part of the bridge was over dry land because ocean storms filled in sand from the opposite side of the island. Administration is about coordination, and twenty-first century coordination is increasingly about bridge-building. The transformation of governance calls for new bridges built in new and imaginative ways—bridges that will cross wide divides and that will endure. Ten principles suggest how to build these bridges:

1. *Hierarchy and authority cannot and will not be replaced, but they must be fitted better to the transformation of governance.* From the earliest days of human history, managers have used hierarchy and authority to coordinate solutions to complex problems. The governance problems of the twenty-first century do not reverse that basic truth. Hierarchy and authority provide enduring strategies for both coordination and accountability in democratic governments.

2. *Complex networks have been layered on top of hierarchical organizations, and they must be managed differently.* Despite the enduring power of hierarchy, managers need to adapt its tools to the interorganizational networks that increasingly drive administrative action. They need to harness their hierarchies to manage those networks, often side by side with traditional programs that continue to be managed through authority-driven structures.

3. *Public managers need to rely more on interpersonal and interorganizational processes as complements to—and sometimes as substitutes for—authority.* Whatever their weaknesses, authority and hierarchy provide stable and useful mechanisms for structuring and controlling the behavior of administrators. The more managers rely on networks, the more they need to find substitutes—or supplements—for coordinating action. The more informal or dynamic those networks are, the more managers need new mechanisms. Traditional administration relied primarily on organizational structure to shape administrative action. The more fluid administrative action becomes, the more administrators are likely to need to shift from structure to process for leverage.

4. *Information is the most basic and necessary component for the transformation of governance.* Many processes, including financial and personnel systems, offer the potential for control and influence. In twenty-first century government, however, information has become essential. As computerized information technology and e-government spread, and as more government work occurs across organizational boundaries, information offers the most effective bridge. Information tech-

nology makes possible instantaneous, boundary-free communication, and that communication is necessary for coordinating twenty-first century work.

5. *Performance management can provide a valuable tool for spanning fuzzy boundaries.* Of the different forms of information, performance-based information can be the most important. When multiple organizations share responsibility for producing public programs, it can become difficult for citizens, government managers, or elected officials to determine who is in charge of what—and who contributes what to the overall outcomes of governmental policy. Performance-based management systems can strengthen administration by allowing administrators to allocate responsibility for broad outcomes among members of the service network, by assessing how the outputs of each part of the network supports the broader goals of public policy, and by encouraging elected officials to examine the links between their policy decisions and the results the system produces. Performance management thus is not only a potential mechanism for managing networks but also a tool for accountability.

6. *Transparency is the foundation for trust and confidence in government operations.* Communication that is transparent—accessible in real time to everyone—can increase the trust and confidence of citizens in governmental work. With the rise of global corporations, many citizens have feared that private power will swamp the public interest. With increasing reliance on devolution, many citizens have worried that the real decisions about managing public programs will be pushed into invisible, nongovernmental nooks and crannies. Both fears have often combined to reduce public trust and confidence in government's work. Information technology, including the Internet and e-government, makes possible rapid and broad distribution of knowledge about what government is doing and how. That, in turn, can help strengthen citizens' relations with an increasingly indirect government.

7. *Government needs to invest in human capital so that the skills of its workers match the jobs they must perform.* Many of these tools, however, require high skill levels, especially in the government managers who must coordinate them. Moreover, these skills are often very different from the ones traditionally developed for command-and-control programs. The bridge-building required to manage the transformation of governance will require, in turn, a retooling of government's personnel systems so that public employees have the skills their jobs require. Many of the tasks of twenty-first century government, especially its critical coordination challenges, are at their core people-based challenges. Solving them will require skilled managers who can negotiate the constantly shifting forces of the administrative systems.

8. *The transformation of governance requires new strategies and tactics for popular participation in public administration.* Although the American republic anticipates top-down administrative accountability through elected officials, citizens increasingly expect more bottom-up responsiveness from public services and the employees who run them. In part, this flows from the customer service movement encouraged in the private sector. In part, it comes from the movement launched through the 1960s Great Society programs to empower citizens and make programs more responsive to their needs. The rise of e-government and other forms of boundary-spanning communication also promotes bottom-up responsiveness. As citizens gain new channels for influence and communication, they can rely less on top officials as problem-solvers and more on going directly to those who manage the programs that affect them. That, in turn, requires a rethinking of the linkages between citizens and governments.

9. *Civic responsibility has become the job of government's nongovernmental partners.* The same holds true for the public's relations with the for-profit and non-profit organizations that increasingly play a central role in service delivery. Government needs more effective mechanisms to ensure that citizens receive the same basic and consistent treatment regardless of whether governments or NGOS provide services. The government's nongovernmental partners are no longer agents-for-hire who can maintain their traditional missions. By becoming partners in public service provision, NGOs assume responsibilities for how they treat citizens. That requires, in turn, the development of mechanisms to promote the responsiveness, flexibility, and efficiency that nongovernmental partners can offer without sacrificing the basic standards that citizens expect from government—and that the Constitution guarantees.

10. *Americans need to devise new constitutional strategies for the management of conflict.* The basic transformation of governance has not so much created brand new paradigms as it has layered new issues on top of old ones. That calls not so much for a new Constitution as for fresh strategies based on the old one. The Constitution has proven remarkably resilient over its history, but periodically new pressures have built up that have required new tactics. The great genius of the founders lay in framing a Constitution that could adapt; the genius of the nation's leaders since has lain in their ability to manage that adaptation as new pressures have demanded. For a century, the patterns devised by the Progressives shaped the relationships between economic and political interests and between administrative and political power. These adaptations have occurred especially when economic power threatened to swamp the public interest. That

spurred the Progressives' reforms of government at the end of the nineteenth century—and the same issues framed the tensions government faced at the end of the twentieth century.

It is always tempting to seize on any new administrative practice and to declare it a revolution, to examine a new theoretical idea and proclaim a new paradigm. In the case of American administrative practice, that is especially dangerous. For centuries, American government and its administrative systems have evolved through endless adaptations. Its basic administrative strategies have grown on foundations that stretch back hundreds, if not thousands, of years. In many ways, therefore, there is nothing really new in the story of the transformation of governance. It simply represents the latest change—one new tide in the waves that constantly have washed across the American political system.[21]

In the transformation of governance, however, lie two basic truths. One truth is that the context truly is new. The rise of globalization and devolution, the stress between government's horizontal and vertical dimensions, and hyperpluralism all combine to create fresh tensions for which government's existing structures and strategies proved a poor match. The other truth is that this transformation plays itself out within the four traditions—Hamiltonian, Jeffersonian, Wilsonian, and Madisonian—that have long shaped America's basic administrative instincts. Neither the context nor the traditions remain stable for long. The system has long been resilient enough to accommodate big changes in context with modest changes in administration. But periodically, the tensions have grown serious. Reformers created new twists on the existing traditions that proved a better and, at least temporarily, more stable fit for the problems they faced. Some of America's most difficult times preceded these adjustments; some of America's most intense periods of economic prosperity and social content have followed these shifts. The new puzzles that emerged at the end of the nineteenth century helped set the stage for America's remarkable twentieth century. The puzzles that surfaced at the end of the twentieth century set the stage for a similar transformation. America's economic prosperity and social welfare depend on cleverly crafting a new match between the emerging policy puzzles and the enduring administrative traditions.

Governance at the Boundaries

A dozen years ago, when the first edition of this book appeared, "hyperpluralism" was a huge and growing threat—a version of Madisonian democracy pumped up on steroids. In *Federalist* 10, James Madison warned of the "mischiefs of faction." In twenty-first century American democracy, factions have become ever more mischievous, creating gridlock, immobilizing government decision-making, and handicapping American democracy's ability to get things done. The first edition ended by asking the questions: Who governs—and how? How can we make and implement effective public policy?

Hyperpluralism became hyperpartisanship, and that has produced depressing answers to these important questions. Who governs? Often, no one. How? With show-stopping conflict. How can we make effective policy? How can we make and implement policy well? The answer strikes a hopeful note, if twenty-first century democracy has the wits to pursue an eleventh principle added to the ten of the first edition: governance, in the United States and around the world, is increasingly a matter of boundary crossing (between the public, private, and nonprofit sectors and between home and abroad). It is driven by increasing interpenetration of government into all aspects of society. Twenty-first century governance requires new strategies for accountability (since blurred boundaries make it difficult not only for anyone to be in charge but also for anyone to know who is in charge) and performance (since government's job has increasingly shifted from delivering services to leveraging action to produce them). This doesn't necessarily mean that government cannot work. It does mean, however, that governance is often harder—and that solutions must be more creative, with fresh and innovative approaches to ensure that government can deliver on its promises while remaining firmly rooted in democratic ideals.

For just one measure of how government has changed, consider the role of the local fire department. There is no older, more important, or more traditional organization in American government. Indeed, a 2011 international survey showed that firefighting is the world's most respected profession.[1] Firefighters are rightly praised for their bravery, and their interactions with the public are mostly positive. Unlike police officers, they don't make traffic stops, pull guns, or arrest citizens. They help people in trouble. But the troubles for which they provide help have changed. According to the National Fire Protection Association, just 4 percent of all fire department responses in 2012 were for fires, down from 19 percent in 1986. False alarms have remained about the same, at about 7 to 8 percent. But calls for medical help have soared from just over half to more than two-thirds of all fire department responses (see figure E.1). Put differently, one of the most traditional and treasured government bureaucracies is increasingly in

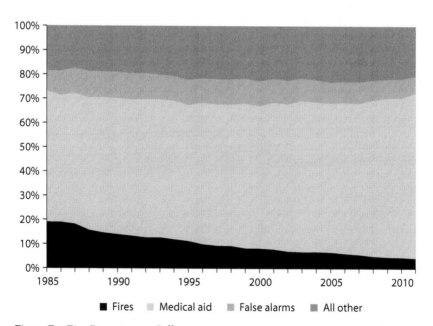

Figure E.1. Fire Department Calls
Source: National Fire Protection Association (2013), at http://www.nfpa.org/research/reports
-and-statistics/the-fire-service/fire-department-calls/fire-department-calls.

the *boundary-crossing* business. When firefighters are dispatched, they often arrive in large trucks equipped with hoses and ladders—and then provide medical help to accident victims, those stricken ill, and others who need their assistance. They deliver babies, treat heart attacks, rescue stranded motorists, and sometimes save pets from deep water or ice floes. They're trained for that, as well as for putting out fires. But on average, firefighters respond to fifteen medical calls for every fire. Their continuous boundary-crossing is not an easy task—and it poses sharp challenges for governance.

Governance Challenges for Twenty-First Century Democracy

American democracy has never been easy. The framers, led by Madison's brilliant leadership of constitution writing in 1787, created a remarkable balancing act among the many forces that threatened to shred the new republic before it had taken root. Just as brilliant was the framers' foresight in devising a system of government that has endured for so long, bending and changing without breaking. Democracy isn't for sissies, and Madisonian democracy is a full-contact sport. It always has been, and it always will be. We've survived the vicious assault of a member of the U.S. Senate by a member of the U.S. House of Representatives on the floor of the Senate itself. We've survived a civil war and a continental expansion. We've survived shouting matches in congressional committee rooms, when committee chairpersons have shut off the microphones of dissenting minority members. We've survived the indictment of mayors and governors and the impeachment of presidents. Despite it all, American democracy is still admired throughout the world. Speechwriters are fond of pointing to a famous quote by Winston Churchill: "Americans will always do the right thing, only after they have tried everything else." Churchill never actually said this, although Sen. Mark Warner (D-Va.) quipped that "if Churchill didn't say it, he should have."[2] However, Churchill did say, in a speech to the House of Commons in 1947, that "democracy is the worst form of government, except for all those other forms that have been tried from time to time." He had that right.

Still, it is impossible to escape the conclusion that American democracy has been sailing of late through especially rocky shoals. The public's trust in government is at historic lows, and Americans' confidence in the government's ability to deliver has declined. Two of America's very best political scientists, Thomas E. Mann and Norman Ornstein, made a powerful argument through the title of their 2012 book, *It's Even Worse Than It Looks: How the American Constitutional System Collided with the New Politics of Extremism.*[3] Hyperpartisanship, driving politics and its politicians into unbridgeable camps, has collided with America's democratic institutions, which are designed to bend toward compromise without breaking. The result of this hyperpartisanship, all too often, has been gridlock.

Hyperpartisanship not only has damaged the ability of America's democratic institutions to make decisions. It has also handicapped the implementation of decisions once they've been made. As noted earlier in this volume, "complex networks have been layered on top of hierarchical organizations."[4] To that can be added the interweaving of government into society, often in ways that citizens and even their elected officials do not recognize. "Keep government's hands off my Medicare" became a running gag on the campaign trail, but underlying the protest signs by demonstrators was a lack of understanding that government, through citizens' tax dollars, pays for and manages Medicare. Critics savaged Barack Obama's Affordable Care Act (ACA) as a "massive government takeover of medicine." Hyperpartisanship has become enmeshed in the battle over the size of government.

The "massive takeover" line tested well in focus groups, but the facts are quite different. In 2012, the federal government provided just 26 percent of all health care spending, mostly through the Medicare and Medicaid programs.[5] The ACA would not affect that total much. The ACA does require all Americans to have health insurance, but the health insurance market is private; almost all health care would continue to be privately provided and most would be privately financed. Why, then, was there such an uproar over the program? A 2013 Heritage Foundation analysis put it accurately: "The Obamacare health insurance exchange system, though often sold as a mechanism to provide consumer choice and competition, is, in fact, a vehicle for the detailed federal regulation of insurance."[6] The fiercest battles have been government mandates over what coverage private employers must provide, such as whether the owners of private companies can decide that their personal religious convictions can permit them to exclude birth-control coverage. The program is thus a prime example of the transformation of governance in the United States—an expansion of government by interpenetrating the public and private sectors.

Government, especially at the state and local levels, still provides a large number of services itself, ranging from police and sanitation to public universities and state prisons. Still more public goods and services are provided through the private sector, with grants, contracts, and tax expenditures. Weaving through everything is a substantial and ever-growing regulatory net. If citizens feel the press of a larger government, it is not because government has more employees reaching deeper into their lives. Rather, there is a growing network of governmental tools, often indirect, that are layered atop hierarchical organizations. Together, this network is taking government increasingly into the lives of Americans. Government surely feels bigger to most Americans because the role of government in their lives has grown.

Moreover, no governmental agency operates on its own. A local government's response to traffic accidents requires police officers, firefighters, and emergency medical technicians. A state government's environmental programs reach across levels of government and deep into the private sector. The federal air-traffic control system is an intricate minuet connecting the National Weather Service, pilots in their cockpits, operations centers for the airlines, and air-traffic centers across the country and around the world. In fact, there is no problem that matters that any single organization can control.[7]

There surely is an epic ongoing debate about government's size and about what new programs the government should create. But there can be no debate about government's increasing reach. Government has increasingly penetrated the private and nonprofit sectors, and there is now no part of any citizen's world that government does not touch. The size-of-government debate is thus about two things: what government ought to do, which is ongoing, and how government ought to do it, which is largely settled. There is no going back on the vast interpenetration of government with the rest of American society.

This development poses a huge problem for trust in institutions. Long-term analysis by the Pew Research Center for the People and the Press shows that 73 percent of Americans surveyed trusted government to do the right thing "just about always" or "most of the time" in 1958. By 2013, the number had dropped to only 13 percent, a historic low. Thirty percent of Americans were "angry" at government in 2013, and another 55 percent were "frustrated."[8] Put together, that is an explosive combination: a government increasingly distrusted, government programs ever more part of every citizen's life, and a strategy of governance likely to worsen the dilemma. Governance has transformed, but it is straining Madisonian democracy in ways that Madison never anticipated and in ways that threaten to cripple the balance he so delicately built.

Strengthening Democracy through Improved Governance

Is there anything that government officials can do to reverse this trend? The problem is huge and difficult to solve. Evidence, however, suggests a strong link between public administration and trust in government. First, citizens tend to trust lower levels of government more than they do the federal government. In 2001, trust in the federal, state, and local governments was about the same, with about two-thirds of poll respondents having a positive view. In the decade that followed, however, trust in state and local governments remained relatively stable, with 63 percent of Americans having a favorable view of local governments and 57 percent having a favorable view of state governments, according to a 2013 poll. That contrasts with the plummeting favorable view of the federal government, which dropped more than forty points.[9] The closer government is to the people, the more the people are likely to trust the government. Some of this stems from hyperpartisanship, but some undoubtedly is also the product of the "don't touch my Medicare" syndrome, in which citizens tend not to trust institutions that they don't see having a direct hand in providing services to them.

Second, research sponsored by the Organisation for Economic Co-operation and Development (OECD) on the world's leading industrialized nations found that citizens were more satisfied with some public services than with government as a whole. For example, the study found that satisfaction was just 40 percent for the overall government, but that satisfaction was 66 percent for the education system, 71 percent for health care, and 72 percent for local police.[10] Citizens discriminate among different kinds of services, and satisfaction is higher the more they directly connect with services they appreciate the most.

The OECD report echoed American surveys, finding that "trust tends to be highest at the local level, where services are delivered and where the link with government performance is most concrete. Trust also tends to be higher for actual users of public services than for non-users."[11] The report concluded that

> a renewed focus on trust in government can bring a new perspective to public governance, enhancing the role of the citizens. At an institutional level, this should reinforce the notion of a social contract between citizens and the state, where the former contribute not only by paying taxes and obeying the law, but also by being receptive to public policies and cooperating in their design and implementation. To gain this support from citizens, however, governments need to be more inclusive, more transparent, more receptive and more efficient.[12]

And that is the core of the governance puzzle. Government's performance and citizens' trust in government to perform is a reciprocal partnership. In fact, it is a new version of the social contract, whose roots go back at least to Rousseau. With the rise of a government whose service delivery is increasingly interconnected, that social contract takes on a vastly important new meaning. Government is not, and cannot be, simply a two-way mechanism for delivering services in exchange for payment of taxes. Government is increasingly a complex and intertwined relationship, in which citizens share responsibility not only for deciding what government ought to do but also sharing responsibility for doing it.

Establishing that relationship and making it work are perhaps the biggest challenges for twenty-first century governance. Elected officials all too often have demonstrated either a lack of understanding about how governmental systems actually work or, in some cases, a disdain for the programs they are responsible for implementing. That, in turn, has even further eroded the trust that must serve as the bedrock of government. As boundary-crossing becomes an even-greater imperative, and because crossing boundaries requires skills and strategies different from those that more traditional hierarchical administration entailed, the strains of government have become more pronounced in the twenty-first century.

The Katrina Syndrome

There is no better example of this problem than the federal government's sluggish response to the near-drowning of New Orleans following Hurricane Katrina in 2005. After the levees failed, most of the city was under water, public services crumbled, most hospitals were inoperative, and the police department struggled to remain operational. Thousands of residents were stranded at the Superdome, with little food, water, or basic sanitation. The country—indeed, the world—watched on televised news, wondering why the federal government seemed dangerously out of touch. President George W. Bush flew over the city in Air Force One, but the photos of him looking out the plane's windows at the devastation below only made him seem more distant. When he visited the region a few days later, he put his arm around Federal Emergency Management Agency administrator Michael Brown and said, "Brownie, you're doing a heckuva job," at a time when it was clear to anyone watching the halting response to the storm that the federal agency was surely not doing a heckuva job. The episode proved devastating to the Bush presidency. There had been rises and falls in the president's approval rating, but Katrina marked the point where Bush's negative ratings exceeded his positives and never recovered (see figure E.2).

The Katrina syndrome—a punishing erosion of public support following a failure to perform—has spilled over to other executives as well.[13] New York Mayor John Lindsay's administration famously stumbled in plowing snow after a 1969 blizzard. He got into a shouting match with furious residents in the

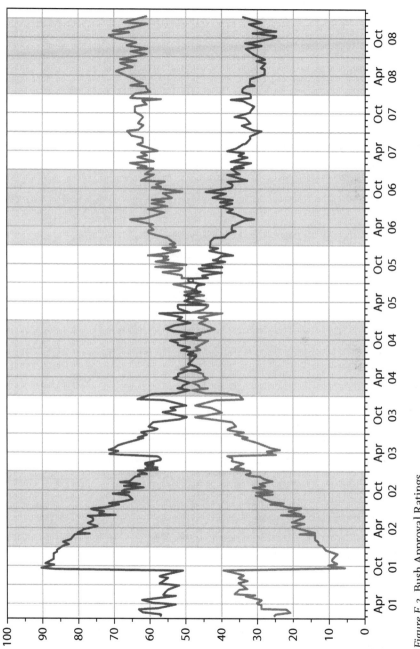

Figure E.2. Bush Approval Ratings
Source: Gallup presidential approval, http://www.gallup.com/poll/116500/presidential-approval-ratings-george-bush.aspx#1.

borough of Queens and, by 1972, six in ten New Yorkers believed that his government's performance was "poor."[14] In the fall of 2013, the launch of President Barack Obama's Affordable Care Act badly stumbled because of failures in the program's website. And like Bush, Obama's approval/disapproval ratings, which had been about even in mid-year 2013, began moving in Bush-like directions. Six months after the initial stumbles, Obama's approval rating had dropped to 42 percent and his disapproval score was 54 percent. These trends match an international comparison by the OECD, which found in 2013 that the biggest drops in trust in the previous five years had occurred in countries that faced the biggest crises—and whose leaders struggled to respond to them.[15] The public expects its government to perform. The bigger the crisis, the higher the expectations for results. The higher the expectation, the greater the potential for disappointment. The larger the disappointment, the greater the impact on public trust.

There is a broader lesson here. Governments—and government officials—have struggled for years to take steps to improve public trust but have made little progress in turning the curve. The Clinton administration's National Performance Review, for example, set out to create a government that "works better and costs less." The "costs less" side of the equation came mainly through cutting the number of government employees, and "works better" side did little to improve trust, despite some truly remarkable accomplishments. In contrast, failures to solve big problems often tend to reduce public trust. In short, there is a political imbalance: improving trust is hard, for it's connected with a vast array of forces beyond the control of government officials, but driving trust down is something public officials can do—and have done.

There is an underlying political logic here. It wouldn't be reasonable to expect citizens to applaud governments for doing what they expect and pay for through taxes. There's never a headline, "Mail Delivered Yet Again Today," or "Tens of Thousands of Planes Land Safely Because of Air-Traffic Control System." But it's equally unreasonable to expect citizens to look the other way when governmental failures are front-page news, from the failure to plow snow after a blizzard to the failure to launch the website needed for a new health care system. Moreover, given the rise of a twenty-four-hour news cycle, with multiple media outlets competing on the airwaves and on the Internet for an audience best attracted by strong ideas and by a highly segmented, often polarized set of values, there's always a ready audience for government failure stories.

That frames a key truth: There is little upside gain to governments that perform well, but there is substantial downside loss for governments that perform poorly. This reality frames an important implication for governance: good results might not improve public trust, but poor ones can quickly feed distrust. Governments, of course, have an ethical responsibility to perform well on behalf of their citizens. That is a bedrock of the social contract. But good performance can also help forestall further erosion of trust, and given the precipitous state of trust in government, that would be an important step.

Good Management for Troubled Programs

No one intentionally wants to manage a program poorly, except in cases where opponents try to smother in failure a program they disagree with. Mayor Lindsay did not intend to leave the residents of Queens stranded. President Bush did not seek to punish the residents of New Orleans, and FEMA director Brown surely did not set to work on the biggest challenge of his career intending to propagate a disaster. President Obama saw the Affordable Care Act as his most important legacy and desperately wanted success. In each case, and in many more, failure occurred despite good intentions.

Obtaining good evidence on these puzzles is difficult, but the U.S. Government Accountability Office's (GAO) "high-risk list" of programs vulnerable to waste, fraud, abuse, and mismanagement offers compelling insights. GAO's original 1990 list contained fourteen programs. By 2013, the list had grown to thirty programs, ranging from Medicare and Medicaid to the Postal Service, and from weather satellite data to food safety.[16] GAO identified the programs most at risk and produced a wide-ranging catalog of problems across the federal government's activities.

An analysis of the factors underlying the list reveals important findings about what ails government programs that aren't working. First, most of the high-risk programs require program managers to work effectively across complex networks. As figure E.3 shows, all the high-risk programs involve networks across organizational boundaries within the federal government and networks across the public, private, and nonprofit sectors. Many of the programs involve managing across federal-state-local and international boundaries. Second, the high-risk programs required managers to develop sophisticated performance metrics, human capital strategies for ensuring they had the right workers for the jobs to be done, sound information systems to provide the management backbone, and the technology needed to tackle complex problems (figure E.4).

These programs are risky because they work through complex networks, sophisticated performance metrics, important human capital puzzles, intricate

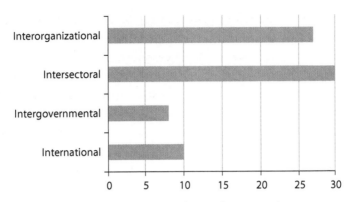

Figure E.3. High-risk Programs and Complex Networks
Source: Content analysis by the author.

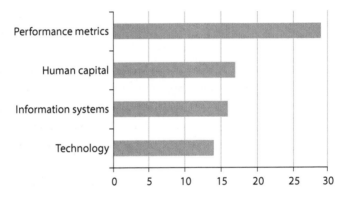

Figure E.4. High-risk Programs and Complex Processes
Source: Content analysis by the author.

information systems, and cutting-edge technology. Of course, that's true for many programs, at the federal, state, and local levels. In the years since the book's first edition, however, those challenges have become greater, the networks have become more complex, the risks of failure have grown, and the consequences for poor performance ripple more widely and more quickly. Performance problems result, and they diminish public trust in government.

Failure is not inevitable, and exemplary government programs conquer these challenges. In 2013, GAO celebrated two programs whose performance had improved enough for them to be removed from the high-risk list: the management of interagency contracting and the business-system modernization at the Internal Revenue Service. Moreover, previous work by GAO showed that these successes were no fluke. There are high-performing organizations in the federal government, GAO concluded, and they share four important characteristics:

1. *A clear, well-articulated, and compelling mission.* High-performingorganizations have a clear, well-articulated, and compelling mission, the strategic goals to achieve it, and a performance management system that aligns with these goals to show employees how their performance can contribute to overall organizational results.

2. *Strategic use of partnerships.* Since the federal government is increasingly reliant on partners to achieve its outcomes, becoming a high-performing organization requires that federal agencies effectively manage relationships with other organizations outside their direct control.

3. *Focus on needs of clients and customers.* Serving the needs of clients and customers involves identifying these needs, striving to meet them, measuring performance, and publicly reporting on progress to help assure appropriate transparency and accountability.

4. *Strategic management of people.* Most high-performing organizations have strong, charismatic, visionary, and sustained leadership, the capability to identify what skills and competencies the employees and the organization need, and other key characteristics, including effective recruiting, comprehensive training and development, retention of high-performing employees, and a streamlined hiring process.[17]

These points lead to important conclusions. Government performance matters, not only in providing value for taxpayers' money but also in shaping public trust in government. A high-performing government might not improve public trust, but it can help prevent its erosion. Some programs perform better than others, and even problem-plagued programs can be improved. What separates high- from low-performing programs is a focus on mission, partnerships, citizens, and the government agency's people. Construction of strong performance metrics and information technology systems provides an essential backbone for good performance. There is strong and growing evidence that these are the principles for public administration in the twenty-first century.

Governance and the State in the Twenty-First Century

At the core of these principles is the need for government's leaders—both its elected officials and its administrators—to guide the fundamental transformation of governance. It is a transformation characterized by boundary-crossing among sectors and between nations, and it is a transformation shaped by government's increasing role in nearly every part of everyday life. Traditional debates about the size of government only begin to capture the trends. In the United States, government has not grown by a vast expansion of the number of government agencies, programs, or public employees. The primary engine for transforming government has been the growth of tools that interweave government more into the very fabric of life, from regulations that require bicycle tires to reflect headlights to tax incentives that encourage home ownership. Government seems big because its presence is everywhere, not because it has turned society into a police state. There is a dilemma built into that transformation: government's presence has grown because citizens want government to do things, but they object to a government that constrains their freedom. It is a dilemma that citizens themselves have constructed, woven into their lives through tools both subtle and far-reaching.

Transforming Steps

The extent of this transformation becomes clear from reading Dwight Waldo's *The Administrative State*, published soon after the end of World War II, which offers one of the most enduring interpretations of public administration.[18] The book is a classic not only because of its insightful analysis but also because, as its title indicates, Waldo discerns the large, mature, administrative apparatus that emerged during the war. For Waldo, government delivered services. Governmental organizations were the primary instrument for service delivery, through a hierarchical structure and with vertical dimensions shaping the execution of public decisions. Elected officials made decisions on behalf of the people, and they delegated responsibility for carrying them out to agency heads, who in turn subdelegated responsibilities through the bureaucracy to the floor, where bureaucrats met citizens. Authority governed accountability, and coordination focused on linkages among elements of the hierarchy. When coordination problems arose, such as when managers in different regions needed to work together or managers in charge of different functions found common problems, the problems were pushed up to the level at which a manager could reach across all the pieces. Administration is rarely tidy, but the theory was clear. Theory focused both on effectively delivering services, since it was clear who was responsible for what, and on ensuring democratic responsibility, since all administrative actions could be traced back to the delegation of authority by elected officials and, ultimately, to the people.

The basic principles of the administrative state continue to drive the way many elected officials, citizens, and reporters think about bureaucracy—and how bureaucracy ought to behave. It's a neat and tidy theory, based on clear boundaries, which addresses the big issues of performance and accountability. Moreover, it offers the basic building blocks of public administration, because the delegations of authority, organization charts, and job descriptions of most public employees have remained relatively unchanged. But the more that government has become a service deliverer by serving as a service coordinator, the more complex administration has become. Policymakers typically focus on policy decisions; they often pay little attention to implementation. In the early days of the administrative state, when policy implementation flowed hierarchically from policy decisions, the challenges to effective and responsible administration were difficult enough.

However, with the transformation of the state from hierarchy and boundaries to networks and boundary-crossing, the challenges have become far larger. The distance from making policy decisions to executing them is often far greater. The linkage from policy deciders to policy implementers is frequently far more indirect. The connections along the chain are often more intricate and prone to breaking, and the leverage of traditional administrative tools is often much weaker. When policies stumble or fail, the consequences for citizens loom larger because government's reach has grown so substantially, and the implications of failure ripple through the interconnected networks. The media are even quicker to pounce—and there is an ever-larger media mouth to feed. Coordination, not surprisingly, falters. Charges of an unaccountable government surface because the levers of administrative power and effectiveness so often seem out of reach. With growing distance and complexity between policymakers and policy implementers, within government and with partners outside, it's little wonder that the grip on accountability and performance seems so slippery and that the implementation of public programs so often runs into trouble. With the transformation of governance, there needs to be as much attention paid to the how as to the what of policy. (See table E.1 for a summary of these forces.)

Getting at the how of policy frames the toughest problems for twenty-first century governance. The models of hierarchical administration served both theory and practice quite well for a very long time. Indeed, they were so successful that they still maintain a powerful hold over the way many Americans conceive of governance and management. But there has been a growing mismatch between administrative realities and these conceptions. It is this gap that feeds

Table E.1   From the "Administrative State" to Twenty-First Century Governance

	Administrative state	Twenty-first century governance
Governmental role	Service deliverer	Service coordinator
Policy instrument	Through government agencies	Through mixed systems
Vertical control	Through hierarchy, from decision to execution	Focus on decision, often neglecting execution through mixed systems
Horizontal coordination	Centralized, through hierarchy	Distributed through networks
Role of government leaders	Strong, through hierarchy, with clear accountability model	Weak, with hierarchy a poor match for strategies of policy execution and uncertain accountability model

the forces weakening government performance and, in turn, undermining the government's ability to engender trust through high-performing programs.

Moreover, the gap has also weakened our democratic institutions. It is clear that many forces, led by growing polarization, are eroding the ability of our legislatures to perform and our executives to work with our legislatures. Moreover, the increasing interpenetration of government into civil society vastly complicates the problem: the increasingly intricate interweaving of governmental programs into every facet of the daily lives of Americans, coupled with the increasing difficulty elected officials have in managing complex policy tools and holding government managers accountable for results that lie outside their immediate control.

This is the fundamental challenge of twenty-first century governance, a challenge large and growing. The problem is difficult, but it is solvable—and worth solving. Although good public administration does not provide a magical solution for the problems of trust and performance in government, good administration can at the very least stem the erosion of trust while enhancing the performance of government. In the difficult and often depressing world in which public programs so often find themselves, that is no mean feat.

Transformative Strategies

What would good administration look like? In an era of transformed governance, solving the challenges posed by the eleventh principle of boundary-crossing requires building bridges. These five elements chart the strategy.

1. *Transforming public law.* The foundation of performance and accountability in government lies in the long—but often overlooked—traditions of public law.

There is a deep reservoir of both theory and practice to guide what administrators do and how they do it. For government programs, the most important pieces are constitutional law, especially the relationships among the executive, legislative, and judicial elements of the government, and the protections afforded citizens against arbitrary use of the state's power and for promoting equitable treatment. In the English-speaking tradition, the roots stretch back to 1215 and King John's signing of the Magna Carta, at the insistence of barons who wanted to limit the king's power and protect their property rights. In the United States, the rule of law has long been at the core of American liberty. In his pamphlet *Common Sense*, published in 1776, Thomas Paine argued that "a government of our own is a natural right," with that right protected in law, because "in America the law is king. For as in absolute governments the king is law, so in free countries the law ought to be king; and there ought to be no other. But lest any ill use should afterwards arise, let the crown at the conclusion of the ceremony be demolished, and scattered among the people whose right it is."[19]

America's transformation of governance, however, is increasingly straining the boundaries of the rule of law. The patterns were becoming clear even before World War II, as John Gaus concluded in 1936: "In a state in which the powers of government intermesh widely with those of industry, commerce, and finance the traditional restraints upon the discretion of the administrator through making him responsible to the electorate, the courts, and the legislators are inadequate."[20]

The state's powers intermeshed even more during World War II, when the government relied heavily on private contractors to supply everything from rations to parts for the atomic bomb. The growth of the modern American state, as we have seen, brought even wider interpenetration of public and private power. That, in turn, pushed both theory and practice further from the historical foundations. As Jody Freeman concludes, this "blended power" system has neither a clear rule of law, to drive administrative accountability, nor a clear model to replace it.[21]

In managing the transformation, government has had to depend on private law, especially contracts and torts, to drive public action. There is a vast body of private law, of course, but it was designed to regulate behavior among equal parties. The preamble to the Constitution makes it clear that government is not just one party among others. Rather, it seeks to "promote the general Welfare." With public law challenged by the rise of blended power and private law limited in its ability to advance the public interest, the transformation of governance requires a new theory of law to ensure accountability.

2. *Transforming public agencies into instruments of leveraged action.* The traditional theory of public administration begins with the presumption that public agencies exist to deliver goods and services to the public. That matches the presumptions of policymakers, who expect to make decisions and delegate responsibility, and of citizens, who presume that government will provide what they need. The basic model is a vending machine: insert tax dollars, push the policy lever, and wait for government agencies to dispense goods and services.[22] That, of course, is a super-simplistic model of how government programs actually work and, as reporters Katherine Barrett and Richard Greene note: "Contractors involved with government products or services often seem to operate under a mask of anonymity—not just in the press, but even in government reports."[23]

For policymakers, however, it's a different story. Citizens expect that policymakers will ensure that tax dollars produce value for money and, if problems crop up, that policymakers will fix them. As governance drifts further from the vending-machine model and the traditional approach of hierarchical, authority-based public administration, it gets harder for policymakers to understand the workings of the systems they are governing—and the greater complexity of the system increases the odds that problems will develop.[24] In fact, the distance between big policy decisions and the intricate details of policy implementation through indirect mechanisms has sometimes crippled policy innovations. Consider a reporter's analysis of the rollout of Barack Obama's signature health care reform initiative in the fall of 2013. White House chief of staff Dennis Mc-Donough told *Time* magazine reporter Steven Brill that before the launch of the ill-fated website, Obama would end by saying, "I want to remind the team that this only works if the technology works." But Brill concludes:

> The problem, of course, was that no one in the meetings had any idea whether the technology worked, nor did the President and his chief of staff have the inclination to dig in and find out. The President may have had the right instinct when he repeatedly reminded his team about the technology. But in the end he was as aloof from the people and facts he needed to avoid this catastrophe as he was from the people who ended up fixing it.[25]

There is an important underlying lesson here: the transformation of governance requires an understanding by policymakers of the tools they are using—and the instincts about how to shift the tools when necessary to get the results they want.

3. *Transforming public leaders into boundary spanners.* In a policy world with more boundaries, policy leaders need to serve as boundary spanners. Policy net-

works are not self-organizing, self-regulating, or self-directing. Indeed, this is a corollary of the point on private and public law: just as private legal traditions can't be counted on to advance the public interest, networks of disparate organizations won't necessarily pursue the public good. Government has increasingly relied on private partners to advance public purposes, but private organizations will only partner if it advances their private interests. That creates a fundamental challenge of how to create complex networks of nongovernmental players whose interactions advance the public interest.

That is a deceptively difficult challenge, both because policymakers often fail to understand the nature of the systems they are building and because administration of these systems often fails to make the public interest supreme. Indeed, many elements of the network approach to governance positions the government as one player among many, instead of the prime player advancing the central issues. Moreover, as Robert F. Durant and Susannah Bruns Ali point out, many of the "bridge-building" theories of administrative reform have taken a fundamentally instrumental approach, focusing on the management of tools, and have looked on citizens as "expertise-challenged," not able to fully engage the governance system.[26] Bridge building is essential to the management of tools that cut across organizational, sectoral, and international boundaries, and citizens are expertise-challenged in understanding these tools.

Of course, citizens don't need to understand the details any more than they need to be able to fathom the way fuel injectors work in their car engines or how an automatic teller machine dispenses cash from their bank accounts. Citizens pay tax dollars for public services; it is not unreasonable for them to expect value for money. But the neglect of the fundamental connections of democracy and administration, as Durant and Ali point out, and the neglect of indirect tools like contracting and grants by elected officials combine to weaken both the effectiveness and the responsiveness of governance. The transformation of governance requires attention to strategies to ensure that public programs perform well—and that the tools be managed in ways that connect, not distance, citizens from their government. In fact, there is considerable evidence that disconnecting citizens from government worsens the already enormous problem of public trust in governmental institutions, both in the United States and around the world.[27] We need new bridge-building strategies that better couple democracy and administration with the emerging tools of governance.

4. *Transforming information into bridging tools.* If government's leaders need to be bridge builders, for both administration and democracy, then they need bridges that will span organizational gaps. The central challenge of the transformation

of governance is that traditional hierarchical theory remains important, but its leverage stops at organizational boundaries. Leaders of transformed governance need management strategies that connect alongside the channels of policy, money, power, and implementation. The most important and promising tool is information, which can connect across the boundaries that often frustrate or stop the flow of authority.[28]

Although it quickly became a cliché to refer to the twenty-first century as the information age, repeating the truism makes it no less true. It's not just the vast amount of information and the proliferation of devices to access it—it's the way that information so easily crosses boundaries, to the point that boundaries evaporate. The dawn of the new century saw the rise of portable devices that made it possible for people everywhere to carry with them information from anywhere. MySpace and AOL, then Facebook and Twitter, and then Instagram and other Internet tools, became enormously popular precisely because they provided social connections independent of time, space, and status. Government was scarcely in the vanguard of the information revolution; the FBI was still asking for individuals undergoing security checks to use fax machines to submit information long after almost everyone else was relying on the Internet. But information has provided vast new opportunities for leveraging networks—and for connecting citizens to government. At the core of these opportunities is the government's underlying reliance on indirect tools, especially contracts with private companies, to provide the infrastructure on which its information connections depended.

Vice President Al Gore saw information as one of the driving forces of his 1993 National Performance Review, designed to transform how the federal government operated. President George W. Bush said in his 2004 State of the Union Address that information technology promised bold advances in health care. President Barack Obama created information and technology czars, put climate change data online for citizens to see, and used information as the central nervous system of his health reform plan. All of these initiatives were, at their core, bridge builders, and all were designed to better connect citizens with their government.

So quickly did information technology transform government's connections with citizens that citizens came to expect that they could avoid trips to the Department of Motor Vehicles by doing business online, that they could file their taxes through private companies like TurboTax, that they could check to see when the next bus was going to arrive by checking an app on their mobile phones, and that they could follow via a website the progress of snowplows after big storms. But this was only the beginning. When the federal government's

Recovery Act of 2009 distributed more than $800 billion to help states and communities dig out of the economic collapse, its management team developed a system to map every project—and to allow any citizen anywhere to track where funds were flowing to which projects. That transparency enhanced confidence in the program and reduced fraud.[29] Communities around the nation created online mapping systems to allow citizens to check everything from the location of dog parks and broken streetlights to hot spots for crime and available parking spots. Information technology, connected with sophisticated mapping software, can increase transparency and better connect citizens with the governments that serve them. Moreover, maps can do what organization charts cannot: maps can display what goods and services citizens receive where they live, work, and travel. It doesn't matter which government agency provides a service—or even whether it's a private contractor or a government worker who provides that service.

Information can flow where authority cannot. The transformation of governance requires a strategy to advance information technology into new functions, provide equitable access to information regardless of a citizen's location or income, drive technology to improve the effectiveness of public services, and use technology to enhance the democratic responsiveness of public programs.

5. *Transforming performance management to drive coordination, results, and accountability.* Closely connected to the rise of information to bridge boundaries is the use of performance management to enhance performance. Reformers have often advanced performance management—the systematic tracking of results against goals, in real time—as a strategy to cut programmatic costs. But it's usually very hard to know what implications to draw from the results of performance management. Is high performance the product of spending money? Would spending a bit more money make performance even better? Is low performance driven by underinvestment? Or would spending more money just be wasting it on a program that doesn't work? The rhetoric surrounding performance management often far exceeds what it produces—and the case for using evidence about performance to make a big difference in spending is thin indeed, both in the United States and around the world.[30]

However, performance management has demonstrated a subtle yet powerful impact on governance, namely, on leadership. As Robert D. Behn has shown, performance management has provided purpose and motivation, has advanced responsibility and discretion, and has improved performance in organizations ranging from the New York City Police Department, the City of Baltimore, and the State of Maryland, to the Department of Housing and Urban Development. Behn argues that performance management is not so much a measurement as a leadership strategy, which helps top agency officials focus the energy of their employees on producing results.[31] So important has performance management become to the federal executive establishment that, since the Clinton administration, presidents have felt compelled to develop and deploy their own strategies, each with its own name and distinctive approach, but all aiming at harnessing data to drive outcomes.

Moreover, performance management has additional boundary-spanning power. Cross-boundary programs inevitably require collaboration, but collaboration often attracts stronger support in the abstract—because few managers would openly decline to work with others—than in practice—because collaboration is often hard, energy-intensive, and distracting from other organizational responsibilities that managers frequently view as more important. But if top leaders can focus managers on issues they all agree are important, as well as define indicators that measure progress in achieving these common goals, then they can improve their odds of success.

For example, through its Performance.gov website, the Obama administration defined a series of cross-agency priority goals that required the collaboration of multiple agencies. The administration committed the government to (1) improved cybersecurity and stronger security clearances; (2) better customer service and smarter IT delivery; and (3) better acquisitions policies and a strong workforce. The Office of Management and Budget developed measures to assess progress and convened the agencies that shared responsibility for these goals to find common ground. In Maryland, the state's BayStat system assessed the health of the Chesapeake Bay and the contributions of different programs toward improving the quality of the water and of the wildlife in it. On the western shore of the Bay, storm water runoff was a major contributor to pollution. On the eastern shore, the problem more often was runoff of animal waste and fertilizer. All of the pollutants flowed into the same body of water; cleaning it required programs on the two shores to work in sync. The BayStat process created measures of success as well as an ongoing management process to improve outcomes. The transformation of governance requires a focus on defining collaboration and boundary spanning, and then driving results to build bridges.

The Transformation of Global Governance

The fundamental transformation of governance is not just an American phenomenon.[32] In fact, the fundamental reform of governance is one of the truly universal, global phenomena since the 1980s. As the Organisation for Economic

Co-operation and Development concluded in its 2013 report, "a new approach to public governance is needed if governments are to meet citizens' expectations with the limited means at hand. This approach should be built around creating strategic capacity, strong institutions, effective instruments and processes and clear measurable outcomes."[33] The economic crisis of the late 2000s quickly spread around the world, leaving no nation untouched. That only further spurred global efforts to strengthen and reform governance—and accelerated the search for a genuinely new strategy to solve the increasingly widespread problems of distrust of governmental institutions and administrative strategies that were struggling, under severe fiscal stress, to deliver the results that citizens expected. This was not just an American effort—it was global.

Governments around the world have developed public-private partnerships to plan, fund, and manage projects, including roads, bridges, airports, waste disposal, housing, and hospitals. Nongovernmental organizations (NGOs) played a critical role in the "Arab spring," which transformed Africa and the Middle East in the early 2010s, and NGOs have become important players in the transformation of governance within China.[34] In fact, Harvard scholars have counted more than one million registered nonprofit organizations in China.[35] The systems of governance are vastly different in China and in the United States, but large transformations are forcing more attention in both countries—and around the world—on managing across sectors. If it's happening in Beijing and Baltimore, there is something very big and very fundamental afoot.

The lessons of the Katrina syndrome likewise are global. The OECD analyzed changes in public confidence in government from 2007 through 2012, during the worst of the economic crisis. In the countries with the steepest drops in public confidence—Greece, Slovenia, Ireland, Spain, Belgium, and Portugal—government officials faced severe political and economic crises with which they struggled mightily to respond.[36] Certainly no government can avoid crises, but the ability of leaders to respond effectively powerfully shapes public confidence in their governments.

In many governments, especially in Europe's advanced democracies, the public sector is still responsible not only for managing but also for delivering public programs. In authoritarian nations like China, the behavior of all organizations, even private companies, is heavily regulated by the state. Governance in the United States is distinctive because it has relied so heavily on indirect mechanisms to expand its reach without substantially growing its governmental structures. But several factors are raising fundamental governance issues for governments around the globe.

First, globalization has created increasing interconnectedness of public problems and solutions. Indeed, in an increasingly globalized world, big problems anywhere can quickly become equally big problems everywhere. Crises can rapidly spread and challenge government officials to respond to problems not of their making and to devise responses beyond their control. The internationalization of the media reinforces these trends. So too is the rise of an interlocking global financial system, in which stock and current markets are open somewhere at any time of the day and night and in which traders can bet on the futures markets. Citizens anywhere can read local newspapers everywhere. No government, and no governmental leader, can put boundaries around problems or solutions.

Second, NGOs have become important forces across national boundaries. Both the State Department's Agency for International Development and the World Bank rely heavily on NGOs for delivering services. More broadly, NGOs have become important political forces that challenge political power.

Third, many governments are developing market-based service-delivery systems that fall outside traditional bureaucratic structures. Many of the same issues with which the United States has grappled are emerging there.

There are vast differences in forms and structures of government around the world, but there is also evidence of convergence in vocabulary, concepts, strategies, and tactics.[37] It is impossible to escape the sense of rapid and dramatic change in governance everywhere. It is likely that, as similar issues emerge around the world, similar solutions based on the transformations of governance will converge: public law redefined to promote public accountability, government agencies seen as instruments of leverage, government leaders seen as boundary spanners, information technology used to make connections that authority cannot, and performance management used to drive collaboration. America's transformation of governance will likely cast a very long shadow around the world. The eleventh principle—the interpenetration of government into vast parts of society and the need for government to develop effective boundary-spanning tools to deal with these forces—is not only likely to become even more widespread. It will also pose a vastly complex set of problems that will, in turn, require truly imaginative bridge-building solutions, not only in the United States but around the world.

Notes

CHAPTER ONE: **Administrative Paradoxes**

1. Judy Newman, "Chee-Tos Lovers May Find Themselves in Puffy Crunch," *Wisconsin State Journal*, 9 December 2000.

2. "Aventis CropScience Is Created in North America," company press release, Aventis CropScience, 15 December 1999. See www.biotech-info.net/aventis.html (accessed January 30, 2001).

3. See Paul P. Van Riper, "The American Administrative State: Wilson and the Founders," in Ralph Clark Chandler, ed., *A Centennial History of the American Administrative State* (New York: Free Press, 1987), 3–36.

4. See Frank J. Goodnow, *Comparative Administrative Law: An Analysis of the Administrative Systems, National and Local, of the United States, England, France, and Germany* (New York: G. P. Putnam's Sons, 1893); and *Politics and Administration: A Study in Government* (New York: Russell and Russell, 1900).

5. Willoughby's central text is *The Government of Modern States* (New York: Century Co., 1919). For Cleveland's work, see *The Budget and Responsible Government* (New York: Macmillan, 1920).

6. Van Riper, "The American Administrative State," 24.

7. On the empowerment of government, see Willoughby, *The Government of Modern States*. For a discussion, see Dwight Waldo, *The Administrative State: A Study of the Political Theory of American Public Administration* (New York: Ronald Press, 1948), 112–13.

8. President's Committee on Administrative Management, *Report with Special Studies* (Washington, D.C.: U.S. Government Printing Office, 1937).

9. For an analysis of these changes, see Barry D. Karl, *Executive Reorganization and Reform in the New Deal* (Cambridge: Harvard University Press, 1963); Paul C. Light, *The Tides of Reform: Making Government Work, 1945–1995* (New Haven: Yale University Press, 1998).

10. Vincent Ostrom, *The Intellectual Crisis in American Public Administration* (Tuscaloosa: University of Alabama Press, 1973).

11. See Goodnow, *Politics and Administration*; see also Goodnow's presidential address at the annual meeting of the American Political Science Association, "The Work of the American Political Science Association," *Proceedings of the American Political Science Association, 1904* (Lancaster, Pa.: Wickersham Press, 1994), 35–46.

12. Roscoe C. Martin, "Political Science and Public Administration: A Note on the State of the Union," *American Political Science Review* 46 (1952): 662.

13. Herbert Simon, *Administrative Behavior* (New York: Macmillan, 1947).

14. Robert Dahl, "The Science of Public Administration: Three Problems," *Public Administration Review* 7 (1947): 1–11.

15. See Frederick W. Taylor, *Principles of Scientific Management* (New York: Harper and Brothers, 1911). For an analysis of the influence of Taylor's work, see Robert Kanigel, *The One Best Way: Frederick Winslow Taylor and the Enigma of Efficiency* (New York: Viking, 1997).

16. See, for example, Herbert Simon, "The Proverbs of Administration," *Public Administration Review* 6 (1946): 53–67.

17. Bernard R. Berelson, Paul F. Lazarsfeld, and William N. McPhee, *Voting: A Study of Opinion Formation in a Presidential Campaign* (Chicago: University of Chicago Press, 1954).

18. Robert A. Dahl, *Who Governs? Democracy and Power in an American City* (New Haven: Yale University Press, 1964).

19. Quoted in Allen Schick, "The Trauma of Politics: Public Administration in the Sixties," in Frederick C. Mosher, ed., *American Public Administration: Past, Present, Future* (University: University of Alabama Press, 1975), 160.

20. See www.maxwell.syr.edu/deans/ (accessed February 5, 2001).

21. Richard E. Neustadt, preface to *Presidential Power: The Politics of Leadership* (New York: John Wiley, 1960).

22. Graham T. Allison, *Essence of Decision: Explaining the Cuban Missile Crisis* (Boston: Little, Brown, 1971).

23. Erwin C. Hargrove, *The Missing Link: The Study of the Implementation of Social Policy* (Washington, D.C.: Urban Institute, 1975).

24. Jeffrey L. Pressman and Aaron Wildavsky, *Implementation* (Berkeley: University of California Press, 1973), 166. In fact, there already was a small but important literature on implementation when Pressman and Wildavsky wrote their pathbreaking book. See, for example, Stephen K. Bailey and Edith K. Mosher, *ESEA: The Office of Education Administers a Law* (Syracuse: Syracuse University Press, 1968); and Jerome T. Murphy, "Title I of ESEA: The Politics of Implementing Federal Educational Reform," *Harvard Educational Review* 41 (1971): 35–63.

25. Robert D. Behn, "Management by Groping Along," *Journal of Policy Analysis and Management* 7 (Fall 1988): 643–63.

26. For an examination of such a battle within sociology, see Emily Eakin, "What Is the Next Big Idea? The Buzz Is Growing," *New York Times*, 7 July 2001, 7(B).

27. Edgar H. Schein, *Organizational Culture and Leadership: A Dynamic View* (San Francisco: Jossey-Bass, 1987), 289.

28. See, for example, Robert D. Behn, *Leadership Counts: Lessons for Public Managers from the Massachusetts Welfare, Training, and Employment Program* (Cambridge: Harvard University Press, 1991).

29. See John Micklethwait and Adrian Wooldridge, *The Witch Doctors: Making Sense of the Management Gurus* (New York: Times Books, 1996).

30. Laurence E. Lynn Jr., *Public Management as Art, Science, and Profession* (Chatham, N.J.: Chatham House Publishers, 1996), 3.

31. See Lynn, *Public Management as Art, Science, and Profession;* and Behn, *Leadership Counts.*

32. See, for example, the "Symposium on the Advancement of Public Administration," *Journal of Public Affairs Education* 5 (April 1999): 119–66.

33. David Osborne and Ted Gaebler, *Reinventing Government: How the Entrepreneurial Spirit Is Transforming the Public Sector from Schoolhouse to Statehouse, City Hall to the Pentagon* (Reading, Mass.: Addison-Wesley, 1992).

34. Personal interview with Elaine Kamarck.

35. See Donald F. Kettl, *The Global Public Management Revolution: A Report on the Transformation of Governance* (Washington, D.C.: Brookings Institution Press, 2000); and Christopher Pollitt and Geert Bouckaert, *Public Management Reform: A Comparative Analysis* (Oxford: Oxford University Press, 2000).

36. Melody Petersen and Greg Winter, "5 Drug Makers Use Material with Possible Mad Cow Link," *New York Times*, 8 February 2001, 1(C), 5(C).

37. Schein, *Organizational Culture and Leadership*, 289.

CHAPTER TWO: **Administrative Traditions**

1. Aaron Wildavsky, *The Nursing Father: Moses as a Political Leader* (Tuscaloosa: University of Alabama Press, 1984).

2. Erna Risch, *Supplying Washington's Army* (Washington, D.C.: Center of Military History, U.S. Army, 1981).

3. Deborah L. Spar, *Ruling the Waves: Cycles of Discovery, Chaos, and Wealth from Buccaneers to Bill Gates* (New York: Harcourt Brace, 2001).

4. David Wessel, "The Market Demands Rules," *Wall Street Journal*, 29 November 2001, 1(A).

5. Wildavsky, *The Nursing Father*, 99–106.

6. Other authors have examined the powerful influence of such traditions on American public administration. In particular, see Richard J. Stillman, chap. 7 in *The American Bureaucracy: The Core of Modern Government* (Chicago: Nelson Hall, 1987).

7. See Leonard D. White, *The Federalists: A Study in Administrative History* (New York: Macmillan, 1948); Lynton K. Caldwell, *The Administrative Theories of Hamilton and Jefferson* (Chicago: University of Chicago Press, 1944); and Van Riper, "The American Administrative State," 34.

8. White, *The Federalists*, 127.

9. See White, *The Federalists*, chap. 8.

10. Richard Brookhiser, *Alexander Hamilton, American* (New York: Free Press, 1999), 101.

11. Ibid., 6.

12. Daniel J. Boorstin, *The Lost World of Thomas Jefferson* (Chicago: University of Chicago Press, 1981), ix, 237.

13. Ibid., 237.

14. See White, *The Federalists*, 222–23. More generally on Jefferson, see Leonard D. White, *The Jeffersonians: A Study in Administrative History, 1801–1829* (New York: Macmillan, 1951).

15. White, *The Jeffersonians*, 4.

16. Ibid., 5.

17. See Brookhiser, *Alexander Hamilton, American*, 70.

18. John A. Rohr, "The Administrative State and Constitutional Principle," in Ralph Clark Chandler, ed., *A Centennial History of the American Administrative State* (New York:

Free Press, 1987), 127–29. See also John A. Rohr, *To Run a Constitution: The Legitimacy of the Administrative State* (Lawrence: University Press of Kansas, 1986).

19. See Van Riper, "The American Administrative State," in Chandler, ed., *A Centennial History of the American Administrative State,* 9. White's textbook is *Introduction to the Study of Public Administration,* 3rd ed. (New York: Macmillan, 1950).

20. Woodrow Wilson, "The Study of Administration," *Political Science Quarterly* 2 (June 1887): 197.

21. Ibid., 200–1.

22. Ibid., 200.

23. Ibid., 201.

24. Ibid., 206.

25. Ibid., 209.

26. Ibid., 210.

27. Ibid., 220.

28. See Frank J. Goodnow, *Politics and Administration: A Study in Government* (New York: Russell and Russell, 1900).

29. Woodrow Wilson, *Congressional Government: A Study in American Politics* (New York: Houghton Mifflin, 1885), xiii; see also Leonard D. White, *The Republican Era: 1869–1901* (New York: Macmillan, 1958), 46–48; and Stephen Skowronek, *Building a New American State: The Expansion of National Administrative Capacities 1877–1920* (Cambridge: Cambridge University Press, 1982), 42–46.

30. Deil S. Wright, "A Century of the Intergovernmental Administrative State: Wilson's Federalism, New Deal Intergovernmental Relations, and Contemporary Intergovernmental Management," in Chandler, ed., *A Centennial History of the American Administrative State,* 233.

31. For a discussion of the Hawthorne experiments and, more generally, of the broader human relations movement, see Charles Perrow, chap. 3 in *Complex Organizations,* 3d ed. (New York: Random House, 1986).

32. See Lester M. Salamon, ed., *The New Governance and the Tools of Public Action: A Handbook* (New York: Oxford University Press, 2001); and Donald F. Kettl, *Government by Proxy: (Mis?)Managing Federal Programs* (Washington, D.C.: Congressional Quarterly Press, 1988).

33. Joseph S. Nye Jr., Philip D. Zelikow, and David C. King, *Why People Don't Trust Government* (Cambridge: Harvard University Press, 1997).

34. Pew Research Center for the People and the Press, *Deconstructing Distrust: How Americans View Government* (Washington, D.C.: Pew Research Center, 10 March 1998).

35. Robert D. Putnam, *Bowling Alone: The Collapse and Revival of American Community* (New York: Simon and Schuster, 2000).

36. Dana Milbank and Richard Morin, "Public Is Unyielding in War against Terror," *The Washington Post,* 29 September 2001, 1(A).

CHAPTER THREE: **Administrative Dilemmas**

1. See Arthur Okun, *Equality and Efficiency: The Big Tradeoff* (Washington, D.C.: Brookings Institution Press, 1975).

2. See, for example, Frederick C. Mosher, "The Changing Responsibilities and Tactics of the Federal Government," *Public Administration Review* 40 (November/December 1980): 541–48; Lester M. Salamon, "Rethinking Public Management," *Public Policy* 29 (Summer 1981): 255–75; and Donald F. Kettl, *Government by Proxy: (Mis?) Managing Federal Programs* (Washington, D.C.: Congressional Quarterly Press, 1988).

3. Lester M. Salamon, "The New Governance and the Tools of Public Action: An Introduction," in Lester M. Salamon, ed., *The Tools of Government: A Guide to the New Governance* (New York: Oxford University Press, 2002), 1–47.

4. Ibid.

5. See also Mosher, "Changing Responsibilities."

6. See E. S. Savas, *Privatization and Public-Private Partnerships* (New York: Chatham House Publishers, 2000); and Jeffrey L. Brudney, Laurence J. O'Toole, and Hal G. Rainey, *Advancing Public Management: New Developments in Theory, Methods, and Practice* (Washington, D.C.: Georgetown University Press, 2000).

7. Statement of David M. Walker, *Managing in the New Millennium: Shaping a More Efficient and Effective Government for the 21st Century*, GAO/T-OCG-00-9 (March 29, 2000), 37.

8. See Harlan Cleveland, "Control: The Twilight of Hierarchy," *New Management* 3 (1985): 14–25.

9. For a review of the New Zealand reforms, see Jonathan Boston, John Martin, June Pallot, and Pat Walsh, *Public Management: The New Zealand Model* (Auckland: Oxford University Press, 1996).

10. New Zealand Treasury, "Introduction," *Government Management: Brief to the Incoming Government, 1987, Vol. 1*, 2–3, at www.treasury.govt.nz/briefings/1987/big87-1-intro.pdf (accessed March 19, 2001).

11. See David Osborne and Peter Plastrik, *Banishing Bureaucracy: The Five Strategies for Reinventing Government* (Reading, Mass.: Addison-Wesley, 1987).

12. See, for example, Arthur M. Schlesinger Jr., *The Imperial Presidency* (Boston: Houghton Mifflin, 1973).

13. Harold Seidman, *Politics, Position, and Power: The Dynamics of Federal Organization* (New York: Oxford University Press, 1998), 142.

14. Ibid.

15. Matthew Holden Jr., "The Competence of Political Science: 'Progress in Political Research' Revisited," *American Political Science Review* 94 (March 2000): 7. Compare Norton Long, *The Polity* (Chicago: Rand McNally, 1962).

16. President's Private Sector Survey on Cost Control, *Report* (Washington, D.C.: GPO, 1983).

17. Al Gore, *Businesslike Government: Lessons Learned from America's Best Companies* (Washington, D.C.: GPO, 1997).

18. See Donald F. Kettl, *Sharing Power: Public Governance and Private Markets* (Washington, D.C.: Brookings Institution Press, 1993).

19. Presidential Commission on the Space Shuttle *Challenger* Accident, *Report to the President* (Washington, D.C.: GPO, 1986); see also Barbara S. Romzek and Melvin J. Dubnick, "Accountability in the Public Sector: Lessons from the *Challenger* Tragedy," *Public Administration Review* 47 (1987): 227–38.

20. James Q. Wilson, *Bureaucracy: What Government Agencies Do and Why They Do It* (New York: Basic Books, 1989), 27–28. The analysis builds on similar work by James D. Thompson, *Organizations in Action: Social Science Bases of Administrative Theory* (New York: McGraw-Hill, 1967); and, ultimately, by Talcott Parsons, *Structure and Process in Modern Societies* (New York: Free Press, 1960). Parsons and Thompson label these layers "technical," "managerial," and "institutional."

21. See Parsons, *Structure and Process in Modern Societies,* 65. Compare Thompson, *Organizations in Action,* 11.

22. Office of Management and Budget, "Workforce Planning and Restructuring," Bulletin 01-07 (May 8, 2001), at www.whitehouse.gov/omb/bulletins/b01-07.html (accessed May 31, 2001).

23. On the layers of government, see Paul C. Light, *Thickening Government: Federal Hierarchy and the Diffusion of Accountability* (Washington, D.C.: Brookings/Governance Institute, 1995).

24. New Zealand State Services Commission and New Zealand Public Service Association, "Partnerships for Quality: Guidelines for Departments and PSA Organisers" (September 2000), at www.ssc.govt.nz/siteset.htm (accessed March 22, 2001).

25. David M. Walker, "Government in the 21st Century," Lecture cosponsored by the PricewaterhouseCoopers Endowment for the Business of Government, the Council for Excellence in Government, and the National Academy of Public Administration (March 23, 1999).

26. Gore, *Businesslike Government,* 7, 11.

27. David Osborne and Ted Gaebler, *Reinventing Government: How the Entrepreneurial Spirit Is Transforming the Public Sector from Schoolhouse to Statehouse, City Hall to the Pentagon* (Reading, Mass.: Addison-Wesley, 1992), 167, and more generally, chap. 6.

28. In addition to the discussion on the National Performance Review cited earlier, see also Evan M. Berman, "Dealing with Cynical Citizens," *Public Administration Review* 57 (March/April 1997): 105–12; and Gerald E. Smith and Carole A. Huntsman, "Reframing the Metaphor of the Citizen-Government Relationship: A Value-Centered Perspective," *Public Administration Review* 57 (July/August 1997): 309–18.

29. The discussion that follows builds on Donald F. Kettl, "Building Lasting Reform," in Donald F. Kettl and John J. DiIulio Jr., *Inside the Reinvention Machine: Appraising Governmental Reform* (Washington, D.C.: Brookings Institution Press, 1995); and John J. DiIulio Jr., Gerald Garvey, and Donald F. Kettl, *Improving Government Performance: An Owner's Manual* (Washington, D.C.: Brookings Institution Press, 1993).

30. See Jonathan Rauch, *Demosclerosis: The Silent Killer of American Government* (New York: Times Books, 1994).

31. George Frederickson, "George and the Case of the Government Reinventors," *PA Times* 17 (January 1, 1994): 9.

32. I am indebted to conversation with Joel Aberbach of the University of Michigan for this point.

33. See James W. Fesler, *Area and Administration* (University: University of Alabama Press, 1949); and Paul C. Light, *The Tides of Reform: Making Government Work, 1945–1995* (New Haven: Yale University Press, 1997).

CHAPTER FOUR: **Boundaries within the Bureaucracy**

1. Norton Long, "Power and Administration," *Public Administration Review* 9 (1949): 257–64.

2. John Merriman Gaus, *Reflections on Public Administration* (University: University of Alabama Press, 1947), 135.

3. Quoted by Herbert J. Storing, "Leonard D. White and the Study of Administration," *Public Administration Review* 25 (1965): 50.

4. Ibid.

5. Leonard D. White, *The Federalists* (New York: Macmillan, 1948); White, *The Jeffersonians* (New York: Macmillan, 1951); White, *The Jacksonians* (New York: Macmillan, 1954); White, *The Republican Era* (New York: Macmillan, 1958).

6. Woodrow Wilson, *The State: Elements of Historical and Practical Politics* (Boston: D.C. Heath, 1898), 631, 633.

7. Lynton K. Caldwell, "Public Administration and the Universities: A Half-Century of Development," *Public Administration Review* 25 (1965): 52–60; and Nicholas Henry, "The Emergence of Public Administration as a Field of Study," in Ralph Clark Chandler, ed., *A Centennial History of the American Administrative State* (New York: Free Press, 1987), 37–85.

8. Frederick W. Taylor, *Principles of Scientific Management* (New York: Harper and Brothers, 1911). For a study of his work and influence, see Robert Kanigel, *The One Best Way: Frederick Winslow Taylor and the Enigma of Efficiency* (New York: Viking, 1997).

9. Roscoe Martin, "Political Science and Public Administration: A Note on the State of the Union," *American Political Science Review* 46 (1952): 667.

10. Barry D. Karl, *Executive Reorganization and Reform in the New Deal* (Cambridge: Harvard University Press, 1963).

11. E-mail to the author from James W. Fesler, 6 April 2001. See also James W. Fesler, "The Brownlow Committee Fifty Years Later," *Public Administration Review* 47 (1987): 291–96.

12. See David H. Rosenbloom, *Building a Legislative-Centered Public Administration: Congress and the Administrative State, 1946–1999* (Tuscaloosa: University of Alabama Press, 2000).

13. Norton Long, "Power and Administration."

14. See, for example, Paul Appleby, *Big Democracy* (New York: Alfred A. Knopf, 1945); Dwight Waldo, *The Administrative State*, 2d ed. (New York: Holmes and Meier, 1984); and James W. Fesler, "The State and Its Study: The Whole and Its Parts," in Naomi B. Lynn and Aaron Wildavsky, eds., *Public Administration: The State of the Discipline* (Chatham, N.J.: Chatham House Publishers, 1990), 84–96.

15. See Orion F. White Jr. and Cynthia J. McSwain, "The Phoenix Project: Raising a New Image of Public Administration from the Ashes of the Past," *Administration and Society* 22 (1990): 3–38.

16. Allen Schick, "The Trauma of Politics: Public Administration in the Sixties," in Frederick C. Mosher, ed., *American Public Administration: Past, Present, Future* (University: University of Alabama Press, 1975), 157.

17. Roscoe C. Martin, "Political Science and Public Administration: A Note on the State of the Union," *American Political Science Review* 46 (1952): 660–76.

18. American Political Science Association, Statement by the Committee on Standards of Instruction of the American Political Science Association, "Political Science as a Discipline," *American Political Science Review* 56 (1962): 417–21.

19. Schick, "The Trauma of Politics," 160.

20. Dwight Waldo, "A Theory of Public Administration Means in Our Time a Theory of Politics Also," in Lynn and Wildavsky, *Public Administration*, 74 (emphasis in original).

21. Herbert Kaufman, "The End of an Alliance: Public Administration in the Eighties," in Lynn and Wildavsky, eds., *Public Administration*, 483–94.

22. Fesler, "The State and Its Study," 85.

23. See Harrison C. White, "Agency as Control," in John W. Pratt and Richard J. Zeckhauser, eds., *Principals and Agents: The Structure of Business* (Boston: Harvard Business School Press, 1985), 187–212.

24. Ronald H. Coase, "The Nature of the Firm," *Economica* 4 (1937): 386–405; and Oliver E. Williamson, *Markets and Hierarchies: Analysis and Antitrust Implications* (New York: Free Press, 1975).

25. See B. Dan Wood and Richard W. Waterman, "The Dynamics of Political Control of the Bureaucracy," *American Political Science Review* 85 (1991): 801–28.

26. Terry M. Moe, presentation at American Political Science Association Annual Meeting, August 31, 2001.

27. Charles Perrow, "Economic Theories of Organization," *Theory and Society* 15 (1986): 41.

28. Terry M. Moe, "An Assessment of the Positive Theory of 'Congressional Dominance,'" *Legislative Studies Quarterly* 12 (1987): 475–520.

29. Donald P. Green and Ian Shapiro, *Pathologies of Rational Choice Theory: A Critique of Applications in Political Science* (New Haven: Yale University Press, 1994), 7; see also Fritz W. Scharpf, *Games Real Actors Play: Actor-Centered Institutionalism in Policy Research* (Boulder, Colo.: Westview, 1997).

30. Kenneth A. Shepsle and Mark S. Bonchek, *Analyzing Politics: Rationality, Behavior, and Institutions* (New York: W. W. Norton, 1997), 8–9. See also Jeffrey Friedman, ed., *The Rational Choice Controversy: Economic Models of Politics Reconsidered* (New Haven: Yale University Press, 1996).

31. William A. Niskanen, *Bureaucracy and Representative Government* (Chicago: Aldine Publishers, 1971).

32. See Gary J. Miller and Terry M. Moe, in Herbert F. Weisberg, ed., *Political Science: The Science of Politics* (New York: Agathon Press, 1986), 167–98.

33. Mathew McCubbins, Roger Noll, and Barry Weingast, "Administrative Procedures as Instruments of Political Control," *Journal of Law, Economics, and Organization* 3 (1987): 243–79; and Mathew McCubbins, Roger Noll, and Barry Weingast, "Structure and Process, Politics and Policy: Administrative Arrangements and the Political Control of Agencies," *Virginia Law Review* 75 (1989): 431–83.

34. David Osborne, *Laboratories of Democracy: A New Breed of Governor Creates Models for National Growth* (Boston: Harvard Business School Press, 1988).

35. David Osborne and Ted Gaebler, *Reinventing Government: How the Entrepreneurial Spirit Is Transforming the Public Sector from Schoolhouse to Statehouse, City Hall to the Pentagon* (Reading, Mass.: Addison-Wesley, 1992), xi.

36. See Donald F. Kettl, *Reinventing Government: A Fifth-Year Report Card* (Washington, D.C.: Brookings Institution Press, 1998).

37. David Rosenbloom, "Editorial: Have an Administrative Rx? Don't Forget the Politics!" *Public Administration Review* 53 (1993): 503–7.

38. Ronald C. Moe, "Let's Rediscover Government, Not Reinvent It," *Government Executive* 25 (June 1993): 46–48; and Ronald C. Moe, "The 'Reinventing Government' Exercise: Misinterpreting the Problem, Misjudging the Consequences," *Public Administration Review* 54 (1954): 125–36.

39. H. George Frederickson, "Painting Bull's-Eyes around Bullet Holes," *Governing* (October 1992): 13.

40. See Donald F. Kettl, *The Global Public Management Reform Revolution: A Report on the Transformation of Governance* (Washington, D.C.: Brookings Institution Press, 2000).

41. See Christopher Hood and Michael Jackson, *Administrative Argument* (Aldershot: Dartmouth, 1991); Christopher Hood, *The Art of the State: Culture, Rhetoric, and Public Management* (Oxford: Clarendon Press, 1998); and Lawrence R. Jones, Kuno Schedler, and Stephen W. Wade, eds., *Advances in International Comparative Management* (Greenwich, Conn.: JAI Press, 1997).

42. See, for example, Sandford Borins, "What the New Public Management Is Achieving: A Survey of Commonwealth Experience," in Jones, Schedler, and Wade, *Advances in International Comparative Management*, 49–70; and Laurence E. Lynn Jr., "The New Public Management as an International Phenomenon: A Skeptical View," in Jones, Schedler, and Wade, *Advances in International Comparative Management*, 105–22.

43. Fred Thompson, "Defining the New Public Management," in Jones, Schedler, and Wade, *Advances in International Comparative Management*, 3.

44. See Hood, *The Art of the State;* B. Guy Peters and Donald Savoie, *Taking Stock: Assessing Public Sector Reforms* (Montreal: McGill-Queens University Press, 1998); Frieder Naschold, *New Frontiers in Public Sector Management: Trends and Issues in State and Local Government in Europe* (New York: Walter De Gruyter, 1996); and Peter Aucoin, *The New Public Management: Canada in Comparative Perspective* (Quebec: Institute for Research on Public Policy, 1995).

45. See Colin James, *The State Ten Years On from the Reforms* (Wellington, New Zealand: State Services Commission, 1998); Graham Scott, Ian Ball, and Tony Dale, "New Zealand's Public Management Reform: Implications for the United States," *Journal of Policy Analysis and Management* 16 (1997): 357–81; Jonathan Boston and June Pallot, "Linking Strategy and Performance: Developments in the New Zealand Public Sector," *Journal of Policy Analysis and Management* 16 (1997): 382–404; Jonathan Boston, John Martin, June Pallot, and Pat Walsh, *Public Management: The New Zealand Model* (Wellington, New Zealand: Oxford University Press, 1996).

46. Scott, Ball, and Dale, "New Zealand's Public Management Reform," 360.

47. Interview with New Zealand Treasury official.

48. See, for example, David Osborne and Peter Plastrik, *Banishing Bureaucracy: The Five Strategies for Reinventing Government* (Reading, Mass.: Addison-Wesley, 1997).

49. Allen Schick, *The Spirit of Reform: Managing the New Zealand State Sector in a Time of Change* (Wellington: New Zealand State Services Commission, 1996), 84, 86, 87.

50. Ibid., 87.

51. Carl J. Friedrich, "Public Policy and the Nature of Administrative Responsibility," in Carl J. Friedrich and E. S. Mason, eds., *Public Policy* (Cambridge: Harvard University Press, 1940).

52. Herman Finer, "Administrative Responsibility in Democratic Government," *Public Administration Review* 1 (1941): 335–50.

53. See Moe, "An Assessment of the Positive Theory of 'Congressional Dominance'"; and Francis E. Rourke, "American Bureaucracy in a Changing Political Setting," *Journal of Public Administration Research and Theory* 1 (1991): 111–29.

54. Barbara Romzek and Melvin J. Dubnick, "Accountability in the Public Sector: Lessons from the *Challenger* Tragedy," *Public Administration Review* 47 (1987): 227–38.

55. Judith Gruber, *Controlling Bureaucracies: Dilemmas in Democratic Governance* (Berkeley: University of California Press, 1987); James L. Sundquist, "Needed: A Political Theory for the New Era of Coalition Government in the United States," *Political Science Quarterly* 103 (1988): 613–35; John P. Burke, *Bureaucratic Responsibility* (Baltimore: Johns Hopkins University Press, 1986); and John Rohr, *To Run a Constitution: The Legitimacy of the Administrative State* (Lawrence: University Press of Kansas, 1986).

56. For an application to contract management, for example, see Phillip J. Cooper, *Governing by Contract: Challenges and Opportunities for Public Managers* (Washington, D.C.: CQ Press, 2002).

57. For example, see Gary L. Wamsley et al., *Refounding Public Administration* (Beverly Hills, Calif.: Sage, 1990); and Charles T. Goodsell, *The Case for Bureaucracy: A Public Administration Polemic,* 3d ed. (Chatham, N.J.: Chatham House Publishers, 1994).

CHAPTER FIVE: **Boundaries outside the Bureaucracy**

1. Jeffrey L. Pressman and Aaron B. Wildavsky, *Implementation* (Berkeley: University of California Press, 1973).

2. See, for example, Martha Derthick, *New Towns In-Town* (Washington, D.C.: Urban Institute, 1972); Eugene Bardach, *The Implementation Game* (Cambridge: MIT Press, 1977); Paul Berman, "The Study of Macro- and Micro-Implementation," *Public Policy* 26 (1978): 157–84; Richard Elmore, "Organizational Models of Social Program Implementation," *Public Policy* 26 (1978): 185–228; and Carl E. Van Horn, *Policy Implementation in the Federal System: National Goals and Local Implementation* (Lexington, Mass.: Lexington Books, 1979).

3. Brian W. Hogwood and B. Guy Peters, *The Pathology of Public Policy* (Oxford: Clarendon Press, 1985).

4. Pressman and Wildavsky, *Implementation,* 107.

5. Morton H. Halperin, *Bureaucratic Politics and Foreign Policy* (Washington, D.C.: Brookings Institution Press, 1974).

6. Bardach, *The Implementation Game.*

7. Erwin C. Hargrove, *The Missing Link: The Study of the Implementation of Social Policy* (Washington, D.C.: Urban Institute, 1975).

8. Randall B. Ripley and Grace Franklin, *Policy Implementation and Bureaucracy,* 2d ed. (Chicago: Dorsey Press, 1986), 12.

9. Calculated by the author from Ripley and Franklin, *Policy Implementation and Bureaucracy.*

10. For example, see Helen Ingram and Dean E. Mann, "Policy Failure: An Issue Deserving Analysis," in Helen Ingram and Dean E. Mann, eds., *Why Policies Succeed or Fail* (Beverly Hills, Calif.: Sage, 1980); Daniel A. Mazmanian and Paul A. Sabatier, *Implementation and Public Policy* (Glenview, Ill.: Scott, Foresman, 1983); and Ripley and Franklin, *Policy Implementation and Bureaucracy.*

11. See Malcom L. Goggin, Ann O'M. Bowman, James P. Lester, and Laurence J. O'Toole Jr., *Implementation Theory and Practice: Toward a Third Generation* (Glenview, Ill.: Scott, Foresman/Little, Brown, 1990).

12. See, for example, the work of Laurence J. O'Toole Jr.: "Policy Recommendations for Multi-Actor Implementation: An Assessment of the Field," *Journal of Public Policy* 6 (1986): 181–210; Laurence J. O'Toole Jr., "Goal Multiplicity in the Implementation Setting: Subtle Impacts and the Case of Wastewater Treatment Privatization," *Policy Studies Journal* 18 (1989): 1–20; Laurence J. O'Toole Jr., "Alternative Mechanisms for Multiorganizational Implementation: The Case of Wastewater Management," *Administration and Society* 21 (1989): 313–39. See also Goggin et al., *Implementation Theory and Practice;* and Helen Ingram, "Implementation: A Review and Suggested Framework," in Naomi B. Lynn and Aaron Wildavsky, eds., *Public Administration: The State of the Discipline* (Chatham, N.J.: Chatham House Publishers, 1990), 462–80.

13. See, for example, Thad E. Hall and Laurence J. O'Toole Jr., "Structures for Policy Implementation: An Analysis of National Legislation, 1965–1966 and 1993–1994," *Administration and Society* 31 (January 2000): 667–86.

14. Laurence E. Lynn Jr., *Managing Public Policy* (Boston: Little, Brown, 1987), 5.

15. John M. Bryson, *Strategic Planning for Public and Nonprofit Organizations* (San Francisco: Jossey-Bass, 1988).

16. Robert Behn, *Leadership Counts: Lessons for Public Managers from the Massachusetts Welfare, Training, and Employment Program* (Cambridge: Harvard University Press, 1991).

17. See Eugene Bardach, *Managerial Craftsmanship: Getting Agencies to Work Together* (Washington, D.C.: Brookings Institution Press, 1998); and Michael Barzelay with Babak J. Armajani, *Breaking through Bureaucracy: A New Vision for Managing Government* (Berkeley: University of California Press, 1992).

18. Laurence E. Lynn Jr., *Public Management as Art, Science, and Profession* (Chatham, N.J.: Chatham House Publishers, 1996).

19. See Laurence E. Lynn Jr., *Managing the Public's Business* (New York: Basic Books, 1981); Lynn, *Managing Public Policy;* Laurence E. Lynn Jr., Carolyn J. Heinrich, and Carolyn Hill, "Studying Governance and Public Management: Why? How?" in Laurence E. Lynn Jr. and Carolyn J. Heinrich, eds., *Governance and Performance: Models, Methods, and Results* (Washington, D.C.: Georgetown University Press, 1999), xx; and Philip B. Heymann, *The Politics of Public Management* (New Haven: Yale University Press, 1987).

20. Behn, *Leadership Counts.*

21. Heymann, *The Politics of Public Management.*

22. Lynn, *Managing the Public's Business;* Lynn, *Managing Public Policy;* and Robert Behn, "The Nature of Knowledge about Public Management: Lessons for Research and Teaching from Our Knowledge about Chess and Warfare," *Journal of Policy Analysis and Management* 7 (1988): 200–12.

23. Michael Barzelay and Linda Kaboolian, "Structural Metaphors and Public Management Education," *Journal of Policy Analysis and Management* 9 (1990): 600.

24. Most notably, see Francis E. Rourke, *Bureaucracy, Politics, and Public Policy,* 3d ed. (Boston: Little, Brown, 1984).

25. See Terry M. Moe, "The Politics of Structural Choice: Toward a Theory of Public Bureaucracy," in Oliver E. Williamson, ed., *Organization Theory: From Chester Barnard to the Present and Beyond* (New York: Oxford University Press, 1995), xx.

26. Jonathan Bendor and Terry M. Moe, "An Adaptive Model of Bureaucratic Politics," *American Political Science Review* 79 (1985): 755–74; Jack H. Knott and Gary J. Miller, *Reforming Bureaucracy: The Politics of Institutional Choice* (Englewood Cliffs, N.J.: Prentice-Hall, 1987); Terry M. Moe, "The Politics of Bureaucratic Structure," in John E. Chubb and Paul E. Peterson, eds., *Can the Government Govern?* (Washington, D.C.: Brookings Institution Press, 1989), 267–329; and Murray J. Horn, *The Political Economy of Public Administration: Institutional Choice in the Public Sector* (Cambridge: Cambridge University Press, 1995).

27. John E. Chubb and Terry M. Moe, *Politics, Markets, and America's Schools* (Washington, D.C.: Brookings Institution Press, 1990).

28. Irwin L. Morris, *Congress, the President, and the Federal Reserve: The Politics of American Policy Making* (Ann Arbor: University of Michigan Press, 1999).

29. David Mayhew, *Congress: The Electoral Connection* (New Haven: Yale University Press, 1974).

30. See Terry M. Moe, "Regulatory Performance and Presidential Administration," *American Journal of Political Science* 26 (1982): 197–224; Barry R. Weingast and Mark J. Moran, "Bureaucracy Discretionary Congressional Control? Regulatory Policymaking by the Federal Trade Commission," *Journal of Political Economy* 91 (1983): 765–800; Terry M. Moe, "Control and Feedback in Economic Regulation: The Case of the NLRB," *American Political Science Review* 79 (1985): 1094–1116; and B. Dan Wood and Richard W. Waterman, "The Dynamics of Political Control of the Bureaucracy," *American Political Science Review* 85 (1991): 801–28.

31. The underlying debate in institutional-choice theory is whether the very nature of bureaucracy creates reservoirs of political power that, in turn, allow bureaucrats to resist attempts by elected officials to control their behavior. In that sense, the institutional-choice movement is an effort to impart more rigor to the arguments initially framed in the implementation movement. Unlike the implementation movement, which focused on programs, institutional-choice theory focuses on the bureaucracy as the unit of analysis.

32. Wood and Waterman, "The Dynamics of Political Control of the Bureaucracy," 801.

33. Michael Lipsky, *Street-Level Bureaucracy: Dilemmas of the Individual in Public Services* (New York: Russell Sage Foundation, 1980).

34. David Osborne and Ted Gaebler, *Reinventing Government* (Reading, Mass.: Addison-Wesley, 1992), chap. 6, esp. 166–67, 186–87.

35. See www.nhq.nrcs.usda.gov/NPR/index.htm (accessed April 11, 2001).

36. See Richard Elmore, "Backward Mapping: Implementation Research and Policy Decisions," in Walter Williams and others, *Studying Implementation: Methodological and Administrative Issues* (Chatham, N.J.: Chatham House, 1982), 18–35.

37. See Frederick C. Mosher, "The Changing Responsibilities and Tactics of the Federal Government," *Public Administration Review* (1980): 541–48; Lester M. Salamon, "Rethinking Public Management: Third-Party Government and the Changing Forms of Government Action," *Public Policy* 29 (1981): 255–75; Donald F. Kettl, *Government by Proxy: (Mis?)Managing Federal Programs* (Washington, D.C.: Congressional Quarterly Press, 1988); and Lester M. Salamon, ed., *The Tools of Government: A Guide to the New Governance* (New York: Oxford University Press, 2002).

38. Christopher C. Hood, *The Tools of Government* (Chatham, N.J.: Chatham House, 1983); Ruth Hoogland DeHoog, *Contracting Out for Human Services: Economic, Political, and Organizational Perspectives* (Albany: State University of New York Press, 1984); Harold Seidman and Robert Gilmour, *Politics, Position, and Power: From the Positive to the Regulatory State*, 4th ed. (New York: Oxford University Press, 1986); and Jeffrey L. Brudney, "Expanding the Government-by-Proxy Concept," *Nonprofit and Voluntary Sector Quarterly* 19 (1990): 62–73.

39. H. Brinton Milward et al., "Managing the Hollow State," paper presented at the 1991 annual meeting of the American Political Science Association, Washington, D.C.

40. Bruce L. R. Smith, "Changing Public-Private Sector Relations: A Look at the United States," *Annals of the American Academy of Political and Social Sciences* 466 (1983): 149–64.

41. See E. S. Savas, *Privatization and Public-Private Partnerships* (New York: Seven Bridges Press, 2000); Laurence J. O'Toole Jr., "Treating Networks Seriously: Practical and Research-Based Agendas in Public Administration," *Public Administration Review* 57 (1997): 45–52; Laurence J. O'Toole Jr., "The Implications for Democracy in a Networked Bureaucratic World," *Journal of Public Administration Research and Theory* 7 (1997): 443–59; H. Brinton Milward and Louise Ogilvie Snyder, "Electronic Government: Linking Citizens to Public Organizations Through Technology," *Journal of Public Administration Research and Theory* 6 (1996): 261–75; H. Brinton Milward and Keith Provan, "A Preliminary Theory of Network Effectiveness: A Comparative Study of Four Mental Health Systems," *Administrative Science Quarterly* 40 (1995): 1–33; H. Brinton Milward and Keith G. Provan, "Principles for Controlling Agents: The Political Economy of Network Structure," *Journal of Public Administration Research and Theory* 8 (1998): 203–21; and Fritz W. Scharpf, *Games in Hierarchies and Networks: Analytical and Empirical Approaches to the Study of Governance Institutions* (Boulder, Colo.: Westview, 1993).

42. See Frank Ostroff, *The Horizontal Organization: What the Organization of the Future Looks Like and How It Delivers Value to Customers* (New York: Oxford, 1999).

43. Charles R. Wise, "Public Service Configurations and Public Organizations: Public Organization Design in the Post-Privatization Era," *Public Administration Review* 50 (1990): 141–55; Harlan Cleveland, "Control: The Twilight of Hierarchy," *New Management* 3 (1985): 14–25; and Donald Chisholm, *Coordination without Hierarchy: Informal Structures in Multiorganizational Systems* (Berkeley: University of California Press, 1989).

44. H. George Frederickson, "The Repositioning of American Public Administration," John Gaus Lecture, American Political Science Association Annual Meeting (September 3, 1999).

45. Lynn, Heinrich, and Hill, "Studying Governance and Public Management."

46. Hall and O'Toole, "Structures for Policy Implementation."

47. Robert Axelrod, *The Evolution of Cooperation* (New York: Basic Books, 1984), 169.

48. Ibid., 170.

49. Ibid., 191.

50. See, for example, Robert Axelrod, *The Complexity of Cooperation: Agent-Based Models of Competition and Collaboration* (Princeton: Princeton University Press, 1997). See also John H. Holland, *Hidden Order: How Adaptation Builds Complexity* (Cambridge: Perseus Books, 1995).

51. Robert Axelrod and Michael D. Cohen, *Harnessing Complexity: Organizational Implications of a Scientific Frontier* (New York: Basic Books, 2000), 159.

52. See, for example, Ralph D. Stacey, *Complex Responsive Processes in Organizations: Learning and Knowledge Creation* (London: Routledge, 2001).

53. Jane Perry Clark Carey, *The Rise of a New Federalism: Federal-State Cooperation in the United States* (New York: Columbia University Press, 1938).

54. See, for example, Frank Smallwood, ed., *The New Federalism* (Hanover, N.H.: Dartmouth Public Affairs Center, 1967); Michael D. Reagan, *The New Federalism* (New York: Oxford University Press, 1972); Timothy J. Conlan, *New Federalism: Intergovernmental Reform from Nixon to Reagan* (Washington, D.C.: Brookings Institution Press, 1988).

55. Laurence E. Lynn Jr., "The Myth of the Bureaucratic Paradigm: What Traditional Public Administration Really Stood For," *Public Administration Review* 61 (March/April 2001): 155.

56. Ibid.

CHAPTER SIX: **Administration and Governance**

1. John Gaus, "Trends in the Theory of Public Administration," *Public Administration Review* 10 (1950): 161–68.

2. Jon Pierre and B. Guy Peters, *Governance, Politics, and the State* (New York: St. Martin's Press, 2000), 7.

3. Robert O. Keohane and John D. Donahue, eds., *Governance in a Globalizing World* (Washington, D.C.: Brookings Institution Press, 2000), 12.

4. Ibid.

5. See Pierre and Peters, *Governance, Politics, and the State*, 1, 7.

6. Robert Cameiro, "A Changing Canon of Government: From Custody to Service," Organization for Economic Cooperation and Development, *Government of the Future* (Paris: OECD, 2001), 92, at www.oecd.org/publications/e-book/420008ie.pdf (accessed March 5, 2001).

7. For a thorough exploration of these issues, see the *New York Times* series on the affair: Matthew Purdy, "The Making of a Suspect: The Case of Wen Ho Lee," *New York Times*, 4 February 2001, 1; and Matthew Purdy with James Sterngold, "The Prosecution Unravels: The Case of Wen Ho Lee," *New York Times*, 5 February 2001, 1.

8. Paul C. Light, *The True Size of Government* (Washington, D.C.: Brookings Institution Press, 1999).

9. U.S. General Accounting Office, *Major Management Challenges and Risks: Department of Health and Human Services*, GAO-01-247 (2001), 7.

10. Ibid., 8.

11. For an overview of the W-2 program, see Thomas Kaplan, "Evaluating Comprehensive State Welfare Reforms: An Overview," *Focus* 18 (Spring 1997): 2.

12. William Fanaras, "Focusing on Outputs: Competition for City Services in Indianapolis" (Washington, D.C.: Brookings Institution Working Paper, 2000); William R. Potapchuk, Jarle P. Crocker, Bill Schechter, "Systems Reform in Two Cities: Indianapolis, Indiana, and Charlotte, North Carolina," *National Civic Review* 87 (Fall 1998): 213; and Jon Jeter, "A Winning Combination in Indianapolis: Competitive Bidding for City Services Creates Public-Private Success Story," *Washington Post*, 21 September 1997, 3(A).

13. Jim Flanagan and Bob Wigenroth, "Phoenix Manages for Performance Results," *PA Times*, 1 March 1996, 1, 3; and Jim Flanagan and Susan Perkins, "Public/Private Competition in the City of Phoenix, Arizona," *Government Finance Review* 11 (June 1995): 7–12.

14. Prime Minister and Cabinet Office, *Modernising Government* (London, 1999), 10, at www.cabinet-office.gov.uk/moderngov/download/modgov.pdf (accessed October 2, 2001).

15. See Frederick C. Mosher, "The Changing Responsibilities and Tactics of the Federal Government," *Public Administration Review* 40 (1980): 541–48; Lester M. Salamon, "Rethinking Public Management: Third-Party Government and the Changing Forms of Government Action," *Public Policy* 29 (1981): 255–75; Lester M. Salamon, ed., *Beyond Privatization: The Tools of Governmental Action* (Washington, D.C.: Urban Institute, 1989); Donald F. Kettl, *Government by Proxy: (Mis?)Managing Federal Programs* (Washington, D.C.: Congressional Quarterly Press, 1988); and Lester M. Salamon, ed., *The Tools of Government: A Public Management Handbook for the Era of Third-Party Government* (New York: Oxford University Press, 2001).

16. Donald F. Kettl, *Sharing Power: Public Governance and Private Markets* (Washington, D.C.: Brookings Institution Press, 1993).

17. Light, *The True Size of Government.*

18. Akira Nakamura and Kosaku Dairokuno, "The Age of Public Management Reform: The Rise of Non-Profit Organizations in Japan's Local Public Administration," in National Institute for Research Advancement and National Academy of Public Administration, *The Challenge to New Governance in the Twenty-First Century: Achieving Effective Central-Local Relations* (Tokyo: National Institute for Research Advancement, 1999), 97–109.

19. Organization for Economic Cooperation and Development, *Government of the Future* (Paris: OECD, 2000), 12.

20. Adrian Croft, "EU, Washington in New Clash over Bananas," March 8, 2001, at http://dailynews.yahoo.com/h/nm/20010308/ts/us_bananas_dc_2.html (accessed March 8, 2001).

21. Anthony Giddens, BBC Reith Lectures, "Lecture 1: Globalisation," at www.lse.ac.uk/Giddens/reith_99/week1/week1.htm (accessed March 8, 2001). See also Anthony Giddens, *Runaway World: How Globalisation Is Reshaping Our Lives* (London: Profile Books, 1999).

22. Ibid.

23. John Micklethwait and Adrian Wooldridge, *A Future Perfect: The Challenge and Hidden Promise of Globalization* (New York: Times Books, 2000).

24. United Nations, *We the Peoples: Executive Summary* (New York: United Nations, 2000), at www.un.org/millennium/sg/report/summ.htm (accessed March 8, 2001).

25. See David Held, Anthony McGrew, David Goldblatt, and Jonathan Perraton, *Global Transformations: Politics, Economics and Culture* (Stanford: Stanford University Press, 1999).

26. Claude Smadja, "Time to Learn from Seattle," *Newsweek International*, 17 January 2000.

27. Jessica Mathews, "Power Shift," *Foreign Affairs* 76 (January/February 1997): 50–66.

28. Ross Gelbspan, "A Good Climate for Investment," *Atlantic Monthly* 281 (June 1998): 22.

29. Mathews, "Power Shift."

30. Quoted in United Nations Research Institute for Social Development, *Report of the UNRISD International Conference: Globalization and Citizenship* (Geneva, 1996).

31. "The Non-Governmental Order," *The Economist* 353 (9 December 1999): 20–21; and Sebastian Mallaby, "Big Nongovernment" *Washington Post*, 30 November 1999, 29(A).

32. Mathews, "Power Shift."

33. See, for example, Giddens, *Runaway World*.

34. Jane Perlez, "Career Diplomat, Yes, but She Shoots from the Hip," *Washington Post*, 26 September 1999, 26(1).

35. Elaine Kamarck, "Homeland Defense Requires Trust, Will," *Newsday*, 26 September 2001, at www.ksg.harvard.edu/news/opeds/kamarck_homeland_defense_nd_092601 .htm (accessed October 3, 2001).

36. Luther Gulick, "Notes on the Theory of Administration," in Luther Gulick and L. Urwick, eds., *Papers on the Science of Administration* (New York: Institute of Public Administration, 1937), 1–45.

37. Ibid., 21.

38. See Donald F. Kettl, ed., *Environmental Governance: A Report on the Next Generation of Environmental Policy* (Washington, D.C.: Brookings Institution, 2002); and Mary Graham, *The Morning after Earth Day: Practical Environmental Politics* (Washington, D.C.: Brookings Institution Press, 1999).

39. Interview with EPA official.

40. Wallace Stegner, *Beyond the Hundredth Meridian: John Wesley Powell and the Second Opening of the West* (New York: Penguin, 1954, 1992).

41. National Academy of Public Administration, *Environment.gov: Transforming Environmental Protection for the 21st Century* (Washington, D.C.: NAPA, 2000), 183. The author served as a member of this NAPA panel.

42. National Academy of Public Administration, *Setting Priorities, Getting Results: A New Direction for EPA* (Washington, D.C.: NAPA, 1995); *EPA: Resolving the Paradox of Environmental Protection* (Washington, D.C.: NAPA, 1997); and *Environment.gov*.

43. NAPA, *Environment.gov*, 11.

44. Ibid., esp. 17–18.

45. See, for example, David Robinson, "Introduction," in David Robinson, ed., *Social Capital in Action* (Wellington, New Zealand: Institute of Policy Studies, Victoria University of Wellington, 1999), 9; and Paul Curry, "Commentary," in Robinson, *Social Capital in Action*, 110. More generally on the issue of social capital, see Robert D. Putnam, *Bowling Alone: The Collapse and Revival of American Community* (New York: Simon and Schuster, 2000).

46. See Donald F. Kettl, Patricia W. Ingraham, Ronald P. Sanders, and Constance Horner, *Civil Service Reform: Building a Government that Works* (Washington, D.C.: Brookings Institution Press, 1996).

47. Daniel Bell, "Previewing Planet Earth in 2013," *Washington Post*, 3 January 1988, 3(B).

48. Jean-Francois Rischard, "High Noon: The Urgent Need for New Global Governance Solutions" (World Bank, 2000), 5, at www.worldbank.org/research/abcde/eu _2000/pdffiles/rischard.pdf (accessed February 4, 2001).

49. Organization for Economic Cooperation and Development, *Managing Across Levels of Government: Executive Summary* (Paris: OECD, 1998), at www.oecd.org//puma/malg /malg97/summary.htm (accessed March 22, 2001).

CHAPTER SEVEN: **Who Governs—and How?**

1. See, for example, Anne M. Khademian, *Working with Culture: How the Work Gets Done in Public Programs* (Washington, D.C.: CQ Press, 2002).

2. Keith Koffler, "White House Defends Increased Federal Role," *Govexec.com Daily Briefing* (October 5, 2001), at www.govexec.com/dailyfed/1001/100401cd1.htm (accessed October 5, 2001).

3. Jeffrey L. Pressman and Aaron Wildavsky, *Implementation* (Berkeley: University of California Press, 1973).

4. Joseph J. Ellis, *Founding Brothers: The Revolutionary Generation* (New York: Alfred A. Knopf, 2001), 5.

5. Ibid., 15, 16.

6. Robert A. Dahl, *Who Governs? Democracy and Power in an American City* (New Haven: Yale University Press, 1961), 1.

7. John Gaus, "Trends in the Theory of Public Administration," *Public Administration Review* 10 (1950): 161–68.

8. Social Security Administration, *Social Security: Performance and Accountability Report for 2000* (Washington, D.C.: GPO, 2000), 25.

9. U.S. Department of Transportation, *DOT Performance Plan (FY 2002) and Report (FY 2000)* (Washington, D.C.: GPO, 2001), 44.

10. See New York City Accountability Program at http://home.nyc.gov/portal/index .jsp?pageID=nyc_stat_reports&catID=1724 (accessed October 5, 2001).

11. Fritz W. Scharpf, "Interdependence and Democratic Legitimation," in Susan J. Pharr and Robert D. Putnam, eds., *Disaffected Democracies: What's Troubling the Trilateral Countries?* (Princeton: Princeton University Press), 115.

12. Dwight Waldo, *The Administrative State* (New York: Ronald Press, 1948), chap. 7.

13. Quoted in ibid., 69n.

14. Ibid., 69.

15. See Donald F. Kettl, *Sharing Power: Public Governance and Private Markets* (Washington, D.C.: Brookings Institution Press, 1993).

16. U.S. General Accounting Office, *GAO's Performance and Accountability Series and High Risk Update 2001: A Governmentwide Perspective* (Washington, D.C.: GAO, GAO-01-241, 2001).

17. David M. Walker, "Government Challenges in the 21st Century" (Speech, National Press Club, April 23, 2001), at www.gao.gov/cghome/ncspch.html (accessed April 23, 2001).

18. Wisconsin Legislative Audit Bureau, *Wisconsin Works (W-2) Program* (April 2001), at www.legis.state.wi.us/lab/Reports/01-7tear.htm (accessed May 14, 2001).

19. See Organization for Economic Cooperation and Development, "E-government for Democracy and Development," *Focus: Public Management Newsletter* (March 2001), at www.oecd.org/puma/focus/num19.pdf (accessed May 14, 2001).

20. See Accenture, *Rhetoric versus Reality: Closing the Gap* (2001), at www.accenture.com/xd/xd.asp?it=enWeb&xd=industries\government\gove_study.xml (accessed May 14, 2001).

21. See Paul C. Light, *The Tides of Reform: Making Government Work, 1945–1995* (New Haven: Yale University Press, 1997).

EPILOGUE: **Governance at the Boundaries**

1. Gfk Group, "Press Release: Trust in Charities and Judges Rising Internationally" (June 17, 2011), at http://www.gfk.com/imperia/md/content/presse/pressemeldungen_2011/20110617_trust_index_efin.pdf (accessed June 17, 2011).

2. Scott Horsley, "A Churchill 'Quote' That U.S. Politicians Will Never Surrender," National Public Radio (October 28, 2013), http://www.npr.org/blogs/itsallpolitics/2013/10/28/241295755/a-churchill-quote-that-u-s-politicians-will-never-surrender (accessed July 7, 2014).

3. Thomas E. Mann and Norman Ornstein, *It's Even Worse Than It Looks: How the American Constitutional System Collided with the New Politics of Extremism* (New York: Basic Books, 2012).

4. Donald F. Kettl, *The Transformation of Governance: Public Administration for Twenty-First Century America* (Baltimore: Johns Hopkins University Press, 2002), 168.

5. Centers for Medicare and Medicaid Services, "National Health Expenditures 2012 Highlights," http://www.cms.gov/Research-Statistics-Data-and-Systems/Statistics-Trends-and-Reports/NationalHealthExpendData/downloads/highlights.pdf (accessed July 9, 2014).

6. Robert E. Moffit and Edmund F. Haislmaier, "Obamacare's Insurance Exchanges: 'Private Coverage' in Name Only" (Heritage Foundation Backgrounder #2846, September 26, 2013), at http://www.heritage.org/research/reports/2013/09/obamacares-insurance-exchanges-private-coverage-in-name-only (accessed July 9, 20140).

7. For an exploration of this issue, please see Donald F. Kettl, *The Next Government of the United States: Why Our Institutions Fail Us and How to Fix Them* (New York: W. W. Norton, 2009).

8. Pew Research Center for People and the Presss, http://www.pewresearch.org/key-data-points/views-of-government-key-data-points/ (accessed July 9, 2014).

9. Ibid.

10. Organisation for Economic Co-operation and Development, Government at a Glance: 2013 (Paris: OECD, 2013), 33.

11. Ibid., 34.

12. Ibid., 36.

13. For an exploration of these issues, see Donald F. Kettl, "The Reluctant Executive," *Government Executive* (May/June 2014), pp. 16–20.

14. Jeff Greenfield, "Hail and Farewell: Reading John Lindsay's Face," *New York Times*, 29 July 1973, at http://query.nytimes.com/mem/archive/pdf?res=F20C14F83C541 77388DDA00A94DF405B838BF1D3.

15. Ibid., chap. 1. See also Geert Bouckaert, "Trust and Public Administration," *Administration* 60 (2012): 91–115; and Geert Bouckaert and Steven van de Walle, "Comparing Measures of Citizen Trust and User Satisfaction as Indicators of 'Good Governance': Difficulties in Linking Trust and Satisfaction Indicators," *International Review of Administrative Sciences* 69 (September 2003): 329–44. More broadly, see Francis Fukuyama, *Trust: The Social Virtues and The Creation of Prosperity* (New York: Free Press, 1995).

16. U.S. Government Accountability Office, High-Risk Series: An Update (February 2013), GAO-13-283, at http://www.gao.gov/assets/660/652133.pdf (accessed July 9, 2014).

17. U.S. Government Accountability Office, High-Performing Organizations: Metrics, Means, and Mechanisms for Achieving High Performance in the 21st Century Public Management Environment (February 2004), GAO-04-343SP, at http://www.gao.gov /assets/250/241451.pdf (accessed July 9, 2014).

18. Dwight Waldo, *The Administrative State: A Study of the Political Theory of American Public Administration* (New York: Ronald Press, 1948).

19. Thomas Payne, *Common Sense*. www.earlyamerica.com/earlyamerica/milestones /commonsense/text.html and http://www.bartleby.com/133/ (accessed July 7, 2014).

20. John M. Gaus, "The Responsibility of Public Administration," in John M. Gaus, Leonard D. White, and Marshall E. Dimock, eds., *The Frontiers of Public Administration* (Chicago: University of Chicago Press, 1936), 37.

21. Jody Freeman, "Extending Public Law Norms through Privatization," *Harvard Law Review* 116 (March 2003): 1339; Laurence E. Lynn, "Restoring the Rule of Law to Public Administration: What Frank Goodnow Got Right and Leonard White Didn't," *Public Administration Review* 69 (September/October 2009): 803–13; and Donald F. Kettl, "Administrative Accountability and the Rule of Law," *PS* (January 2009), 13–14.

22. Donald F. Kettl, *The Next Government of the United States: Why Our Institutions Fail Us and How to Fix Them* (New York: W. W. Norton, 2009).

23. Katherine Barrett and Richard Greene, *Governing Management*, March 20, 2014, at http://now.eloqua.com/es.asp?s=1222&e=620854&elq=d4a9e3672a5442209a51ad5cb ad3112c.

24. Substantial scholarship has emerged bringing complexity theory to public administration. See Robert Geyer and Samir Rihani, *Complexity and Public Policy: A New Approach to 21st Century Politics, Policy and Society* (New York: Routledge, 2010); and Göktuğ Morçöl, *A Complexity Theory for Public Policy* (New York: Routledge, 2012).

25. Steven Brill, "Code Red," *Time*, March 10, 2014, 26 ff.

26. Robert F. Durant and Susannah Bruns Ali, "Repositioning American Public Administration? Citizen Estrangement, Administrative Reform, and the Disarticulated State," *Public Administration Review* 73 (March/April 2013): 278–89.

27. Organisation for Economic Co-operation and Development, *How's Life: Measuring Well-Being* (Paris: OECD, 2013); and *Government at a Glance: 2013* (Paris: OECD, 2013).

28. See, for example, Chris Ernst and Donna Chrobot-Mason, *Boundary Spanning Leadership: Six Practices for Solving Problems, Driving Innovation, and Transforming Organizations* (New York: McGraw-Hill, 2011); Natalia Levina and Emmanuelle Vaast, "Turning a Community into a Market: A Practice Perspective on Information Technology Use in Boundary Spanning," *Journal of Management Information Systems* 22 (Spring 2006): 13–37; and Gary Noble and Robert Jones, "The Role of Boundary-Spanning Managers in the Establishment of Public-Private Partnerships," *Public Administration* 84 (December 2006): 891–917.

29. U.S. Government Accountability Office, Recovery Act: Grant Implementation Experiences Offer Lessons for Accountability and Transparency, GAO-14-219 (January 2014).

30. For a careful look at the performance management movement, see Donald P. Moynihan, *The Dynamics of Performance Management: Constructing Information and Reform* (Washington, D.C.: Georgetown University Press, 2008).

31. Robert D. Behn, *The PerformanceStat Potential: A Leadership Strategy for Producing Results* (Washington, D.C.: Brookings Institution Press, 2014).

32. For a thorough review of these reforms, see Christopher Pollitt and Geert Bouckaert, *Public Management Reform: A Comparative Analysis—New Public Management, Governance, and the Neo-Weberian State*, 3d ed. (Oxford: Oxford University Press, 2011).

33. OECD, *Government at a Glance: 2013*, 9. At http://www.keepeek.com/Digital-Asset -Management/oecd/governance/government-at-a-glance-2013_gov_glance-2013-en #page11 (accessed July 9, 2014).

34. Ann Florini, Hairon Lai, and Yeling Tan, *China Experiment: From Local Innovations to National Reform* (Washington, D.C.: Brookings Institution Press, 2012).

35. Hauser Institute for Civil Society, John F. Kennedy School of Government, at http://www.hks.harvard.edu/centers/hauser/programs/past-programs/nonprofits-in -china (accessed March 21, 2014).

36. OECD, *Government at a Glance: 2013*, 25–27.

37. Christopher Pollitt, "Clarifying Convergence: Striking Similarities and Durable Differences in Public Management Reform," *Public Management Review* 3:4 (2001): 471–92.

Index

Page numbers in *italics* refer to figures and tables.